# Critical Conversation Analysis

# CRITICAL LANGUAGE AND LITERACY STUDIES

*Series Editors*: **Professor Alastair Pennycook** (*University of Technology, Sydney, Australia*) and **Professor Brian Morgan** (*Glendon College/York University, Toronto, Canada*) and **Professor Ryuko Kubota** (*University of British Columbia, Vancouver, Canada*)

Critical Language and Literacy Studies is an international series that encourages monographs directly addressing issues of power (its flows, inequities, distributions, trajectories) in a variety of language- and literacy-related realms. The aim with this series is twofold: (1) to cultivate scholarship that openly engages with social, political, and historical dimensions in language and literacy studies, and (2) to widen disciplinary horizons by encouraging new work on topics that have received little focus (see below for partial list of subject areas) and that use innovative theoretical frameworks.

All books in this series are externally peer-reviewed.

Full details of all the books in this series and of all our other publications can be found on http://www.multilingual-matters.com, or by writing to Multilingual Matters, St Nicholas House, 31–34 High Street, Bristol, BS1 2AW, UK.

**Other books in the series**
Ethnography, Superdiversity and Linguistic Landscapes: Chronicles of Complexity
*Jan Blommaert*
Power and Meaning Making in an EAP Classroom: Engaging with the Everyday
*Christian W. Chun*
Local Languaging, Literacy and Multilingualism in a West African Society
*Kasper Juffermans*
English Teaching and Evangelical Mission: The Case of Lighthouse School
*Bill Johnston*
Race and Ethnicity in English Language Teaching
*Christopher Joseph Jenks*
Language, Education and Neoliberalism: Critical Studies in Sociolinguistics
*Mi-Cha Flubacher and Alfonso Del Percio* (eds)
Scripts of Servitude: Language, Labor Migration and Transnational Domestic Work
*Beatriz P. Lorente*
Growing up with God and Empire: A Postcolonial Analysis of 'Missionary Kid' Memoirs
*Stephanie Vandrick*
Decolonising Multilingualism in Africa: Recentering Silenced Voices from the Global South
*Finex Ndhlovu and Leketi Makalela*
English Learners' Access to Postsecondary Education: Neither College nor Career Ready
*Yasuko Kanno*
English Linguistic Imperialism from Below: Moral Aspiration and Social Mobility
*Leya Mathew*
The Power of Voice in Transforming Multilingual Societies
*Julia Gspandl, Christina Korb, Angelika Heiling and Elizabeth J. Erling* (eds)
Redoing Linguistic Worlds: Unmaking Gender Binaries, Remaking Gender Pluralities
*Kris Aric Knisely and Eric Louis Russell* (eds)

CRITICAL LANGUAGE AND LITERACY STUDIES: 31

# Critical Conversation Analysis

Inequality and Injustice in Talk-in-Interaction

Edited by
**Hansun Zhang Waring
and Nadja Tadic**

MULTILINGUAL MATTERS
Bristol • Jackson

DOI https://doi.org/10.21832/WARING5393
Names: Waring, Hansun Zhang, editor. | Tadic, Nadja, editor.
Title: Critical Conversation Analysis: Inequality and injustice in Talk-in-Interaction/
Edited by Hansun Zhang Waring and Nadja Tadic.
Description: Bristol, UK; Jackson, TN: Multilingual Matters, [2024] |
   Series: Critical Language and Literacy Studies: 31 | Includes
   bibliographical references and index. | Summary: "This book presents the
   first collection of conversation analytic studies addressed exclusively
   to issues of inequality and injustice. The chapters produce a forensic
   analysis of how participants enact discriminatory ideologies, negotiate
   systemic power imbalances, and pursue social change in and through the
   nuances of their interactions"—Provided by publisher.
Identifiers: LCCN 2023048897 (print) | LCCN 2023048898 (ebook) | ISBN
   9781800415386 (paperback) | ISBN 9781800415393 (hardback) | ISBN
   9781800415416 (epub) | ISBN 9781800415409 (pdf)
Subjects: LCSH: Racism in language—United States. | Discrimination in
   language—United States. | Conversation analysis—United States. |
   Racism—United States. | Social justice—United States.
Classification: LCC P120.R32 C75 2024 (print) | LCC P120.R32 (ebook) |
   DDC 408.9—dc23/eng/20231204
LC record available at https://lccn.loc.gov/2023048897
LC ebook record available at https://lccn.loc.gov/2023048898

Library of Congress Cataloging in Publication Data
A catalog record for this book is available from the Library of Congress.

British Library Cataloguing in Publication Data
A catalogue entry for this book is available from the British Library.

ISBN-13: 978-1-80041-539-3 (hbk)
ISBN-13: 978-1-80041-538-6 (pbk)

**Multilingual Matters**
UK: St Nicholas House, 31–34 High Street, Bristol, BS1 2AW, UK.
USA: Ingram, Jackson, TN, USA.

Website: https://www.multilingual-matters.com
Twitter: Multi_Ling_Mat
Facebook: https://www.facebook.com/multilingualmatters
Blog: https://www.channelviewpublications.wordpress.com

Copyright © 2024 Hansun Zhang Waring, Nadja Tadic and the authors of individual chapters.

All rights reserved. No part of this work may be reproduced in any form or by any means without permission in writing from the publisher.

The policy of Multilingual Matters/Channel View Publications is to use papers that are natural, renewable and recyclable products, made from wood grown in sustainable forests. In the manufacturing process of our books, and to further support our policy, preference is given to printers that have FSC and PEFC Chain of Custody certification. The FSC and/or PEFC logos will appear on those books where full certification has been granted to the printer concerned.

Typeset by SAN Publishing Services.

# Contents

|  | Contributors | vii |
|---|---|---|
|  | Acknowledgements | xiii |
|  | Foreword | xv |
|  | Series Editors' Preface | xxxiii |
| 1 | Introduction<br>Nadja Tadic and Hansun Zhang Waring | 1 |

**Part 1: Reproducing Inequality and Injustice**

| 2 | Investigating Raciolinguistic Ideologies in Interaction<br>Nadja Tadic, Hansun Zhang Waring<br>and Elizabeth Reddington | 27 |
|---|---|---|
| 3 | Racist Renditions: Mock Language in Interaction<br>Elliott M. Hoey and Chase Wesley Raymond | 49 |
| 4 | Talk in Local News Broadcasts: Reinforcing Negative<br>Views towards the Hawaiian Language<br>Scott Saft | 71 |
| 5 | Inequality in Action: Granting Emergency Service<br>Requests in a Highly Resource-Constrained Context<br>Catherine L. Tam, Kevin A. Whitehead<br>and Geoffrey Raymond | 91 |
| 6 | Delegitimizing the 'Other' at US Congressional<br>Town Hall Meetings<br>Di Yu | 115 |

**Part 2: Resisting Inequality and Injustice**

| 7 | Negotiating Power Inequalities in Joint Decision-Making<br>in a Faculty Meeting<br>Innhwa Park and Santoi Wagner | 133 |
|---|---|---|

8  *I'm Just Saying:* Being Explicit in a Mixed-Race
   Conversation about Racism                                      155
   *Sarah Chepkirui Creider*

9  Using Racial Incompetence as a Comedic Device
   and Tacit Method of Anti-Racist Education                      174
   *Lillian Cheeks and Kevin A. Whitehead*

**Part 3: A Final Argument**

10 'Just a Method in Search of a Problem?'
   The Power of Conversation Analysis                             197
   *Elizabeth Stokoe and Saul Albert*

   Index                                                          224

# Contributors

**Saul Albert** is a Lecturer in Social Science (Social Psychology) in Communication and Media at Loughborough University. His research explores the technology of social interaction at two ends of the spectrum of formalization. At one end, his work on conversational AI asks which features and mechanisms of human social action can be represented and modeled computationally. At the other, he studies how people make aesthetic judgements and interact while dealing with underdetermined cultural objects and situations. This program spans multiple, often incompatible disciplines, so his work builds methodological interfaces between them.

**Lillian Cheeks** is a graduate of the University of California, Santa Barbara with a double major in Sociology and Linguistics. Her research uses ethnomethodological and conversation analytic approaches to study how television comedy writers and actors use race in their shows, especially in relation to portrayals of asymmetries of common-sense racial knowledge between characters of different racial categories.

**Sarah Chepkirui Creider** is a Lecturer in the Applied Linguistics & TESOL program at Teachers College, Columbia University. Her work, as a researcher, teacher and activist, is focused on what she calls a 'microrevolution' – the possibilities for change inherent in each moment of everyday conversations. As a conversation analyst, Sarah works in two primary areas: teacher–student interaction; and political conversations, particularly among mixed-race groups. Her work has been published in *Linguistics & Education;* the *Journal of Contemporary Foreign Language Studies; Learning, Culture & Social Interaction; Discourse Studies; Language and Information Society;* and the *Journal of Applied Linguistics and Professional Practice.* Her book (co-authored with Hansun Waring), *Micro-reflection on Classroom Communication: A FAB framework,* was published by Equinox in 2021. Sarah has a doctorate in Applied Linguistics from Teachers College, Columbia University.

**Elliott M. Hoey** (PhD, 2017, Radboud University) is Assistant Professor of Language and Communication at the Vrije Universiteit Amsterdam. In his research he examines the multimodal orchestration of everyday activities. Recent work has focused on construction site interactions and palliative care settings. He is the author of *When Conversation Lapses* (Oxford University Press, 2020).

**Innhwa Park** (PhD, Applied Linguistics, UCLA) is Associate Professor of TESOL in the Department of Languages and Cultures at West Chester University of Pennsylvania. She uses conversation analysis to examine language and social interaction, together with its applications in the fields of applied linguistics and education. Her research interests include meeting interaction, educational discourse and second language use. She has recently published in *Discourse Studies*, *Journal of Pragmatics*, and *Language and Communication*.

**Anne Warfield Rawls** is Professor of Sociology at Bentley University, Research Professor University of Siegen, Germany, and Director of The Garfinkel Archive. Focusing on theories of constitutive practice in classical and contemporary social theory, Professor Rawls has written extensively on the history of sociology with a focus on Durkheim, Du Bois and Garfinkel, with particular application to issues of social justice, race and racism. Publications include *Tacit Racism* (co-authored with Waverly Duck, University of Chicago, 2020); *Black Lives Matter: Ethnomethodological and Conversation Analytic Studies of Race and Systemic Racism in Everyday Interaction* (edited and co-authored with Kevin Whitehead and Waverly Duck, Routledge, 2020); *La Division du Travail Revisited: Vers une Théorie Sociologique de la Justice* (Trans. Francesco Callegaro and Philip Chanial. Le Bord de l' Eau, 2019); *Durkheim's Epistemology* (Cambridge University, 2009); editor of Garfinkel's *Parsons Primer* (Springer, 2019); co-author with Jason Turowetz of '"Discovering Culture" in Interaction: Solving Problems in Cultural Sociology by Recovering the Interactional Side of Parsons' Conception of Culture' (*American Journal of Cultural Sociology*, 2019); and 'Race as an Interaction Order Phenomenon: W.E.B. Du Bois's "Double Consciousness" Thesis Revisited' (*Sociological Theory*, 2000).

**Chase Wesley Raymond** (PhD, 2014, UCLA; PhD, 2016, UCLA) is Associate Professor of Linguistics at the University of Colorado, Boulder. His research interests lie at the intersection of language and (different facets of) social identity and normativity, in both ordinary and institutional contexts, with a particular emphasis on grammar. Much of his work in both research and teaching is geared toward questions of methodology in the study of social interaction. Recent publications have appeared in journal outlets across the fields of linguistics, sociology, psychology, communication studies and medicine, and he is author (with Luis Manuel Olguín) of *Análisis de la Conversación: Fundamentos, metodología y alcances* (Routledge, 2022).

**Geoffrey Raymond** is a Professor of Sociology at the University of California, Santa Barbara. His research interests include conversation analysis, the role of talk-in-interaction in the organization of institutions, and qualitative research methods.

**Elizabeth Reddington** holds an EdD in Applied Linguistics from Teachers College, Columbia University and is Lecturer of ESL at Kean University. A language educator and discourse analyst, her research interests include classroom interaction, teacher education and communication in the public sphere. Her single- and co-authored work has appeared in edited volumes and in journals such as *Classroom Discourse*, *Discourse & Communication* and *Linguistics and Education*. She is the editor, with Hansun Zhang Waring, of *Communicating with the Public: Conversation Analytic Studies* (Bloomsbury, 2020).

**Scott Saft** is a Professor of Linguistics at the University of Hawai'i at Hilo. His research interests include conversation analysis, institutional discourse, multilingualism, and pidgins and creoles.

**Elizabeth Stokoe** is Professor in the Department of Psychological and Behavioural Science, The London School of Economics and Behavioural Science. She uses conversation analysis to understand how talk works – from first dates to medical communication and from sales encounters to hostage negotiation. She has worked as an industry fellow at Typeform and is currently on secondment with Deployed. Outside the university, she runs research-based communication training for practitioners using the method she developed called 'CARM'. She is a *Wired* Innovation Fellow, and her research and biography were featured on the BBC Radio 4's *The Life Scientific* and *Word of Mouth*. In addition to her academic publishing, she is passionate about science communication, and has given talks at TED, New Scientist, Google, Microsoft and The Royal Institution, and performed at Latitude and Cheltenham Science Festivals. Her book, *Talk: The Science of Conversation*, was published by Little, Brown (in 2018), and her co-authored book on *Crisis Talk* was published by Routledge in 2022.

**Nadja Tadic** (EdD, Applied Linguistics, Columbia University) is Assistant Professor in the Linguistics Department at Georgetown University. Her research examines issues of diversity, discrimination and social (in)justice through the lens of critically motivated conversation analysis and membership categorization analysis. Her work has been published in edited volumes and in journals such as *Applied Linguistics, Language in Society, Language and Education* and *Linguistics and Education*.

**Catherine L. Tam** is a PhD in the Department of Psychology and a Lecturer in the Faculty of Humanities Teaching and Learning Unit at the University of the Witwatersrand, Johannesburg. Using an ethnomethodological and conversation analytic approach, she investigates the interactional mechanisms that underpin asymmetries and inequities in social relations with a focus on parent-child, lecturer-learner and emergency medical services interactions.

**Santoi Wagner** (EdD, Applied Linguistics, Columbia University) is Senior Lecturer in Educational Linguistics and Associate Director of TESOL at the University of Pennsylvania's Graduate School of Education. Her scholarly interests are in applying conversation analysis to issues within language education. Her current projects include teacher–mentor interactions in post-observation meetings and the development and use of authentic materials for second language teaching. She has recently published in *Journal of Pragmatics, Language Assessment Quarterly* and *English Teaching & Learning*.

**Hansun Zhang Waring** is Professor of Linguistics and Education at Teachers College, Columbia University and founder of *The Language and Social Interaction Working Group* (LANSI). As an applied linguist and conversation analyst, Hansun is the author of over 60 journal articles and book chapters in addition to seven books on social interaction across a variety of contexts, including *Theorizing Pedagogical Interaction: Insights from Conversation Analysis* (2016), *Discourse Analysis: The Questions Discourse Analysts Ask and How they Answer them* (2018) and *Communicating with the Public: Conversation Analytic Studies* (2020; co-edited with E. Reddington).

**Kevin A. Whitehead** is an Associate Professor in the Department of Sociology at the University of California, Santa Barbara, and a Visiting Associate Professor in the School of Human and Community Development at the University of the Witwatersrand, Johannesburg. His research uses ethnomethodological and conversation analytic approaches to study recorded talk-in interaction, focusing in particular on practices through which social categories are used, reproduced and resisted.

**Di Yu** holds an EdD in Applied Linguistics from Teachers College, Columbia University and served as a past president of *The Language and Social Interaction Working Group* (LANSI). Her research interests include political discourse, humor and multimodality in interaction. Her co-authored work has appeared in journals including R*esearch on Children and Social Interaction, Discourse & Communication* and *Language Learning Journal,* along with a few edited volumes. Di currently oversees the program operations team at the Executive Education department of Columbia Business School.

# Acknowledgements

Many thanks to Anna Roderick at Multilingual Matters for her enthusiasm about this project from the outset and to the three anonymous reviewers for their expertise and insights. Our gratitude also goes to Steven Talmy for his thought-provoking discussion on Critical Conversation Analysis at the 2022 American Association for Applied Linguistics (AAAL) conference and to the audience at our panel for helping us think through the many issues surrounding our endeavor. We are so lucky to have worked with this amazing group of stellar authors. As seasoned scholars and rising stars, they have not only opened our eyes to the astounding possibilities of putting CA to its critical use, but also shown us a tremendous amount of patience, grace and good will as they journeyed with us over the past two years to bring you – here at last – '*Critical Conversation Analysis*'.

HZW: This project was inspired by Nadja's 2020 conversation analytic dissertation on diversity in the adult ESL classroom. Known as the 'diversity diva' among the #lansibunch, Nadja embodies 'critical' as a scholar, a teacher and a human being. She asks, 'why not?' and pursues, not what is prescribed, but what is possible. Hers is the kind of fresh voice that moves conversations and pushes fields forward. While I have more or less played the role of a curator, Nadja is, without a doubt, the soul of this volume.

NT: This project would not have been possible without the generosity that permeates Hansun's scholarly work. Her wholehearted dedication not only sparked the idea for our critical CA venture but also turned what might have remained wishful thinking into the reality that is this volume. I am eternally grateful for her mentorship and collaboration.

# Foreword

Over the course of two centuries of racialized slavery in the US and another 160 plus years of racial segregation (both *de facto* and *de jure*), inequalities of Race[1] became deeply embedded in our daily life interactions and were then exported around the world. Other inequalities are similarly embedded in structures of interactional expectation such that in ordinary interaction people are often producing inequality unintentionally. Nevertheless, we tend to treat inequality as if it were a matter of institutional rules and individual attitudes, and thus attempts at reform tend to focus on either changing rules and laws or on sensitizing individuals to personal bias. To the extent that the pervasive forms of exclusion that produce inequality do their work through social interaction, in focusing on individuals and explicit organized forms of exclusion, the actual processes through which we continue to produce Race and other forms of inequality together in daily social interaction tend to be overlooked. Because such instances of exclusion are 'social facts', produced like other social facts through the tacit taken-for-granted practices of ordinary social interaction, they cannot be explained in terms of individual attitudes and formal institutions. Nor can such inequalities be eradicated by convincing people to become anti-racist, or anti-sexist, or anti-ableist – although that is certainly necessary. Even people who are thoroughly committed to achieving equality will continue producing social facts in ways that exclude if they continue to participate in unexamined social practices in which inequality has become embedded. The dynamics of the tacit social practices through which we create inequality together every day must be understood, and ordinary people must develop an awareness of these tacit taken-for-granted social processes before change is possible (Rawls & Duck, 2020).

In this timely book on *Critical Conversation Analysis,* Hansun Zhang Waring and Nadja Tadic have brought together conversation analytic (CA) research that takes a critical stance toward revealing the tacit taken-for-granted underpinnings of racism and other inequalities in conversational interaction so that we can understand how these processes of

Othering work. They present this research under the umbrella of what they call 'Critical CA' in 10 illuminating chapters that analyze interaction across ordered sequences of talk to reveal contemporary inequalities of Race, Gender, Power and Politics at work in social interaction (discussed in more detail below). There is a false belief among many social scientists that to illuminate *big* issues like racism and exclusion we need to start with *big* conceptual ideas. The research in this book challenges that premise, each contribution in its own way showing how the analysis of interaction in sequential details reveals processes of Race and inequality at work line-by-line, sometimes explicitly, sometimes tacitly. When the so-called big ideas ignore how things actually work, they need to take a back seat to a detailed analysis of social interaction.

In their opening discussion, Tadic and Waring context their critical CA approach in what they refer to as the 'oft-cited debate on the relationship between critical analysis and CA' (p. 4), which comprised a series of articles by Emanuel Schegloff, Margaret Wetherell and Michael Billig, featured in *Discourse & Society* between 1997 and 1999. The point at issue was the claim – consistent with the 'big ideas' position – that empirical research on the details of language use cannot lead to better theory or social change. In refuting this charge, Schegloff emphasized a crucial difference between CA and conventional research: political and social categories are typically the starting point of analysis – chosen *a priori* – for researchers not using CA, which makes critique based on them circular. Whereas for CA researchers, categories and their relevance are an emergent property that can be tracked empirically by sequential analysis. This 'emergent' quality makes the difference (Rawls, 1987, 1990).

Racism and other inequalities require being enacted, one might say 'performed', in situated social contexts to be experienced. However, because the social processes through which racism and inequality are enacted/achieved as social facts are largely tacit and interactional, even when backed by racist beliefs or formal legal mandates, they are difficult to pin down: obvious to those excluded by them – but not to those doing the excluding. Thus, those who do not experience racism and exclusion tend to know little about it, while those who do experience racism are rarely listened to. For Harold Garfinkel and Harvey Sacks, the founders of ethnomethodology (EM) and conversation analysis (CA), Jewish scholars in a US social science founded largely by the White male sons of Protestant ministers, the relationship between marginality and trouble in interaction was clear. Working together in the early 1960's, their heightened awareness of interaction as a setting for the 'doing' of marginality, coupled as it was to their own marginality and alignment with other marginalized categories of person, set them against the mainstream (Duck & Rawls, 2023) or what they might have called the 'normals' (Rawls, 2023) who then further marginalized their message.[2]

To do a better job of understanding racism it is necessary to determine how – just how – interactional practices are being used to enact expectations and presuppositions about Race, Gender and Other marginalized categories. Lacking such an understanding we have failed over and over again to address problems of racialization and marginalization, often mistakenly believing that they have been overcome. This particular failure to identify racism in action has made the US vulnerable to racialized appeals that are being used to amplify divisions between citizens and threaten the US democratic experiment. EM and CA have essential roles to play in generating the understanding we need to meet the moment – a bit like the role of Newton and Galileo in grounding the natural sciences in empirical demonstrations of things like gravity, the fragmentation of light, and inertia: findings to which we now give big names like 'laws' but were originally small demonstrations of matter in action.

Critical CA is an appropriate name for this important research. It is important to note, however, that even when EM and CA focus on establishing how ordinary social facts are made when there is no trouble or inequality, they are still involved in *an inherently critical enterprise* that promises to rewrite the foundations of many disciplines. Garfinkel and Sacks were both explicit about this in collaborating to launch their joint challenge to Sociology and Linguistics through a series of five meetings at UCLA in 1962 and 1963 funded by Garfinkel's AAF grants.[3]

On top of this intrinsic challenge of EM/CA to mainstream disciplines, when their focus is on what interactional troubles reveal about how social inequalities are being produced, as in this book, the research also has a direct relevance to practical political and moral issues. In his first published article in 1940, Garfinkel reported on an ethnographic observation of racism he made as a 22-year-old graduate student traveling on a segregated bus in the US South. The article documented how tacit presuppositions were used to maintain segregation on the bus and how things fell apart when those tacit presuppositions were questioned.[4] Garfinkel realized from the beginning that *making what is tacit explicit is a critical enterprise* that can reveal how inequalities are created and maintained, and he based EM on that premise (Rawls, 2022a, 2022b). Sacks, working with Garfinkel in the early 1960's, realized that making what was tacit about the achievement of conversational meaning explicit would reveal the social interaction – the sociology – that is hiding at the heart of linguistics (as Durkheim's exposure of the

Individual as a social fact had revealed the sociology hiding at the center of philosophy and psychology). Garfinkel and Sacks launched EM and CA together in the early 1960's with the idea of doing this critical work of revealing what is ordinarily taken for granted and changing the way we approach both social and technical research (see Eisenmann et al., 2023).

Unfortunately, for most of the past century a prejudice against social interactionism has worked against the reception of such studies (Rawls, 2018) and their critical potential has not been recognized. Tadic and Waring touch on this problem. EM/CA researchers who make critical contributions to understanding racism and injustice endure unfounded criticisms by those who attack their methods as 'unscientific', while those same critics blithely adhere to positions that hide and even reinforce the social inequalities they claim to be addressing.

When Lewis Coser, for instance, in his 1974 Presidential Address, referred dismissively to EM as a 'Method in Search of a Substance' – implying that EM/CA were engaged in observing trivia to no purpose – he aligned himself with theoretical and conceptual models and against the possibility of progress through detailed research that is not grounded in such models. For Coser, concepts and models come first and define the substantive problems a researcher then tries to 'measure'.[5] Coser (following Whitehead, 1927) called attempts to prioritize empirical data over conceptual models a 'fallacy of misplaced precision'. By contrast, this prioritizing of concepts and models by Coser and most mainstream thinkers is in my view a 'Fallacy of Misplaced Abstraction' (Rawls, 2004).

The assumption that concepts take precedence over and precede empirical observations is precisely what EM and CA challenge. How can concepts come first if, as social facts, they are an interactional achievement (an argument Durkheim (1912) intended as the grounding for sociology as a discipline: practices he argued create concepts (Rawls, 2009)). There is certainly no lack of substance; EM and CA have been clear from the beginning about the problem – or substance – they targeted. That target is the theoretical models that those like Coser insist must be *allowed to stand in for the world as it is*: models, which can only be as good as the assumptions they rest on, are supposed to take precedence over the way society is actually organized move-by-move, turn-by-turn. That those models hide how social processes actually work (what Garfinkel and Sacks called 'glossing' the actual practices) – that they hide how people cooperate to use practices to make social facts – did not interest Coser and those he aligned with. They considered the 'real world' too messy to deal with and treated empirical contingencies as an irrelevant part of that mess, which should be reduced – or cleaned up – through conceptual generalization/glossing.

While others imagined that such 'clean' conceptual representations are needed to do real 'scientific' research, Garfinkel's experience with the deficiency of models during WWII told him otherwise. Working for the Army Air Force (AAF), Garfinkel prepared a report on how the AAF went about training airplane mechanics (Garfinkel, [1943] 2019). At the beginning of the war, everything was in short supply. There were no planes or engines for the mechanics to train on. Even simple tools were hard to come by. The AAF generals nevertheless insisted that those doing the training throw out the books (conceptual models), and crude physical models were built to support the training.

In commenting on the difference between airplane mechanics and sociologists in 1963, Garfinkel told a story about an airplane mechanic who finally climbed into a real airplane for the first time and found that the plane was very different from the model. Garfinkel's point was that the mechanic did not fault the plane for not meeting the criteria of the model. The mechanic saw that the fault was with the model. The sociologist, however, as Garfinkel told it, would complain about the world that it did not meet the criteria of the model (Garfinkel, 1988; Rawls & Lynch, [1943] 2019).

By contrast with a mainstream sociology that faulted the social world for being less orderly than their conceptual models, Garfinkel and Sacks intended EM/CA to reveal what those models were hiding, arguing that what the models were treating as irrelevant contingencies are actually the key to how things work. Imagine if natural scientists had kept approaching the details of elements, atoms and electrons as irrelevant contingencies, as they had in the age of Copernicus. Research that begins with conceptual models of society is similarly problematic, reflecting the beliefs and biases of those who constructed the model, while saying nothing about the order properties of the actual social world – the target of the research.

The 10 chapters in this book investigate issues that are central to creating a diverse, equitable and inclusive democratic society, and they do so using CA analysis of how the design and placement of turns in talk implicate conversational moves that either indicate that participants are already orienting to such issues as a problem in the interaction, or make such issues a problem through the placement of those turns in the talk. Finding inequality embedded in social practices across a wide range of interactions, each chapter in different detailed ways specifies how unequal power relations are produced, reproduced, resisted and problematized by ordinary people doing what we all take for granted in our daily lives.

## How this Book Delivers on the Promise of Critical Conversation Analysis

In giving their Chapter 10 the title '"Just a Method in Search of a Problem?" The Power of Conversation Analysis', Elizabeth Stokoe and Saul Albert allude to and challenge the Coser critique – pushing back against the insinuation that EM/CA has no substance, with a powerful demonstration that CA has indeed *found its problem* in studies of embedded power and preference. After first showing what more can be learned from doing CA analysis of two public controversies for which audio was available (one involving Race, the other Gender), Stokoe and Albert discuss a range of problems that CA analysis has located within policing and health care organizations. Focusing on a gap between guidance and practice in police training and evaluation and in health diagnosis and evaluation, they explain how CA analysis reveals that in actual interrogations and diagnostic interviews practitioners deviate from the protocols in ways that matter, both for the services clients receive and for their own careers, arguing that: 'CA has the power to reveal the inadequacy of standardization and written guidance' (p. 208). Their analysis shows how performance assessments based on role-playing and other conceptual 'tools' differ from what actually happens in ways that make assessments based on such tools deeply flawed, and demonstrates that CA has the 'power' to reveal that such misunderstandings about the way interaction works have become embedded in social institutions and their methods of evaluation in ways that add to the burden of disadvantage.

It should be added that EM/CA is/are not a method, as Coser assumed, but many methods driven by a theoretical insight, the whole of which had its problem clearly in view from the beginning. That problem was always at one level focused on social inequality and the particular racial inequalities and heightened awareness of them that were experienced by its first Jewish authors (Duck & Rawls, 2023). Garfinkel's early realization that the way inequality is reproduced in social interaction was being hidden by conventional approaches fueled a broad challenge – to rewrite social science and sociology in particular – such that the processes of social fact making that are hidden by conventional methods and theories can be brought out into the light of day – inspected – and understood. Sacks extended the challenge to rewriting linguistics as an enterprise reliant on interaction and hence also inherently sociological.

This book delivers on the promise of critical CA to demonstrate how inequalities are embedded in talk and interaction, in many different ways. Chapter 8, '*I'm Just Saying*: Being Explicit in a Mixed-Race Conversation about Racism', by Sarah Chepkirui Creider, takes a close look at conversations about racism that took place in 2020 as people all over the world inspired by BlackLivesMatter protests tried to come to terms with the murder of George Floyd and other Black men and women by the police in the US. We learn that a CA analysis of the turns of Black speakers in such conversations indicates that they orient to the reality that the White participants they are talking to do not share their experience of the world. When they talk about their experiences of Race with White people, this awareness is marked through the placement of accounts and formulations that would be unnecessary between participants who can assume they share the same social experiences. Creider formulates this as a visible marker that participants are not able to achieve what Garfinkel called 'Trust Conditions', leading to troubles in the talk.

That aspects of turn-taking can be analyzed to reveal difficulties in talk about racism, because accounts and formulations only appear when speakers orient the proximity of trouble, or a lack of shared understanding, is important. For White speakers who are not sure when they are being naïve about Race, being on the lookout for such occurrences and *taking them seriously as evidence of a problem* would be one quick and easy way of being less naïve and incompetent and more successfully anti-racist in such encounters.

From Chapter 9, 'Using Racial Incompetence as a Comedic Device and Tacit Method of Anti-Racist Education', by Lillian Cheeks and Kevin Whitehead, we learn that sitcoms can be a useful tool for teaching anti-racism. The authors demonstrate how comedy sketches can accomplish this through the enactment of sequences of talk in which actors perform White incompetence. Audiences learn to recognize this interactional incompetence through its humorous juxtaposition with the responses of Black performers. Again, the analysis makes use of CA detail to illuminate what is going on in these episodes and show how they illustrate the racism embedded in ordinary everyday sequences as performed by White actors.

We also learn in Chapter 2, 'Investigating Raciolinguistic Ideologies in Interaction', by Nadja Tadic, Hansun Zhang Waring and Elizabeth Reddington, about ways in which raciolinguistic ideologies work to position non-White speakers as inferior/not-American – and as inferior speakers of English. CA analysis reveals that second language learners have different experiences in the US depending on whether they are White or non-White, because Americans take for granted that White people are American (speakers of English), and that non-White people are not-American (and therefore not speakers of English). This creates many absurdities that second language teachers must explain to their students, involving them in awkward explanations, e.g. of why, because Americans will assume that White Europeans *can* speak English, they will need to explain that they do *not* speak English or Americans will assume they do. Whereas non-White speakers will find that no matter how proficient in English they become, Americans will likely treat them as if they cannot speak English – often even speaking to them loudly and slowly as if they could not hear. This of course involves the teacher in giving explanations like '[you are White] you look American', which replicate US racism in an effort to help students manage it.

A detailed analysis of how 'mocking repeats' and nonsense syllables are being used in aggressive racial confrontations in ways that make use of the sequential obligations relevant to 'repair' appears in Chapter 3, 'Racist Renditions: Mock Language in Interaction', by Elliott Hoey and Chase Raymond. The details of 'mock language' are treated by Hoey and Raymond '*as an interactional practice* – that is, as produced and understood in the service of action' (p. 51). Using data from a corpus of racist/racialized altercations on video that are circulating on social media, the authors use CA, as they put it, 'to uncover how mock-language practices can emerge within, and be fitted to, the particulars of their interactional environments…within the immediacy of heated exchanges…to maintain "White public space"' (p. 51). Preserving White public spaces is a White supremacist objective that the CA analysis in this chapter shows can be achieved by mocking repeats.

How does this work? There is, the authors note, a 'family resemblance with the sequential organization of repair' (p. 66) that enables the aggression. Repair is, they point out, considered a 'priority activity' (Schegloff *et al.*, 1977: 720) in that '[i]ts actions can supersede other actions, in the sense that they can replace or defer whatever else was due next … It is the only action type that we know of now which has this property' (Schegloff, 2000: 208). Repair can be inserted anywhere. 'Whatever is said', they argue, 'a next speaker can always say "Pardon?", for example, thereby initiating repair and halting – albeit momentarily – the trajectory of action in progress' (p. 66). A mocking repeat, which takes the form of other-initiated repair is thus a powerful interactional move *that obligates those being mocked to respond*. According to Hoey and Raymond, these 'racist renditions … resemble other-initiated repair in both its action context non-specificity, as well as in the sequence-/action-halting power it wields' (p. 66). In other words, mocking renditions can be used almost anywhere to trap persons of color in sequences of interaction in which they are 'visibly constrained by rigid norms of linguistic purity, but white linguistic disorder goes unchallenged' (Zentella, 2003: 53, as cited in Hoey & Raymond, this volume, p. 66).

While the authors argue that the practice is 'usable "anywhere"', 'part of its power as a tool of domination is that it is not usable by "anyone" (cf. "true" other-initiated repair). Rather, it is asymmetrically available to members of the relational pair dominant language speaker–subordinate(d) language speaker' to create White linguistic disorder (p. 66). In the data they analyzed, the device is 'used by speakers of "standard" US English against those who are raciolinguistically categorized as e.g. Spanish(-speaking) and Chinese(-speaking) – members who are unable to deploy the same devices in return' (pp. 66). In other words, it is a device for use by White speakers of standard English against non-White non-standard English speakers (who are often assumed not to be speaking standard English even when they are). The authors argue that this use 'recalls Sacks' (1992: 394) description of certain membership categories as "protected against induction", such that evidence to the contrary (i.e. Target's use of "standard" English) does not foreclose the usability of a (raciolinguistic) category' (p. 66). The analysis demonstrates how conversational preference orders, which are ordinarily used to structure talk to create shared meaning, can be misused by people to marginalize Others – trapping them into preferred responses that further enable their own marginalization. It would certainly be helpful to be able to recognize such aggressive strategies and develop ways of responding or not responding (Rawls & Duck, 2017) that could neutralize the aggression.

CA analysis of how news reports can present the use of nonstandard English speech (in this case Hawaiian speech) as deficient, presented by Scott Saft in Chapter 4, 'Talk in Local News Broadcasts: Reinforcing Negative Views towards the Hawaiian Language', shows how the sequential organization of news presentations, combined with the choice of descriptors, and formulations of Hawaiian speech, are used to construct the use of Hawaiian speech in public as rebellious and bad – instead of recognizing that such speech exercises a right to use one of the two official languages of the state of Hawaii. According to Saft, news reports are candidates for such CA analysis because, 'Although the news reports considered in this chapter do not center on exchanges of interaction, there is a parallel with talk radio in that the sequential organization of the reports derives directly from the fact that representatives of the institution, anchors, reporters, producers, etc. possess the institutional power to control how the reports are organized' (p. 88).

It is this ability to organize information sequentially, Saft argues, 'including the strategic insertion of voice-overs with practices such as categories, formulations and reported speech that construct content that reinforces power asymmetries in society' (pp. 88–89) which creates the appearance that speaking Hawaiian in public is 'controversial' and 'rebellious' – thus devaluing the speech of legislators and other public figures when they do speak Hawaiian in public. Without appearing to take a side on the political issues, such practices of news presentation, according to Saft, 'make it possible to portray attempts to speak Hawaiian as problematic and to avoid devoting significant time and space to consideration of rights', while at the same time allowing news organizations to claim that they are not taking sides: 'These practices, in sum, help to reinforce the current asymmetrical relationship between Hawaiian and English' (p. 89).

Chapter 5, 'Inequality in Action: Granting Emergency Service Requests in a Highly Resource-Constrained Context', by Catherine Tam, Kevin Whitehead and Geoffrey Raymond, looks closely at the role of turn-taking in managing trust in the context of emergency and service calls, finding that (1) a 'caller's willingness to end the call and await the arrival of the service reflects their trust that institutional actors will fulfill the obligations entailed by the call-taker's granting of the service' (pp. 91–92). This is consistent with previous research that shows (2) callers 'displaying "trust" that the emergency service institution will function as expected as a background condition for the accomplishment of the actions of requesting and providing services (cf. Garcia & Parmer, 1999; Heritage, 1984; Watson, 2009)' (p. 91). By contrast, where callers may not trust the service providing institution – which is common for those who experience marginalization – and where they 'may have grounds to anticipate that the fulfillment of this "social contract" may be so substantially delayed as to call into question its status as an *emergency* service' (p. 92), calls are marked with 'indications of contingency', 'tag questions' and other practices *to manage this lack of trust*. In other words, callers who lack trust in the service provider mark that lack of trust with indications of their reluctance to end the call.

Tam, Whitehead and Raymond maintain that the solution to the problem of trust in service calls is not for call-takers to speak differently to callers, but rather, to *deal with the underlying inequalities* in the society that lead to this lack of trust in the first place. The point of the CA analysis of the calls is to establish that such lack of trust *does interfere* with business as usual – and that when the business as usual is emergency services *the consequences can be dire.*[6]

Chapter 6, 'Delegitimizing the "Other" at US Congressional Town Hall Meetings', by Di Yu, demonstrates that a prevalent strategy used in such political meetings is very much at odds with the stated democratic purposes of those meetings. The strategy is to delegitimize the opponent – often a marginalized Other – and if they are not already marginalized, to marginalize them through the talk – which can be done to almost anyone.

Yu observed in these meetings 'instances of citizens delegitimizing the "other" who come from different backgrounds or hold opposing views by portraying them as threats' (p. 127). Apparently, such 'citizens are often joined by the MOC [Member of Congress] or other attendees to collaboratively delegitimize the "other"' (p. 127). In doing this work of Othering, Yu found that 'citizens use categorical shorthands (e.g. gender movement, AOC, Muslim interest, Pelosi) to encode the "other" as threatening, dangerous, uninformed, biased or potentially harmful', and that 'such portrayals of the "other" can also be used as bases for requesting political action against them' (p. 127).

Many emphasize the role of such meetings in making politics democratic, arguing according to Yu that 'inclusivity of diverse perspectives in deliberation and policy making can facilitate the achievement of more equitable outcomes', which leads to the perception that they are 'a required component of public deliberation forums such as congressional town halls' (pp. 127–128). However, Yu notes that what often occurs in such meetings has the opposite effect, concluding that: 'practices exemplifying deeply rooted differences among citizens abound, and those who have access to the town hall floor have the potential opportunity to assert power over the "other" and even enact political actions against them' (p. 128), thus nullifying the potential benefits of a town meeting forum.[7]

Finally, Chapter 7, 'Negotiating Power Inequalities in Joint Decision-Making in a Faculty Meeting', by Innhwa Park and Santoi Wagner, uses a CA analysis to demonstrate how power differentials conferred by privilege can be neutralized through turn-taking in a meeting between high school teachers and administrators. Park and Wagner note that meetings are essential to the work of many organizations, but that they often involve power relations that can make participation difficult. They explain that with regard to faculty meetings (at a high school not a university, which would be quite different): 'In particular, faculty meetings, the context of this study, constitute a large amount of work time for many teachers and are a significant channel of organizational communication. Effective faculty meetings play a central role in improving professional competence, fostering communication and building community' (p. 133).

As Park and Wagner note, teachers know the most about the classroom but have the least power to make decisions in such meetings: 'Thus, decision-making at faculty meetings can involve an ongoing power struggle ... among participants with varying levels of institutional authority and domain-specific knowledge' (p. 134). The authors do a turn-by-turn analysis of how such power relations are managed in an actual meeting during which decisions about teaching are made, through the lens of what they call 'deontic authority' (Stevanovic, 2018; Stevanovic & Peräkylä, 2012). In so doing, they demonstrate ways that a teacher with less institutional power than others in the meeting can design and position her turns sequentially to 'balance compliance and resistance' to the authority displayed by higher ranking participants and 'move her proposal forward'. This balance is accomplished through small details of turn construction that would be missed by a non-CA analysis. The authors note that the teacher in their data 'shows compliance by acknowledging the broader issues raised by the assistant superintendent and/or the department head and affiliating with their stance towards these issues', while also conveying 'resistance by challenging the relevance of the broader issues to her specific proposal and moving to close the sequences concerning them' (p. 151). Indications of compliance are followed by returns to her proposal.

Overall, Park and Wagner argue that the sequential design of these turns is critical to their success, noting that 'the teacher orients to her display of resistance as delicate: she delivers disagreements in a dispreferred manner with mitigations and self-repairs (Pomerantz, 1984) and/or rejects problematizations by aligning with the more powerful institutional voice (Ford, 2008: 53–91)' (p. 151). This 'balancing act' helps get the other participants refocused on her own proposal. The placement of the hesitations, mitigations and self-repair in her turns is critical to her success but would either be 'cleaned up' (not transcribed) and thus not appear at all, or be considered irrelevant, in most non-CA analysis of these meetings.

### The Theoretical/Political Relevance of Interactional/Sequential Detail

When ethnomethodology and conversation analysis began making their mark – and were so roundly attacked in the late 1960's and early 1970's – the US was at an inflection point. The Civil Rights Act had passed in 1965, Title IX became law in 1972, and Vietnam veterans spurred on the passage of two Disabilities Acts in 1973 and 1974. In addition to Race and Gender, these new laws guaranteed equal rights to many categories of marginalized and disabled people. In formal law, the US made a great leap forward. But progress foundered in the face of a concerted and organized White conservative effort to evade and undermine equal rights in combination with deeply embedded differences in how people in different categories experience social interaction. The possibilities for a new era of equality were endless. Making that a reality, however, would have required a broad and meaningful acknowledgment that US society is shot through and through with social practices and expectations that embed racism, power and inequality. That did not happen.

A book that showcases the relevance of CA to issues of Race, Power and Marginality more generally, as this one does, is very timely: we are at another inflection point with regard to racism and civil rights – this time worldwide. Whether we go forward or back depends a great deal on whether we have learned anything about how Race and inequality work through social interaction in the meanwhile and whether we are ready to listen to marginalized voices with awareness of those processes (Rawls, 2000). There is the social will in this moment (again) to do something about racism and inequality. But, without coming to terms with the tacit racism being taken for granted in interaction every day, we will keep repeating the cycles of denial and repression we have been through so many times.

First and foremost, the confrontation with racism we so desperately need to have requires recognizing that and how racism is embedded in ordinary interaction. Unless we accept that every one of us in 'doing being ordinary', as Sacks put it, engages in tacit embedded practices that marginalize and racialize – unless we stop searching for individual racists and take a good look at ourselves and our own daily social practices – the future will not only be like the past, but active attempts to suppress change will continue to grow. Nostalgia for the days when Black people 'knew their place', Women 'stayed at home' and the Disabled were 'neither seen nor heard', now animates enough US citizens to threaten the stability of the nation.

For those who are aware of the role Race and inequality have played in US history and scholarship, this will not be altogether surprising. The White predominantly male sons of Protestant ministers, members of a society that worships Individualism, took a Social Contract Theory of society from Durkheim (a marginalized Jewish man), which established sociology as the study of social facts created by the collective efforts of members bound by an implicit social contract, and reduced it to an approach in which the individual and individual agency are said to face off in a perennial struggle against social structure: as if the social Self and social Institutions were not both the result of cooperative social interaction. That the prominent students of these early sociologists led an effort during WWII (that carried over into the post-war and beyond) to strip social science of any interest in social interaction and social fact making processes (Rawls, 2018), literally stripping it of 'the social', is also not surprising.

That those invested in defending the conceptual models laid down by this tradition made a point of criticizing EM/CA was predictable. The CA studies represented in this book challenge the most basic assumptions of their critics. EM/CA follow Durkheim (1893) in arguing that the Individual and Individual Reason are social achievements – social facts – and therefore cannot be the starting points for argument (as they are in many disciplines) (Rawls, 2022b).

Although the CA argument that meaning making can be documented in the relationship between turns in sequences of interaction is entirely new, the argument that meaning making can be studied empirically has a venerable history. Durkheim used detailed empirical descriptions to argue that the concepts that comprise human reason (cause, force, etc.) are created in interaction through the use of what he called 'constitutive practices' (Durkheim, 1912; Rawls, 1996, 2009). It was also Durkheim's (1893) position that processes of social fact making leave empirical evidence of their requirements. What he called 'self-regulating constituitive practices' would self-sanction when their implicit social requirements are not met, leaving sanctions as empirical markers. His most important argument, however, was that sets of self-regulating constitutive practices would develop in diverse modern societies around occupations and sciences as a new way of making social facts and organizing society – and that sociology should study them (Rawls, 2021).

EM/CA has led the way in following up on what Garfinkel (2002) called 'Durkheim's Aphorism': that the processes of making social facts is sociology's fundamental subject. Self-regulating practices have prerequisites – implicit conditions of contract – that include the need for reciprocity. Durkheim spoke of equality and justice. And when those prerequisites are not met, the practices self-sanction, marking them visibly as troubled in ways that can be empirically documented. Accounts, formulations, justifications and other evidence of trouble mark such failures. As Creider shows in Chapter 8, when prerequisites cannot be met between Black and White speakers because they don't experience the same social world, and therefore cannot be talking about the same thing, troubles are obvious and evident in their talk and marked by Black speakers as such with accounts and formulations. Because they don't share the same expectations, trust conditions cannot be met.

It is important to underscore Stokoe and Albert's point that rather than accepting that CA should be held accountable to the rhetoric of 'big questions', those who pose those so-called big questions should be held accountable to the findings of EM/CA – to what we have discovered about how things actually work – and to an informed understanding of just how much tacit inequality framed those 'big questions' that we need to escape from (p. 218).

The conventional argument seems to be that reasoning on the basis of general ideas is valid – but that it is not valid to find out how things actually work and then demonstrate how inequalities can get in the way and create trouble. The latter addresses a huge question. Why the fact that it does so on the basis of empirical description, and/or what people like to call 'micro' data, should be a problem is strange. The size of the data has never been an issue in the natural sciences. No one dismisses research on molecules because they are small.

EM/CA launched a stiff challenge to most existing disciplines – including sociology and linguistics – and they did so on the basis of a heightened awareness of interaction that was not familiar to the majority. A lot was and still is at stake, so it is not too surprising that the challenge was resisted. At this point, however, it is past time to recognize the power of EM/CA. As Sacks argued in 1967–68 (unpublished manuscript, Garfinkel Archive), if a response by a second person to something said by a first person achieves its sense only as a display of understanding of the first utterance and not from grammar or syntax, and if such displays are expected and even preferred, then something is going on in conversation that cannot be explained by linguistics. The upshot, according to Sacks, is that talk is fundamentally interactional. What words mean and sentences/utterances signify is a situated interactional achievement – and therefore conversation and talk are a proper subject of sociology – which the chapters in this book demonstrate, in addition to showing the utility of CA for addressing questions of Race and inequality.

The chapters in this book show that CA and the detailed analysis it delivers can reveal how Race and racism are produced in social interaction. They also reveal the subtleties of Power and how it can be neutralized in talk. They reveal ways in which asymmetries in society can make trouble in talk and how the use of models/generalizations can amplify disadvantage. Social meaning is created through the use of practices bound by tacit Social Contract. Living in the world unequally makes sharing the Trust Conditions of that tacit agreement all but impossible to achieve. Words and sequences literally mean different things for people with contrasting racialized experiences and differential social access, and that this is the case is marked in the talk and can be empirically documented. How this order has been overlooked for so long is something of a puzzle, but the refusal to look at what people are doing in conversation and interaction, criticizing those who do look, and insisting that concepts and ideas should stand in as models of reality, certainly has a lot to do with it.

*Anne Rawls*

## Notes

(1) I have adopted the practice of capitalizing terms for key social facts such as Race, Self and Other marginalized categories in all my publications to indicate the socially made, contingent, social fact status of those categories.

(2) There is something important to be said here about Goffman's argument in *Stigma* about passing and marginality – basically that everyone is passing and consequently anyone can be marginalized. Most people don't know that Goffman was working with Garfinkel on this question, and while many know he was working with Sacks, they don't typically make much of it. But Goffman and Garfinkel were working together in 1963 to make an important argument 'on passing' that is relevant to the argument of this chapter (Rawls, 2023). Goffman argued that because social identities need to be performed to social criteria – and no one perfectly fits the criteria – we are all to some degree passing to achieve identity. In other words, because we are all orienting to categories that are somewhat idealized in order to achieve social identities (or roles) that no one really ever exactly fits, we are all engaged in passing. The difference is that some of us succeed in 'passing' and avoid the stigma, while those who cannot pass become stigmatized, and are therefore more aware of what they do. This makes research on the marginalized (or deviant) central to key sociological questions about the rest of us whom Goffman and Garfinkel called 'normals'. Garfinkel called those with heightened awareness 'perspicuous settings' for learning about what is normally taken for granted. Furthermore, because we all pass to some extent, and are subject to the same contradictions in trying to distinguish ourselves from others to emphasize our better fit to the norm, seeing past what we take for granted is not only necessary in order to stop Othering people – it is necessary to stop living in a state of self-contradiction.

(3) Materials from these meetings are in the Garfinkel Archive.

(4) Often mistakenly called a short story, this early article by Garfinkel was an ethnography of an incident he had observed (see Rawls, 2022a).

(5) Of course, when Coser refers to the quantitative measurement of 'variables' that are defined *a priori*, then he is correct that theory must come first, and that letting such methods drive theory has been a highly problematic and circular process. However, his identification of EM/CA as a method is incorrect, and his claim that it lacks theory is also wrong. EM/CA is an inherently theoretical approach that generated many different methods and findings. The big problem for Coser and many others is that the theoretical premise of EM/CA, that meaningful social facts are the end product of ordering practices used in social interaction (that are self-sanctioning in Durkheim's sense), conflicts with their own mainstream theory that social action is inherently disorderly in its own right – and only rendered orderly through the application of social theory and its derivative methods (by the practices of professional sociologists), which Garfinkel (1988) referred to as the 'Parsons' Plenum' approach.

(6) Prior research has also documented that dispatchers tend not to trust minority callers, and that this lack of trust often results in lack of service in response to those calls (Manning, 2000).

(7) Yu recommends a solution: 'To move citizens out of the extreme divisiveness, those hosting such events can consider instituting deliberative structures to facilitate citizens' participation toward productive, inclusive outcomes and creating opportunities for further civic education for citizens (Knobloch & Gastil, 2015)' (p. 128). The problem with this hope is that it is a current GOP strategy to maximize divisiveness because it gets them votes. The findings of the chapter, in other words, are not

evidence of a failure – but are in fact a successful outcome of political strategy to divide the American population by Race and marginalized categories. There is a history that explains this. It is called *The Southern Strategy*.

## References

Duck, W. and Rawls A. (2023) Black and Jewish: 'Double consciousness' inspired a qualitative interactional approach that centers Race, marginality, and justice. *Qualitative Sociology* 46 (2), 163–198.

Eisenmann, C. and Rawls A. (2023) The continuity of Garfinkel's approach: Seeking ways of 'making the phenomena available again' through the experience and usefulness of trouble. In P. Sormani and D. Vom Len (eds) *The Anthem Companion to Harold Garfinkel* (pp. 19–41). Anthem Press.

Eisenmann, C., Mlynář, J., Turowetz, J. and Rawls, A. (2023) 'Machine down': Making sense of human-computer interaction – Garfinkel's research on ELIZA and LYRIC from 1967 to 1969 and its contemporary relevance. *AI & Society*.

Durkheim, E. (1893) *de la Division du Travail Social*. Alcan. (English Translation: *The Division of Labor in Society, Translated 1933 by Simpson*. Free Press).

Garfinkel, H. (1940) Color trouble. *Opportunity*, May.

Garfinkel, H. (1963) A conception, of and experiments with, 'trust' as a condition of stable concerted actions. In O.J. Harvey (ed.) *Motivation and Social Interaction: Cognitive Determinants* (pp. 187–238). Ronald Press Company.

Garfinkel, H. (1967) *Studies in Ethnomethodology*. Prentice-Hall.

Garfinkel, H. (1988) Evidence for locally produced, naturally accountable phenomena of order, logic, reason, meaning, method, etc. in and as of the essential quiddity of immortal ordinary society, (I of IV): An announcement of studies. *Sociological Theory* 6 (1), 103–109.

Garfinkel, H. (2002) *Ethnomethodology's Program: Working Out Durkheim's Aphorism* (edited and with an introduction by A. Rawls). Rowman and Littlefield.

Goffman, E. (1963) *Stigma: Notes on the Management of Spoiled Identity*. Simon & Schuster.

Rawls, A. (1987) The interaction order sui generis: Goffman's contribution to social theory. *Sociological Theory* 5 (2), 136–149.

Rawls, A. (1990) Emergent sociality: A dialectic of commitment and order. *Symbolic Interaction* 13 (1), 63–82.

Rawls, A. (1996) Durkheim's epistemology: The neglected argument. *American Journal of Sociology* 102 (2), 430–482.

Rawls, A. (2000) Race as an interaction order phenomenon: W.E.B. Du Bois's 'double consciousness' thesis revisited. *Sociological Theory* 18 (2), 239–272.

Rawls, A. (2004) Le falace de l'abstraction mal place (Situated practice and modernity: Practice vs concepts. Not published in English). *The Mauss Review* 24.

Rawls, A. (2009) *Epistemology and Practice: Durkheim's the Elementary Forms of Religious/Life*. Cambridge University Press.

Rawls, A. (2018) The wartime narrative in US sociology 1940–1947: Stigmatizing qualitative sociology in the name of 'science'. *The European Journal of Social Theory* 59 (1).

Rawls, A. (2021) The structure of social facts: Self, objects and action as products of reciprocity and cooperation in constitutive practices. *Mauss Review International – Anti-Utilitarian Interventions in the Social Sciences* 1, 181–200.

Rawls, A. (2022a) Harold Garfinkel's focus on racism, inequality, and social justice: The early years 1939–1952. In D. Maynard and J. Heritage (eds) *The Ethnomethodology Program: Legacies and Prospects* (pp. 90–113). Cambridge University Press.

Rawls, A. (2022b) Situating Goffman's "Interaction Orders" in Durkheim's social fact lineage. Grounding an alternate sociology of modernity in heightened awareness of interaction. *Etnografia e ricerca qualitativa, Rivista quadrimestrale* 2022 (1), 27-62. https://doi.org/10.3240/103744

Rawls, A. (2023) The Goffman-Garfinkel correspondence: Planning 'on passing'. *Etnografia e ricerca qualitativa* March (1), 173–215.

Rawls, A. and Duck, W. (2017) 'Fractured reflections' of high status Black male presentations of self: Non-recognition of identity as a tacit form of institutional racism. *Sociological Focus* 50 (1), 36–51.

Turowetz, J. and Rawls, A. (2021) The development of Garfinkel's 'trust' argument from 1947 to 1967: Demonstrating how inequality disrupts sense and self-making. *Journal of Classical Sociology* 21 (1), 3–37.

# Series Editors' Preface

A number of years ago, one of us (AP) was on an interdisciplinary panel discussing aspects of medical communication. After the panel, we reflected on the apparently odd state of affairs where the 'linguist', who might have been expected to deal with close linguistic data – detailed analysis of some form of medical communication – instead looked at broad sociological and political matters to do with the global spread of English. Looking at Hong Kong (a case of a doctor omitting the word for 'acute' in a referral letter because he couldn't think of the English term), South Africa (where nurses acted as translators between patients and English-speaking doctors) and Malaysia (where patients struggled to be understood by their English-trained doctors), the concern was with the role English played in the inequitable access to medical provision around the world. The 'sociologist', by contrast, used close analysis of the language of medical encounters to show how patients arrived at a point where they felt their concerns were being taken seriously and were potentially treatable (doctorable). Both seemed important concerns – the one a broad analysis using Foucault and theories or globalization among others (though arguably rather light on analysis), the other close textual accounts drawing on conversation analysis of doctor-patient recordings – but the fact that the linguist looked at wide social and political questions while the sociologist focused on key moments in spoken interaction seemed to go against common expectations.

The sociologist was John Heritage, who had taken over the mantle of the ethnomethodological interests of Harold Garfinkel at UCLA (Heritage 1984). The seemingly odd aspects of this panel debate interestingly reflect the origins of Garfinkel's own research while a doctoral student at Harvard. Garfinkel was concerned with identifying the 'Trust Conditions' (see Rawls' foreword to this book) needed to mitigate the types of inequalities in medical encounters the panel was discussing. As a young Jewish scholar, Garfinkel was acutely aware of the restrictive quota system limiting the number of Jews into post-WWII professional schools in the USA. His research sought to reproduce the discourse conditions of pre-medical school interviews and examine the additional anxiety they produced in minority candidates hyper-sensitive to the 'uncommon' expectations of the majority gatekeepers in these high-stakes interactions. The heightened anxiety and societal inequalities (re)produced in these institutional encounters also reflected what Du Bois described as a 'double consciousness' (Du Bois, [1903] 2007), in which the pressures of conformity to dominant norms served to undermine the bonds of racialized or ethnic minority community membership (Turowitz & Rawls, 2021). Identifying the language and discourse-embedded Trust Conditions necessary for more equitable encounters was thus a 'bottom-up' research agenda explcitly directed towards broader social justice goals that underpin the chapters of this book.

As Heap (1984: 169) succinctly notes, 'ethnomethodology is the study of how reasoning and activities are organizable, within the limits and resources of a culture, as rational, identifiable events and occurences'. Ethnomethodology thus eschews the large abstractions common to sociology – class, gender, race and so on – in favor of an understanding of practical everyday reasoning in face-to-face interaction. There are some parallels here (not often acknowledged) between ethnomethodology and Bourdieu's (1977) interest in *practice*: How do our everyday practices relate to wider social effects and how do such social relations in turn affect our practices? The notion of the *habitus* was developed to account for these processes. How, for example, are broader social inequalities realized in the everyday cultural practices of schooling? As conceived by Harvey Sacks, Emanuel Schegloff and Gail Jefferson, conversation analysis (CA) developed as a crucial means to investigate everyday social action by looking at conversations in close detail. A key theoretical principle of CA is that social order is produced and reproduced in apparently unimportant details of spoken interaction (Birkner *et al.*, 2020).

For applied linguists who encounter CA only as an apparently obsessive concern with adjacency pairs and a very time-consuming approach to transcription conventions for close analysis of data, it may come as a surprise that the origins of CA are in sociology, that some of its major figures (such as Heritage) are sociologists, and that it claims to deal with major social issues while engaging with the minutiae of conversational interaction. It is important to understand, therefore, that CA is not principally interested in analyzing conversations as the end point. In their book on spoken language – *conversational English* – aimed at language educators, Thornbury and Slade (2006) only devote a fairly small amount of space to conversation analysis: Not only is it one amongst several ways of looking at spoken data, but its central goal is not, in the end, to describe conversations but to shed light on wider social orders through this analysis. In his book on *spoken discourse*, by contrast, Rodney Jones (2016) has much more space for CA (and a clear explanation of these issues) because he is interested in the *consequentiality* of spoken discourse – the close analysis and larger implications, for example, of 'coming out' discourse – and thus the careful analysis of spoken discourse and its wider social effects.

The attention to detailed analysis in CA means that it appears on the radar of some applied linguists principally as a potential methodology: student/researchers ask us if CA might be a useful methodology for dealing with their research data, and we rightly caution them against its adoption for particular tasks: it's more detailed than you need, it takes too long, no reason to go into all that detail. Try critical discourse analysis (CDA) instead (both are often seen in these methodological terms) because you can get there more quickly without all the fiddly details. In his book on research methods in applied linguistics, Dörnyei (2007) only mentions CA once, as a type of highly specialized analysis of language data. CA is sometimes seen in the same light as Alison Lee's (1997) description of Systemic Functional Linguistic (SFL)-based genre literacies as a 'pedagogy of deferral': just as you're not literate until you've mastered the important genres, so CA asks us to wait, to be patient, to refrain from jumping to unwarranted conclusions until we've done the analysis properly. Like SFL, CA also seems at times open only to those who have done the intitiation ceremonies and are prepared to spend the hours following the prescribed forms of analysis. The point, however, as Schegloff (1997: 180) explains in a response to CDA critics who saw CA as blind to larger social forces, is that that although CA can lead to 'impatience in those who aspire to more global claims and assertions', detailed analysis of interactions that might at first sight seem unremarkable or easily characterizable, 'turn out to yield rather more complex, and differently complexioned, understandings'. This goes to the heart of a continuing concern in (critical) discourse analysis (Schegloff's comment is part of a series of exchanges over several years in the journal *Discourse and Society*): how much do we read into texts from our prior assumptions and how much can we read out of texts without prior assumptions?

It is a pity if CA is considered only in largely methodological terms, as a means to describe conversations in close detail. There are a number of ways that CA needs to be understood as a much broader enterprise, even if one does not share the same ethnomethodological framework and the tendency to suspend analysis of broader sociological categories. The questions that are basic to CA – how do we understand how the wider forces of the social order and the local practices of interaction are related? – remain crucial for an area such as applied linguistics. McNamara (2019) gives the example of road rules to explain this: on the one hand the explicit and codified rules of the road (which side to drive on, how fast to go, when you can overtake and so on), on the other hand the everyday practices of driving (adapting to other drivers, local conditions, passengers in the car). The question is how these interact. McNamara (2019) argues that this kind of understanding can be very useful for seeing how gender and sexuality are performatively realized. If we want to take Butler's (1997) understanding of how gender is produced in social life seriously, we can use CA to show these interactions at work on an everyday level. Like Hacking's (2004) argument that we need not just Foucault and not just Goffman but the two together – one to show us the macro-operations of discourse and power, the other to show us how this works at the micro-level of language – McNamara (2019) brings together CA with Butler's (1997) idea of performativity: if we want to see how subjectivities are called into being, we have to look at the micro-politics of language use to see how this actually works, how the 'turn-by-turn enactment of social positioning...closely parallels the notion of the endlessly iterated performativity of discourse' (McNamara, 2019: 220).

What makes this book particularly important – for this book series (where we have not published CA work previously) as well as for applied linguistics more generally – is that editors and authors have sought to extend these arguments by showing explicitly how the big issues of critical analysis – racism, for example – need to be understood through close analysis of daily interactions, to show how and why CA can indeed be a tool for critical analysis. While not from a CA lens, analyses of the interconnections between wider societal order and local practices have shed light on race and racism in previous books in this series. One example is Christopher Jenks' (2017) monograph, which draws on studies that through close readings of such data as advertisements, legal documents and interviews with language teachers help us to understand the normalization of inequity and subsequent production of racism. Similarly, Andrea Sterzuk was able to look carefully (again not CA, but certainly a detailed and revealing analysis) at the discourses of teachers in her (2011) study. Her participants were unaware of the concept of English language variation as applied to indigeneity and instead used terms such as 'deficit', 'lower language skills' and 'improper' (2011: 97–99) to describe the Indigenous English of their First Nations and Métis students, offering an easily identifiable connection to the formation of race and racial discrimination. Other books in the series have addressed dimensions of racial identity and identification in relation to being considered 'half' (young people of mixed backgrounds able to trade on their novel status in Japan but also denigrated as less than whole) (Kamada, 2010) or the intersectional relations between gender and race in English language learning in Japan and Australia (Takahashi, 2013).

This book is a welcome addition to our series because it helps tie these levels of analysis together, showing why close analysis of data is always important while we also maintain our focus on major processes of inequality and exclusion. As we consider the range of potential approaches to studying language and society, we wonder about the degree to which our understandings of injustice are better informed when we move our analysis from a broader lens to the fine-grained detail of CA. If there is a close CLLS series comparison to this discussion to be made, it would be in the recently published afterword by Rampton *et al.* (2023) and their advocacy for the 'Total Linguistic Fact' as a more complete frame of reference for understanding the micro-macro elements of sociolinguistic interaction and their potential adoption for transformative (additional) language pedagogies. CA, we should also note, has been used in many applied projects: Heritage's (2009) work on medical communication (the idea of doctorability, for example) being but one example. Conversation matters: 'every conversation we have involves issues of identity, agency and group affiliation; every conversation involves us in some way "putting ourselves on the line"; and every conversation demands from us that we *respond* to other people, not just in terms of what they are saying, but also in terms of who they are being' (Jones, 2016: 181). It is our hope, therefore that this book will be read not just by conversation analysts interested in seeing good examples of analysis, or in how the tenets of ethnomethodology can be challenged by bringing in social categories early in the analysis, but by a much broader range of people interested in questions such as racism that these chapters address, and in the challenge that these analyses pose across a wide range of institutional settings: unless we look closely at the data, our sweeping assertions may rest on fragile ground.

*Alastair Pennycook*
*Brian Morgan*
*Ryuko Kubota*

## References

Birkner, K., Auer, P., Bauer, A. and Kotthoff, H. (2020) *Einführung in die Konversationsanlayse*. Walter de Gruyter.

Bourdieu, P. (1977) *Outline of a Theory of Practice*. Cambridge University Press.
Butler, J. (1997) *Excitable Speech: A Politics of the Performative*. Routledge
Dörnyei, Z. (2007) *Research Methods in Applied Linguistics*. Oxford University Press.
Du Bois, W. E. B. ([1903] 2007) *The Souls of Black Folk*. Oxford University Press.
Hacking, I. (2004) Between Michel Foucault and Erving Goffman: Between discourse in the abstract and face-to-face interaction. *Economy and Society* 33 (3), 277–302.
Heap, J.L. (1984) Ethnomethodology and education: Possibilities. *Journal of Educational Thought* 18, 168–171.
Heritage, J. (1984) *Garfinkel and Ethnomethodology*. Polity Press.
Heritage, J. (2009) Negotiating the legitimacy of medical problems: A multi-phase concern for patients and physicians. In D. Brashers and D. Goldsmith (eds) *Communicating to Manage Health and Illness* (pp. 147–164). Routledge.
Jones, R. (2016) *Spoken Discourse*. Bloomsbury.
Kamada, L.D. (2010) *Hybrid Identities and Adolescent Girls: Being 'Half' in Japan*. Multilingual Matters.
Lee, A. (1997) Questioning the critical: Linguistics, literacy and curriculum. In S. Muspratt, A. Luke and P. Freebody (eds) *Constructing Critical Literacies: Teaching and Learning Textual Practice* (pp. 409–432). Allen & Unwin.
McNamara, T. (2019) *Language and Subjectivity*. Cambridge University Press.
Rampton, B., Cooke, M., Leung, C., Bryers, D., Winstanley, B. and Holmes, S. (2023) Afterword: Localising (socio)linguistic citizenship. In J. Gspandl, C. Korb, A. Heiling and E.J. Erling (eds) *The Power of Voice in Transforming Multilingual Societies* (pp. 211–228). Multilingual Matters.
Schegloff, E. (1997) Whose text? Whose context? *Discourse and Society* 8, 165–187.
Sterzuk, A. (2011) *The Struggle for Legitimacy: Indigenized Englishes in Settler Schools*. Multilingual Matters.
Takahashi, K. (2013) *Language Learning, Gender and Desire: Japanese Women on the Move*. Multilingual Matters.
Thornbury, S. and Slade, D. (2006) *Conversation: From Description to Pedagogy*. Cambridge University press.
Turowitz, J. and Rawls, A.W. (2021) The development of Garfinkel's 'Trust' argument from 1947 to 1967: Demonstrating how inequality disrupts sense and self-making. *Journal of Classical Sociology* 21, 3–37.

# 1 Introduction

Nadja Tadic and Hansun Zhang Waring

For many, the trademark of conversation analysis (CA) is its preoccupation with the details of social interaction – its power of micro-analysis. Likewise for many, this 'micro' reputation has limited CA's ability to tackle 'macro' issues such as inequality and injustice, or the unequal and ultimately unfair treatment of groups with (historically) restricted access to sociocultural resources and power. By launching the critical CA program, we wish to challenge this assumption and demonstrate otherwise. Our endeavor is by no means an innovation. Engaging critical issues has been part of CA's DNA since its inception, although such efforts have typically been made on isolated terrains and often recognized as notable exceptions. Our goal is to consolidate these efforts and invigorate a comprehensive movement towards solidifying CA's statute as a uniquely revelatory approach to illuminating how issues of inequality and injustice are (re)produced, resisted and/or transformed in talk-in-interaction. Importantly, we do not proffer 'critical CA' as a distinct methodological framework. Rather, we aim to illustrate how CA – as it was originally envisioned – can be used to explore critical research questions. This endeavor may be characterized by researchers, including by the authors in this volume, in various ways, ranging from 'ethnomethodological CA' to 'critically informed CA'. At times, authors also complement their sequential analyses with other relevant frameworks, most notably membership categorization analysis (MCA), which readily lends itself to investigations of social categories such as race and gender – the 'usual suspects' in critical research. Such rich and exciting analytic diversity notwithstanding, we intend this to be overall, and first and foremost, a *CA* volume on critical research. In this introduction chapter, we first introduce CA in its original, uncaricatured form. To further contextualize CA's critical potential, we review the debates surrounding CA's limitations over the years as well as a burgeoning body of research that uses CA to engage issues of a critical nature. We end this introduction with an overview of this volume, highlighting the specific ways in which each chapter furthers our agenda in solidifying CA as a not only legitimate but also compelling tool for investigating important societal problems.

## Conversation Analysis

Founded by sociologists Harvey Sacks, Emmanuel Schegloff and Gail Jefferson in the 1960s, CA is the study of social interaction as it *actually* happens in its natural habitat. More importantly, it is the study of such happenings in participants' terms, not via analysts' theorizing. As conversation analysts, we are interested in excavating the tacit methods and procedures participants deploy to get things done in social interaction, be that getting the floor to tell a story, launching a complaint, responding to a compliment or exiting a conversation. As a form of ethnomethodology (Garfinkel, 1967), CA rests on a set of assumptions that prioritize analytic induction (ten Have, 2007) and participant orientations (Schegloff & Sacks, 1973): (1) social interaction is orderly at all points, i.e. no detail can be dismissed *a priori*; (2) order is constituted by the participants, not conceptualized by the analysts; (3) such order is discoverable and describable through close scrutiny of the details of interaction. These assumptions permeate and govern various aspects of CA's methodology.

First, a CA investigation does not typically begin with a specific research question, which would necessarily dismiss certain details *a priori*. Rather, a research focus or question would emerge from detailed observations of interactions. To further avoid dismissing any details *a priori*, we would also need to obtain audio/video recordings of those interactions for repeated inspection. In a similar vein, our transcripts would need to capture, to the greatest extent possible, a full range of interactional features, such as volume, pitch, pace, intonation, overlap, inbreath, smiley voice, and the length of silence (see Appendix) as well as embodied conduct (see Appendices of individual chapters). Second, a CA investigation does not involve interpreting or fitting preformulated concepts or categories to specific instances in the data. After all, order is constituted by the participants themselves, not conceptualized by the analysts. Rather than engage in the exercise of coding then, 'our job is to crack the codes of social interaction' (Waring, 2016: 47) – codes oriented to by the participants themselves. As such, any pre-existing finding such as 'X does Y' is not grounds for claiming that this X in this particular case also does Y. Finally, a CA investigation entails discovering and describing the codes or order through a close look at the minute details of everyday life to see things that 'we could not, by imagination, assert were there' (Sacks, 1984: 25). It is in these minute details that evidence is located for how social actions such as requesting or complaining are produced and understood by the participants themselves. We may come to understand, for example, that 'Do you know what happened?' in a particular instance works as a pre-announcement rather than a solicitation of information because it is preceded by some pre-telling of an event, delivered with a particular prosodic package, and responded to with 'what' rather than a report of what happened. In other words, by inspecting a full range of details of X in its sequential context, we obtain a glimpse into the 'order' in the participants' own terms. As Schegloff and Sacks (1973) famously write:

> in so far as the materials we worked with exhibited orderliness, they did so not only to us, indeed not in the first place for us, but for the co-participants who had produced them.
>
> (1973: 290)

As can be seen, these methodological features of CA neither explicitly nor implicitly exclude its deployment to engage 'macro' issues. In fact, the details to be documented and attended to on their own terms, as constituted by the participants themselves, are precisely where the macro resides. In Leiter's (1980) words:

> [ethnomethodology] is the study of the basis of social structure as it exists for the layman and the social scientist. ... it brings macro processes back to where they really count – people's everyday lives. Ethnomethodologists are interested in social forces at the level of everyday life and take the position that if they cannot be found there, they are found only in the imagination of sociologists.
>
> (1980: 34)

By taking a great deal of power out of the analysts' hands and replacing it with a tremendous amount of responsibility – to discover and describe, not catalog and interpret – the CA mentality is utterly anti-elitist and radically democratic, in that every single turn is an opportunity to revolutionize the participants' understanding of the interaction so far and of the social world, including such matters as epistemics, morality and ethics. In fact, one might find some lovely symmetry between this sentiment and Garfinkel's roots as a Jewish boy growing up in a marginalized community in New Jersey, whose 1940 ethnographic observation of passengers on a bus negotiating racial segregation with the driver and police was subsequently published twice in collections of short stories (Anne Rawls, personal communication, 01/30/2023; vom Lehn, 2014: 19). It is not by coincidence then that ethnomethodology, as the people's methods, has always treated the minute details of everyday life as the locus for a wide range of social problems (Maynard, 1988).

## Critical Analysis and CA: The Classic Debate

Even though everyday life is permeated by critical issues of inequality and injustice, researchers have long debated CA's ability to examine such issues in the details of everyday social interaction. One oft-cited debate on the relationship between critical analysis and CA consisted of a series of articles by Emanuel Schegloff, Margaret Wetherell and Michael Billig featured in *Discourse & Society* between 1997 and 1999. While these exchanges seemed to be sparked off by Schegloff's (1997) paper on CA's possible contributions to critical analysis, they were also part of larger discussions on the (in)compatibility between 'formal' and 'political' approaches to discourse analysis. In fact, Schegloff's (1997) paper 'Whose text? Whose context?' was initially prepared for one such discussion – a colloquium, organized by Claire Kramsch and Ruth Wodak for the 1996 American Association of Applied Linguistics conference, the purpose of which was to 'elicit a public debate' on the potential various discourse analytic approaches have for bringing about social change (see Schegloff, 1997: 185–186). The ongoing nature of this debate notwithstanding, here we briefly review its *Discourse & Society* rendition, which addressed some key, though not insurmountable, issues in pursuing critical CA: the starting point, scope and ideological presuppositions of the analysis.

In comparing critical analysis and CA, Schegloff (1997) points to a fundamental difference in their research goals and procedures: critical analysis places sociopolitical categories (e.g. gender, race, ethnicity) and themes (e.g. inequality, exclusion, oppression) 'at the start or the center of inquiry, and as its guiding concern' (1997: 185), while CA treats the interactional event as the object of inquiry, aiming to understand it '*in its own terms*' (1997: 171). For the former, sociopolitical issues become analytically relevant *a priori*, and for the latter, they can become analytically relevant only if and when they emerge in the interaction being studied. When considering how the two might be brought together, Schegloff proposes first conducting a formal, CA analysis[1], so as to 'understand the object – the conversation episode – in its endogenous constitution', and then considering 'what forms a critical approach to it might take' (1997: 168). Schegloff (1999a: 568, n. 2) frames this sequential ordering of the two approaches as merely *one* form of their possible 'co-existence' and suggests that a critical approach may also become relevant fairly early in the analysis, when political issues emerge as 'a constitutive element of the object in the first instance' (1997: 170). However, he also repeatedly stresses the importance of starting with a formal, CA analysis and *'only then* explor[ing]…what political issue *if any* it allows us to address' (1997: 168, emphasis added). According to Schegloff, starting with a critical analysis could lead us to (inadvertently) examine data for results we already know we will or *should* find; and an initial formal analysis would introduce safeguards against this potential imposition of our own preoccupations onto the data.

For Wetherell (1998) and Billig (1999a, 1999b), this apparent insistence on prioritizing CA in the research process is both impractical – unnecessarily delaying and complicating a critical analysis (Wetherell, 1998: 402) – and ultimately ineffective as a 'safeguard' against analysts' *a priori* preoccupations. The authors argue that, just as critical analysts, CA analysts will inevitably make some 'prior judgements…at least provisionally', if only to consistently identify the 'type of talk being studied' (Billig, 1999b: 574). What's more, it is CA-specific concerns (e.g. with phenomena such as turn-taking) that will guide the data collection process and then 'restrict the analyst's gaze' to a selected turn or conversational fragment, at the expense of broader social discourses and interactional histories (Wetherell, 1998: 403). Thus, rather than serving as a safeguard, an initial CA analysis will itself skew the research, all the while also hampering a critical approach to it. One possibility for overcoming this 'impractical' sequencing may be found in a more iterative or, in Wetherell's (1998: 405) terms, 'synthetic approach'. Instead of CA strictly preceding a critical analysis, the two could inform each other throughout the research process.

A more synthetic approach can still, however, be vulnerable to centering analysts' critical preoccupations and sidelining participants' displayed, nuanced understandings and practices, which, importantly, may be 'uncomfortably at variance with commonsense understanding or ideological predilection' of the analyst (Schegloff, 1997: 180). To ensure that we are, in fact, examining participants' preoccupations and not (merely) pursuing our own, Schegloff (1997: 182–183) argues for restricting the analytic scope to issues which are demonstrably relevant for participants in the course of the analyzed interaction. As he points out, interactions could be characterized with reference to many different sociopolitical categories and themes which are technically accurate or true. Parties to an interaction can, for instance, be characterized in terms of their age, gender, race, ethnicity, occupation, etc. However, 'none of these characterizations can get an adequate warrant by saying that it was employed because it is *true* – even though it *is* true. They are *all* true' (1997: 166). If our aim is indeed to uncover participants' understandings and practices and examine *their* concerns, we would need to refrain from treating any sociopolitical categories or themes 'as given and as inescapably relevant' simply because they are true (Schegloff, 1999b: 577); instead, we would need to only treat as analytically relevant those categories and themes that the participants themselves demonstrably orient to.

Although Wetherell (1998: 403) finds the requirement for demonstrating participant orientation in the data 'unacceptably narrow' and inadequate even for answering CA's own 'why that now?' question, Schegloff notably seems to allow for flexibility in terms of how this requirement can be met. He namely accepts Wetherell's argument for a more comprehensive understanding of interaction, which would entail examining both what is observably present and what is absent in the data and considering how broader discourses as well as local contingencies might shape what transpires in the data. Schegloff (1998) notably treats this wider analytic scope as not necessarily incompatible with CA, since sociopolitical concerns of relevance for the participants can be located and explicated at different (not necessarily sequential) levels of granularity, which analysts are encouraged to be sensitive to, search for and draw on. In his words: 'It is because anything can in principle be a locus of order for parties – something which invokes 'why that now?' – that analysts are well-advised to remain open to any order of detail they can notice' (1998: 414). And in terms of demonstrating participant orientations, he explains that analysts should by no means be restricted to explicit mentions of (sociopolitical) issues or practices, since these may be oriented to by participants in various, still-to-be discovered ways (Schegloff, 1997: 182). Unlike Wetherell, however, Schegloff maintains that an analysis which is primarily driven by data-extrinsic sociopolitical issues – those identified in 'academic and political literature or...inquirer's sympathies' (Schegloff, 1998: 414) – would go beyond the scope of CA. For a more synthetic approach to remain consistent with CA's participant-oriented focus, therefore, critical research literature might be a resource for raising analysts' awareness of *potentially,* but not 'inescapably', relevant issues in the data.

Interestingly, even though Schegloff (1997: 183) treats the focus on observable participant (rather than analyst) preoccupations as a defining feature of CA and as a buffer against a 'merely ideological' critical analysis, Billig (1999a, 1999b) argues that CA itself has ideological assumptions and preoccupations which it imposes onto its data and participants. As he explains, while CA's 'naïve methodology and epistemology' entails examining social reality directly, 'in the participants' own terms' (1999b: 573), participants' terms and concerns are regularly supplanted by those of the analyst. Conversation analysts use technical terminology that interactants themselves do not use (e.g. 'adjacency pairs'), disattend topics of talk that interactants ostensibly attend to, and refer to interactants in ways suggestive of roles potentially irrelevant and inapplicable to those interactants (e.g. first-name references, which give a sense of 'informality'). Billig adds that CA's foundational 'participatory rhetoric' similarly does more than 'merely label what actually exists' (1999a: 547): The terms 'conversationalist' and '(co)participant' imply interactants' equal conversational rights and agency, while the under-explicated term 'member' in CA implies interactants' shared group membership and knowledge. As Billig (1999a: 545) concludes, these 'traditional' CA terms and practices not only prioritize analysts' *a priori* concerns over the observable concerns of the participants, but they also 'convey a particular and contestable image of social order' – one of equality and commonality, where co-membership, equal rights and agency, and informal conversations are the presumed norm.

Billig sees these 'traditional' CA practices as 'not ideologically neutral' and thus challenges Schegloff's claims of any firm, ideology-based distinctions between CA and critical analysis (Billig, 1999b: 576). However, he also sees these practices as 'socially uncritical' (Billig, 1999a: 552) and questions whether, as such, they are even suitable for analyzing critical issues of inequality, exclusion and oppression. Using CA for critical analysis, as he suggests, might require some modifications, such as abandoning CA's 'participatory rhetoric' and replacing its 'naivety' with an explicit critical awareness (Billig, 1999a: 556) – modifications which Schegloff (1999a) finds unnecessary, claiming that they target positions *attributed* rather than intrinsic to CA (1999a: 568, n. 4). Schegloff (1999a: 567, n. 1) clarifies, for instance, that: (1) conversation analysts do not claim to be free from *a priori* assumptions; (2) 'conversation does not *presume* an equalitarian society, it *allows* for one' (1999a: 564); and (3) analyzing interaction in 'participants' own terms' does not assume limiting the analysis to words explicitly used by participants (1999a: 570, n. 8). Upon offering these clarifications, Schegloff concludes that 'there is no ideological veil in CA that precludes analysts finding in a strip of interaction what is going on there' (1999a: 567), and he proposes CA's participant-oriented approach as a resource for discovering and showing precisely how issues of inequality, exclusion and oppression may be realized in interaction (1999a: 562).

Although important points of contention in this debate should not be denied and might not so easily be overcome, we would like to highlight some key points of agreement as well. Each of these authors claimed that critical issues of power could be observed in talk-in-interaction. Each stressed the importance of conducting close examinations of interactional data to *show how* power inequality might be (re)produced. Finally, each argued that CA, in one form or another, can be a valuable resource in these examinations. As Schegloff (1999b: 581) notes, CA can offer critically motivated discourse analysts tools for 'observing [interaction] carefully, closely, seriously, open-mindedly; observing – over and over again – to find what the natural world may be "telling you" that you did *not* know before, that you had not thought about *that way* before, that you had not entertained before'.

In fact, despite these seeming tensions, CA has been pursuing critical questions from its beginnings. In the 1960s and 1970s, Sacks was showing how inequality may be tacitly reproduced as a by-product of participants' mundane actions (Sacks, 1984, 1992); and in the 1980s, a special issue of *Social Problems* put front and center CA's potential to address issues of power and conflict (Maynard, 1988). As work in this vein continued, it was recognized as 'social-problem applied CA', wherein CA's 'micro approach is applied to the understanding of macro-social issues' (Antaki, 2011: 1). As Anataki (2011) pointed out, however, this work was overall rare and often only indirectly concerned with critical questions. Although more explicitly critical CA studies did emerge – most notably as 'feminist' CA, focused on sexism and heteronormativity (Kitzinger, 2000; see also Speer, 2002b; Stokoe & Smithson, 2002) and 'motivated' CA, focused on prejudices and inequalities more broadly (Talmy, 2009, 2023) – such studies were generally seen as, at times controversial (e.g. Wowk, 2007; see also Kitzinger, 2008), exceptions within the field.

With this volume, we aim to build on this long and complex history of critical CA research, too often done on the margins and with apprehension. As mentioned at the outset of this chapter, we do not propose 'critical CA' as a distinct framework; we see it instead as a steppingstone toward the uncontroversial and unequivocal use of CA in examining inequality and injustice. Such work might tackle feminist (Kitzinger, 2000) and various other societal issues; it might arise from somewhat 'motivated' (Talmy, 2009) and entirely 'unmotivated' looking; and it might contribute to pure CA – concerned with uncovering basic and general principles of talk-in-interaction – or to any of the six types of applied CA (Antaki, 2011), which are dedicated to illuminating different areas of study and aspects of social life (i.e. foundational, social-problem oriented, communicational, diagnostic, institutional and interventionist applied CA). Researchers might, in other words, locate the 'critical' aspect of their work in theoretical intentions, analytical data, and/or social outcomes as they adopt CA's detail-oriented, emic approach. This conceptual diversity runs through the chapters featured in this volume, and we see it not as a shortcoming but as an asset: a means of rendering, piece by piece, a more comprehensive, and ever-changing, picture of social interaction. Before introducing the chapters in more detail, we provide an overview of studies which have paved the way for CA to be recognized and embraced as a viable approach to critical research questions.

## Prior CA Studies on Inequality and Injustice

In this section, we review prior CA work which explored inequality and injustice. Much of this work also notably draws on membership categorization analysis (MCA) (Hester & Eglin, 1997) and discursive psychology (DP) (Edwards & Potter, 1992). This integration is not entirely surprising: given their respective concerns with local, potentially inequitable, instantiations of social types and interpersonal dispositions, MCA and DP lend themselves particularly well to critical analysis; and CA's granular, sequential and emic perspective allows for a nuanced exploration of such instantiations moment-to-moment in interaction. While these, as well as other frameworks within the field of language and social interaction, continue to generate important critical research, here we confine our focus to studies that explicitly employ CA. We first outline work examining power imbalances through the lens of speakers' interactional asymmetries – i.e. their differential access to managing turn-taking and sequence development. We then consider research on prejudiced talk – i.e. practices of expressing and resisting hearable prejudices in speakers' references, descriptions and categorizations. This review is certainly not exhaustive, nor is it meant to ascribe a critical perspective to the featured studies. It rather synthesizes some key concerns in examining inequality and injustice using CA and illustrates approaches which critically motivated researchers might find informative.

### Inequality and interactional asymmetry

One of CA's initial pathways to addressing inequality was through analyses of speakers' differential access to turn-taking and sequence control. Among the classic studies in this domain were those conducted by Candace West and Don Zimmerman in the 1970s and 1980s – a period of burgeoning research on language and gender inequality. In light of prominent work on women's interactional and sociopolitical 'powerlessness', West and Zimmerman approached gender and inequality as local, interactional accomplishments (West, 1979; West & Garcia, 1988; West & Zimmerman, 1977, 1987; Zimmerman & West, 1975; see also Duneier & Molotoch, 1999). Their close analyses uncovered gender-based asymmetries in turn-taking and topic management: men more frequently interrupted women, showed lack of support for women's topic development, and initiated unilateral topic shifts, thus reproducing their sociopolitical dominance.

These classic gender-inequality studies have at times been criticized for establishing false correlations between interactional practices and sociopolitical categories, as well as for essentializing and imposing gender categories as *a priori* relevant (see Speer & Stokoe, 2011; Wilkinson & Kitzinger, 2008). However, they also made significant contributions by dismantling commonly held beliefs about 'women's language' being 'powerless'. Classic, and more recent, studies have shown that practices believed to display (women's) 'inferiority' – e.g. tag questions and acquiescence to interruptions – may in fact display orientations to alignment and sequence progression (West, 1979, 1995), and presumably 'submissive' interactants may in fact engage in more assertive interactional practices than their presumably more 'aggressive' counterparts (Clayman et al., 2020).

Still, since it runs the risk of essentializing and imposing analysts' concerns onto the data, work tying power inequality to interactional practices of different 'transportable identities' (Zimmerman, 1998) or potentially omni-relevant categories, such as gender and race, has admittedly been rare in CA. There have been growing calls to explicitly acknowledge speakers' identities and explore their potential relevance in interaction (Koening et al., 2022) across expanded data collections (Whitehead, 2020), as well as to critically consider how participants' and analysts' identities might shape the research process (Koening et al., 2022; Sciubba et al., 2021; Talmy, 2023). Relatively 'safer' (and, so far, more productive), however, has been an analytic focus on power in institutional settings, where participants routinely orient to their 'differential distribution of knowledge, rights to knowledge, access to conversational resources, and to participation in interaction' (Drew & Heritage, 1992: 49). It should be noted that this work has often 'shied away' from explicit references to power inequality, 'preferring the more neutral – or agnostic – term asymmetry' (Hutchby, 1999: 89). Nevertheless, these detail-oriented sequential analyses have greatly helped explicate the 'shifting distribution of resources which enable some participants locally to achieve interactional effects not available to others' (Hutchby, 1996b: 481), generating invaluable tools and insights for critical CA.

Institutional CA research has, for instance, shown that interactants often collaboratively reproduce local power asymmetries as they 'talk institutions into being' (Heritage & Clayman, 2010). Across contexts – e.g. in legal (Atkinson & Drew, 1979), medical (Maynard, 1991), classroom (McHoul, 1979) and media interactions (Clayman & Heritage, 2002; Hutcbhy, 1996b) – experts and their 'lay' interlocutors have been found to jointly treat the former as having entitlements that the latter do not, with experts routinely and unproblematically (re)establishing their control over lay persons' floor access and actions (e.g. Hutchby, 1996b; Park, 2012; Thornborrow, 2001; Waring, 2013; Waring *et al.*, 2016; Weiste *et al.*, 2016). Detail-oriented sequential analyses have also helped to elucidate the scope and implications of such power asymmetries: CA has shown how interactants might use and reduce asymmetries to pursue (shared) institutional goals (e.g. Ong *et al.*, 2021; Paoletti & Fele, 2004; Smoliak *et al.*, 2022; Waring, 2014) and how (apparently asymmetrical) interaction might be shaped by participants' various concerns, including those not necessarily related to issues of power (Schegloff, 1980).

Importantly, rather than treating it as static, monolithic or unilateral, CA approaches power, in Hutchby's (1996a: 114) words, as 'a set of potentials which, while always present, may be varyingly exercised, resisted, shifted around, and struggled over by social agents'. With this in mind, studies have helped illuminate how inequality might not only be reproduced but also renegotiated. Interactants whose actions are relatively constrained in institutional discourse – e.g. lay persons, patients, students – might enact their authority by resisting the expert's and initiating their own courses of action (e.g. Ehrlich & Sidnell, 2006; Ekberg & LeCouteur, 2015; Galatolo & Drew, 2006; Gill *et al.*, 2010; Tadic, 2019; Thornborrow, 2001; Waring, 2011). Although these 'power struggles' might undermine smooth completion of institutionally relevant tasks (Ong *et al.*, 2021; Waring & Hruska, 2011), they can also foster 'nonexperts' agency and create new paths toward accomplishing institutional goals (Tadic, 2019).

CA has additionally shown how institutional practices of turn allocation and sequence organization can reinforce broader inequalities. Research has revealed that racism and sexism can be tacitly (re)produced through differential speaker selection (Kilby & Horowitz, 2013; Stivers & Majid, 2007) and response uptake (Garcia & Fisher, 2011; Janusz *et al.*, 2018). In the context of call-in radio and television shows, the control that hosts have over floor access can, for example, result in the privileging of exclusionary views and ideologies such as sexism and nationalism (Kilby & Horowitz, 2013; Ohara & Saft, 2003). Even institutions which mandate equal speaker rights (e.g. through strict speaking time limits) can be vulnerable to abuses of discursive power. Analysis of US Senate Judiciary Committee hearings, for instance, found that procedures aimed at promoting egalitarianism also allowed the party-affiliated chairperson to insert partisan commentary as a matter of fact, thus compromising the Committee's goals of impartiality (Raymond et al., 2019). These various power imbalances subtly creep into institutions through speakers' mundane practices; and it is CA's nuanced approach to turn-taking and sequence development that can help faithfully uncover and transform them (Kitzinger & Frith, 1999; Tennent & Weatherall, 2019).

## Injustice and prejudiced talk

Another productive line of CA research has explored how social injustices are (re)produced and resisted through interactants' management of hearable prejudices. While this area of work rapidly expanded in the aftermath of the *Discourse & Society* debate – particularly within the realm of feminist CA – its roots can be traced further back to Harvey Sacks' lectures. Most notably, in his lecture on doing 'being ordinary', Sacks (1984) examines the implicit prejudices in one woman's telling about seeing police cars in front of a local store. The teller describes the police as solving rather than (potentially) creating the observed trouble, portrays a woman of color as an involved party-to-the-scene, and positions herself as clearly uninvolved, and in no way vulnerable to being seen as involved, in the scene. The version of events (not) reported, or even considered, reveals the teller's 'massive comfort in her innocence, and in the legitimate audience status that she has' (1984: 422) – i.e. it reveals her unrecognizably biased vision of the world. Importantly, as Sacks notes: 'This lady is not designing a right-wing report. All she is doing is reporting what she saw' (1984: 422); and this question of how, while pursuing mundane actions (such as reporting what they saw), interactants (re)produce prejudices has been quite compelling for CA researchers.

A sizable body of work in this area has focused on participants' potentially prejudicial references, descriptions and categorizations (Berard, 2005; Edwards, 1998; Hansen, 2005; Kitzinger & Wilkinson, 2017; Stokoe, 2012; Stokoe & Smithson, 2002; Stokoe & Edwards, 2012; Whitehead 2009, 2020; Whitehead & Lerner, 2009). Studies have shown that proterms and category references which support participants' interactional goals may tacitly reproduce heteronormativity, sexism, racism and ageism (e.g. Artamonova, 2018; Garcia & Fisher, 2011; Kitzinger, 2005a, 2005b; Ostermann, 2017; Previtali *et al.*, 2023; Raymond, 2019; Speer, 2005;

Tadic, 2023; Tadic & Yu, 2020; van de Weerd, 2019). Exclusionary ideologies may also be reinforced through stereotypical expectations and portrayals of minoritized speakers' language use (Ehrlich, 2007; Raymond, 2013; Rawls & Duck, 2020; Romaniuk, 2016). Prejudicial references and portrayals can certainly be resisted as well – e.g. through counters and corrections (Ekberg & Ekberg, 2017; Kitzinger, 2000; Land & Kitzinger, 2005; Tadic, 2024; Weatherall, 2015), transformed speaker portrayals (Li *et al*., 2022) and subversive categorizations (Land & Kitzinger, 2007; Raymond, 2013; Robles & Kurylo, 2017; Tadic, 2024; Talmy, 2009); however, as studies have noted, such resistance may be limited, ambiguous and even potentially counterproductive (Land & Kitzinger, 2007; Robles & Kurylo, 2017; Talmy, 2009).

While some work has examined overtly prejudiced talk, for instance in (violent) confrontations (Alfahad, 2016; Whitehead *et al*., 2018; see also Stokoe & Edwards, 2007), researchers have observed that prejudices are often, and more 'safely', expressed under the radar – with an ambiguity and defeasibility making them difficult to pin down. In line with these observations, conversation analysts have also focused on so-called 'possible -isms', i.e. possibly racist, sexist or otherwise prejudiced utterances whose (non)prejudiced nature may be re-negotiated *in situ* (Stokoe, 2015; Whitehead, 2015). This area of work has helped shine a light on potential prejudices that may otherwise be obscured behind a veil of hints, allusions and innuendos (Durrheim *et al*., 2015), non-serious absurdities (Antaki, 2003), invitations to laughter (Blain & Diskin-Holdaway, 2023; Jefferson *et al*., 1987; Lobban *et al*., 2022; Tadic, 2023), innocent mistakes (Burford-Rice & Augoustinos, 2018) and claims of impartiality (Edmonds & Pino, 2022; Speer, 2002a, 2005; Speer & Potter, 2000; Whitehead, 2013, 2015).

CA research has notably also explored how prejudices might be challenged (or inadvertently reinforced). Studies have shown that designedly ambiguous, defeasible and 'non-serious' -isms can impede challenging responses by (potentially) rendering them as overreactions (Durrheim *et al*., 2015) and by inviting, and often receiving, recipient laughter, extensions and agreement (Kurylo & Robles, 2015; Pagliai, 2009; Tadic, 2023). When recipients do challenge -isms, they often do so delicately, with tacitly undercutting mitigations and delays (Robles, 2015; Stokoe, 2015; Tadic, 2023; Whitehead, 2015; Zhang & Okazawa, 2022). Even reports of personally experienced prejudice tend to be treated as problematic – reduced to instances of individual ignorance (Wilkes & Speer, 2021; Xie *et al*., 2021) and invalidated through highly antagonistic or merely acquiescing responses (Rafaely & Barnes, 2020; Romaniuk, 2015; Zhang, 2023). Importantly, however, researchers have found that accusations of and challenges to prejudice can be strengthened with persistent, experience-based and evidence-based arguments, displaying that 'discourse can be used...to dismantle the very forms of oppression that it creates' (Rafaely & Barnes, 2020: 84; see also Edmonds & Pino, 2022; Joyce *et al.*, 2021; Xie, 2023).

Overall, this rich research corpus illustrates CA's ability to illuminate critical issues in the intricacies of social interaction: it is through nuanced analysis of interaction as it unfolds that CA can uncover (un)equal participation rights and resources, hearably (non)inclusive references and descriptions, and orientations to these and other instantiations of inequality and injustice as (un)problematic and (non)repairable. The studies reviewed here also reveal how CA can 'bind' the analysis of inequality and injustice to the data without strictly 'limiting' it. With an awareness that explicit mentions are neither necessary nor sufficient for addressing critical questions, these studies show how broader social concerns can tacitly seep into interaction (e.g. Garcia & Fisher, 2011; Rawls & Duck, 2020), as well as how local, rather than (solely) 'political', contingencies can shape apparent interactional inequalities (e.g. Kitzinger & Wilkinson, 2017). They, relatedly, deepen our understanding of participant orientations to socio-political categories and issues, uncovering their, at times, designedly ambiguous and defeasible nature (e.g. Stokoe, 2015; Whitehead, 2015). And they demonstrate how CA can be used to examine sociopolitical issues when participant orientations to them are ostensibly lacking: acknowledging and drawing on their own member knowledge (e.g. Stokoe & Smithson, 2002) and expanding the context of analysis (e.g. Whitehead, 2020), CA researchers have explored *potentially relevant* sociopolitical issues in interaction, arguing that it is precisely participants' apparent lack of orientation to them that can help illuminate their routine (re)production and transformation (Kitzinger, 2000; Whitehead, 2020). As this line of work continues to grow, we hope that this volume will encourage researchers to embrace, rather than shy away from, CA as an approach with great potential to contribute to our collective understanding of injustice and inequality in interaction.

**Overview of the Volume**

The chapters in this volume variously address how conversation analysis can be engaged to investigate how inequality and injustice are (re)produced (Chapters 2–6), resisted (Chapters 7–9) or both (Chapter 10).

In Chapter 2, Tadic, Waring and Reddington demonstrate how raciolinguistic ideologies are (re)produced in family interaction and classroom discourse as the participants ascribe English proficiency to Whiteness, assess White American English as superior, and respond to non-white

English as deviant. In Chapter 3, drawing on videos from institutional security cameras and private citizens' smartphones, Hoey and Raymond describe how the specific practice of 'racist rendition' (i.e. hearably mocking adoption of a language variety) is utilized to exercise language policing and discrimination in the public space. This refrain of linguistic discrimination resurfaces in Chapter 4, as Saft reveals how negative views toward the Hawaiian language are reinforced in local news broadcasts through sequencing information in particular ways and inserting voice-overs with practices such as categorizations, formulations and reported speech. (Re)producing inequality and injustice also becomes evident outside this focus of raciolinguistic ideologies. In Chapter 5, Tam, Whitehead and Raymond unveil how inequality is made evident as participants manage trust in granting service requests (e.g. by indicating contingency) and closing emergency calls (e.g. by treating contingent granting as non-problematic) in a highly resource-constrained context – an emergency service call center in South Africa. Finally, in Chapter 6, turning her focus to US congressional town hall meetings, Yu documents how participants collaboratively delegitimize the 'other' by using categorial shorthands (e.g. Muslim interest) to construct the 'other' as biased, uninformed and dangerous, and how such portrayals can be weaponized to request political actions against the 'other'.

In addition to uncovering many tacit manifestations of inequality and injustice, CA can also play a powerful role in capturing the subtle interaction work towards combating such discriminatory tendencies. In Chapter 7, Park and Wagner delineate how, during a faculty meeting in a US K-12 public school district, a member with less institutional power, despite the organizational hierarchy that often yields unequal opportunities with regard to whose voice gets heard and which opinion prevails, manages to pursue her interactional agenda by balancing compliance and resistance. In Chapter 8, based on a Zoom conversation about racism among a mixed-race group of community members from a rural county in the Midwestern United States, Creider calls attention to how the work of anti-racism can be accomplished simply by being explicit as the participants use definitions and formulations to dismantle the fiction of shared experiences and understandings. The work of anti-racism is also found in the unlikely space of television situational comedies ('sitcoms'), as demonstrated by Cheeks and Whitehead in Chapter 9. Through humorously exaggerated portrayals of white characters' incompetence with respect to common-sense knowledge about people of color, the writers and actors manage to tacitly deliver lessons of antiracism beyond laughter and entertainment. Our volume ends, fittingly, with Stokoe and Albert's all-encompassing chapter offering a wide range of exhibits that showcase the power of CA in exposing and combating inequality and injustice.

Collectively, the chapters in this volume offer a panoramic exhibition of inequality and injustice in contexts from local to global, in settings from ordinary to institutional, in spaces from private to public, and in tenors from serious to comedic. While many of the chapters foreground issues of race and racism, the volume overall addresses a wider scope of critical issues, including institutionalized constraints and inequalities, political (il)legitimacy and divisiveness, and inequitable communication standards and assessments. These tales of unfairness are often deeply rooted in the most routine, taken-for-granted, exchanges we experience – a prime terrain of investigation for the conversation analytic interest in the seen but unnoticed. We thus hope to have rendered visible, through the featured chapters, that much of the work of combating inequality and injustice can be accomplished, in the signature conversation analytic style, in the micro-details of social interaction – one word, one turn and one sequence at a time.

## Note

(1) Schegloff (1997: 179) identifies the following steps in a formal analysis: (1) specifying the discursive practices within an interaction, (2) explicating how those practices are designed and used, and (3) showing how their design and use are oriented to by the participants.

## Appendix: Transcription Notations

| | |
|---|---|
| . (period) | falling intonation |
| ? (question mark) | rising intonation |
| , (comma) | level or semi-rising intonation |
| - (hyphen) | abrupt cut-off |
| :: (colon(s)) | prolonging of sound |
| word (underlining) | stress |
| WORD (caps) | loud speech |
| °word° (degree symbols) | quiet speech |
| ↑word (upward arrow) | raised pitch |
| ↓word (downward arrow) | lowered pitch |
| >word< (more than and less than) | quicker speech |
| <word> (less than & more than) | slowed speech |

| | |
|---|---|
| < (less than) | jump start or rushed start |
| (words) (parentheses) | uncertain transcription |
| ( ) (empty parentheses) | non-transcribable segment of talk |
| $word$ | smiley voice |
| #word# | creaky voice |
| hh (series of h's) | aspiration or laughter |
| .hh (h's preceded by period) | inhalation |
| [ ] (lined-up brackets)<br>[ ] | beginning and ending of<br>simultaneous or overlapping speech |
| = (equal sign) | latch or contiguous utterances of the same speaker |
| (2.4) (number in parentheses) | length of a silence in 10ths of a second |
| (.) (period in parentheses) | micro-pause, 0.2 second or less |
| ((words)) | transcriber comment |

## References

Alfahad, A. (2016) Professionalism vs. popularity: The shift in ethics of interviewing in Arab media. *Global Media Journal: Canadian Edition* 9 (2), 99–113.

Antaki, C. (2003) The uses of absurdity. In H. Van den Berg, M. Wetherell and H. Houtkoop-Steenstra (eds) *Analyzing Race Talk: Multidisciplinary Perspectives on the Research Interview* (pp. 85–102). Cambridge University Press.

Antaki, C. (2011) Six kinds of applied conversation analysis. In C. Antaki (ed.) *Applied Conversation Analysis: Intervention and Change in Institutional Talk* (pp. 1–14). Palgrave Macmillan UK.

Artamonova, O. (2018) Teacher's ethnic teasing: Playing with ambiguity and exploiting in-group communication. *Discourse & Society* 29 (1), 3–22.

Atkinson, J.M. and Drew, P. (1979) *Order in Court*. Springer.

Berard, T.J. (2005) On multiple identities and educational contexts: Remarks on the study of inequalities and discrimination. *Journal of Language, Identity, and Education* 4 (1), 67–76.

Billig, M. (1999a) Whose terms? Whose ordinariness? Rhetoric and ideology in conversation analysis. *Discourse & Society* 10 (4), 543–558.

Billig, M. (1999b) Conversation analysis and the claims of naivety. *Discourse & Society* 10 (4), 572–576.

Blain, H. and Diskin-Holdaway, C. (2023) Destabilizing racial discourses in casual talk-in-interaction. *Applied Linguistics* 44 (4), 631–657. https://doi.org/10.1093/applin/amac064

Burford-Rice, R. and Augoustinos, M. (2018) 'I didn't mean that: It was just a slip of the tongue': Racial slips and gaffes in the public arena. *British Journal of Social Psychology* 57 (1), 21–42.

Clayman, S. and Heritage, J. (2002) *The News Interview: Journalists and Public Figures on the Air*. Cambridge University Press.

Clayman, S.E., Heritage, J. and Hill, A.M.J. (2020) Gender matters in questioning presidents. *Journal of Language and Politics* 19 (1), 125–143.

Drew, P. and Heritage, J. (1992) *Talk at Work: Interaction in Institutional Settings.* Cambridge University Press.

Duneier, M. and Molotch, H. (1999) Talking city trouble: Interactional vandalism, social inequality, and the 'urban interaction problem. American Journal of Sociology 104 (5), 1263–1295. https://doi.org/10.1086/210175

Durrheim, K., Greener, R. and Whitehead, K.A. (2015) Race trouble: Attending to race and racism in online interaction. *British Journal of Social Psychology* 54 (1), 84–99.

Edmonds, D.M. and Pino, M. (2022) Designedly intentional misgendering in social interaction: A conversation analytic account. *Feminism and Psychology.* https://doi.org/10.1177/09593535221141550

Edwards, D. (1998) The relevant thing about her: Social identity categories in use. In C. Antaki and S. Widdicombe (eds) *Identities in Talk* (pp. 15–33). Sage.

Edwards, D. and Potter, J. (1992) *Discursive Psychology.* Sage Publications, Inc.

Ehrlich, S. (2007) Legal discourse and the cultural intelligiblity of gendered meanings. *Journal of Sociolinguistics* 11 (4), 452–477.

Ehrlich, S. and Sidnell, J. (2006) 'I think that's not an assumption you ought to make': Challenging presuppositions in inquiry testimony. *Language in Society* 35 (5), 655–676.

Ekberg, K. and LeCouteur, A. (2015) Clients' resistance to therapists' proposals: Managing epistemic and deontic status. *Journal of Pragmatics* 90, 12–25.

Ekberg, K. and Ekberg, S. (2017) Gendering occupations: Persistence and resistance of gender presumptions about members of particular healthcare professions. *Gender & Language* 11 (1), 100–120.

Galatolo, R. and Drew, P. (2006) Narrative expansions as defensive practices in courtroom testimony. *Text & Talk* 26 (6), 661–698.

Garcia, A.C. and Fisher, L.M. (2011) Being there for the children: The collaborative construction of gender inequality in divorce mediation. In S.A. Speer and E. Stokoe (eds) *Conversation and Gender* (pp. 272–293). Cambridge University Press.

Gill, V.T., Pomerantz, A. and Denvir, P. (2010) Pre-emptive resistance: Patients' participation in diagnostic sense-making activities. *Sociology of Health & Illness* 32 (1), 1–20.

Hansen, A.D. (2005) A practical task: Ethnicity as a resource in social interaction. *Research on Language and Social Interaction* 38 (1), 63–104.

Heritage, J. and Clayman, S. (2010) *Talk in Action: Interactions, Identities, and Institutions.* Wiley-Blackwell.

Hester, S. and Eglin, P. (1997) *Culture in Action: Studies in Membership Categorization Analysis.* University Press of America.

Hutchby, I. (1996a) *Confrontation Talk: Arguments, Asymmetries and Power on Talk Radio.* Lawrence Erlbaum Associates, Inc.

Hutchby, I. (1996b) Power in discourse: The case of arguments on a British talk radio show. *Discourse & Society* 7 (4), 481–497.

Hutchby, I. (1999) Beyond agnosticism?: Conversation analysis and the sociological agenda. *Research on Language & Social Interaction* 32 (1–2), 85–93.

Janusz, B., Józefik, B. and Peräkylä, A. (2018) Gender-related issues in couple therapists' internal voices and interactional practices. *Australian and New Zealand Journal of Family Therapy* 39 (4), 436–449.

Jefferson, G., Sacks, H. and Schegloff, E. (1987) Notes on laughter in the pursuit of intimacy. In G. Button and J.R.E. Lee (eds) *Talk and Social Organisation* (pp. 152–205). Multilingual Matters.

Joyce, J. B., Humă, B., Ristimäki, H.-L., Almeida, F. F. and Doehring, A. (2021) Speaking out against everyday sexism: Gender and epistemics in accusations of 'mansplaining'. *Feminism & Psychology* 31 (4), 502–529. https://doi.org/10.1177/09593535 20979499

Kilby, L. and Horowitz, A.D. (2013) Opening up terrorism talk: The sequential and categorical production of discursive power within the call openings of a talk radio broadcast. *Discourse & Society* 24 (6), 725–742.

Kitzinger, C. (2000) Doing feminist conversation analysis. *Feminism & Psychology* 10 (2), 163–193.

Kitzinger, C. (2005a) Heteronormativity in action: Reproducing the heterosexual nuclear family in after-hours medical calls. *Social Problems* 52 (4), 477–498.

Kitzinger, C. (2005b) 'Speaking as a heterosexual': (How) does sexuality matter for talk-in-Interaction? *Research on Language and Social Interaction* 38 (3), 221–265.

Kitzinger, C. (2008) Developing feminist conversation analysis: A response to Wowk. *Human Studies* 31, 179–208.

Kitzinger, C. and Frith, H. (1999) Just say no? The use of conversation analysis in developing a feminist perspective on sexual refusal. *Discourse & Society* 10 (3), 293–316.

Kitzinger, C. and Wilkinson, S. (2017) Referring to persons: Linguistic gender and gender in action – (when) are husbands men? In G. Raymond, G.H. Lerner and J. Heritage (eds) *Enabling Human Conduct: Studies of Talk-in-interaction in Honor of Emanuel A. Schegloff* (pp. 189–204). John Benjamins.

Koenig, C.J., DiDomenico, S.M., Robles, J.S., Williamson, F., Park, I., Katila, J., Ibnelkaïd, S., Shrikant, N., Goico, S., Hoey, E. and Brohi, H. (2022) *Interrogating Ethnomethodology and Conversation Analysis (EMCA) for Racial Justice: Preliminary Insights from a Meta-synthesis of EMCA Articles Rddressing Race, Racism, and Ethnicity Published between 2001–2020*. Paper presented at the National Communication Association (NCA) 108th Annual Convention, 17 November, New Orleans, LA.

Kurylo, A. and Robles, J.S. (2015) How should I respond to them? An emergent categorization of responses to interpersonally communicated stereotypes. *Journal of Intercultural Communication Research* 44 (1), 64–91.

Land, V. and Kitzinger, C. (2005) Speaking as a lesbian: Correcting the heterosexist presumption. *Research on Language and Social Interaction* 38 (4), 371–416.

Land, V. and Kitzinger, C. (2007) Contesting same-sex marriage in talk-in-interaction. *Feminism & Psychology* 17 (2), 173–183.

Leiter, K. (1980) *A Primer on Ethnomethodology*. Oxford University Press.

Li, H., Liu, H. and Liu, D. (2022) Gender/power relationships in fictional conflict talk at the workplace: Analyzing television dramatic dialogue in The Newsroom. *Journal of Pragmatics* 187, 58–71.

Lobban, R., Luyt, R. and McDermott, D. (2022) (Hetero)sexist microaggressions in practice. *Gender and Language* 16 (2), 125–148.

Maynard, D. (1988) Language, interaction, and social problems. *Social Problems* 35 (4), 311–334.

Maynard, D. (1991) Interaction and asymmetry in clinical discourse. *American Journal of Sociology* 97 (2), 448–495.

McHoul, A. (1978) The organization of turns at formal talk in the classroom. *Language in Society* 7 (2), 183–213.

Ohara, Y. and Saft, S. (2003) Using conversation analysis to track gender ideologies in social interaction: Toward a feminist analysis of a Japanese phone-in consultation TV program. *Discourse & Society* 14 (2), 153–172.

Ong, B., Barnes, S. and Buus, N. (2021) Downgrading deontic authority in open dialogue reflection proposals: A conversation analysis. *Family Process* 60 (4), 1217–1232.

Ostermann, A.C. (2017) 'No mam. You are heterosexual': Whose language? Whose sexuality? *Journal of Sociolinguistics* 21 (3), 348–370.

Pagliai, V. (2009) Conversational agreement and racial formation processes. *Language in Society* 38 (5), 549–579.

Paoletti, I. and Fele, G. (2004) Order and disorder in the classroom. *Journal of Pragmatics* 14 (1), 69–85.

Park, I. (2012) Seeking advice: Epistemic asymmetry and learner autonomy in writing conferences. *Journal of Pragmatics* 44 (14), 2004–2021.

Previtali, F., Nikander, P. and Ruusuvuori, J. (2023) Ageism in job interviews: Discreet ways of building co-membership through age categorisation. *Discourse Studies* 25 (1), 25–50.

Rafaely, D. and Barnes, B. (2020) African climate activism, media and the denial of racism: The tacit silencing of Vanessa Nakate. *Community Psychology in Global Perspective* 6 (2/2), 71–86.

Rawls, A.W. and Duck, W. (2020) *Tacit Racism*. The University of Chicago Press.

Rawls, A.W., Duck, W. and Turowetz, J. (2020) The White self-interested 'strong man' ideal vs. the Black practice of 'submissive civility': In a Black/White police encounter. In *Tacit Racism* (pp. 129–161). The University of Chicago Press.

Raymond, C.W. (2013) Gender and sexuality in animated television sitcom interaction. *Discourse & Communication* 7 (2), 199–220.

Raymond, C.W. (2019) Category accounts: Identity and normativity in sequences of action. *Language in Society* 48 (4), 585–606.

Raymond, C.W., Caldwell, M., Mikesell, L., Park, I. and Williams, N. (2019) Turn-taking and the structural legitimization of bias: The case of the Ford-Kavanaugh hearing by the United States Senate Committee on the Judiciary. *Language & Communication* 69, 97–114.

Robles, J.S. (2015) Extreme case (re)formulation as a practice for making hearably racist talk repairable. *Journal of Language and Social Psychology* 34 (4), 390–409.

Robles, J.S. and Kurylo, A. (2017) 'Let's have the men clean up': Interpersonally communicated stereotypes as a resource for resisting gender-role prescribed activities. *Discourse Studies* 19 (6), 673–693.

Romaniuk, T. (2015) Talking about sexism: Meta-sexist talk in presidential politics. *Journal of Language and Social Psychology* 34 (4), 446–463.

Romaniuk, T. (2016) On the relevance of gender in the analysis of discourse: A case study from Hillary Rodham Clinton's presidential bid in 2007–2008. *Discourse & Society* 27 (5), 533–553.

Sacks, H. (1984) On doing 'being ordinary'. In J.M. Atkinson and J. Heritage (eds) *Structures of Social Action: Studies in Conversation Analysis* (pp. 413–429). Cambridge University Press.

Sacks, H. (1992) *Lectures on Conversation* (vol. 1 & vol. 2) Blackwell.

Schegloff, E.A. (1997) Whose text? Whose context? *Discourse & Society* 8 (2), 165–187.

Schegloff, E.A. (1980) Preliminaries to preliminaries: 'Can I ask you a question?'. *Sociological inquiry* 50 (3–4), 104–152.

Schegloff, E.A. (1998) Reply to Wetherell. *Discourse & Society* 9 (3), 413–416.

Schegloff, E.A. (1999a) 'Schegloff's texts' as 'Billig's data': A critical reply. *Discourse & Society* 10 (4), 558–572.

Schegloff, E.A. (1999b) Naivete vs sophistication or discipline vs self-indulgence: A rejoinder to Billig. *Discourse & Society* 10 (4), 577–582.

Schegloff, E.A. and Sacks, H. (1973) Opening up closings. *Semiotica* 8, 289–327.
Sciubba, E., Shrikant, N. and Williamson, F. (2021) Guest Blog: EM/CA for Racial Justice. *Research on Language and Social Interaction*, 2 June. https://rolsi.net/2021/06/02/guest-blog-em-ca-for-racial-justice/
Smoliak, O., MacMartin, C., Hepburn, A., Le Couteur, A., Elliott, R. and Quinn-Nilas, C. (2022) Authority in therapeutic interaction: A conversation analytic study. *Journal of Marital and Family Therapy* 48 (4), 961–981.
Speer, S.A. (2002a) Sexist talk: Gender categories, participants' orientations and irony. *Journal of Sociolinguistics* 6 (3), 347–377.
Speer, S.A. (2002b) What can conversation analysis contribute to feminist methodology? Putting reflexivity into practice. *Discourse & Society* 13 (6), 783–803.
Speer, S.A. (2005) The interactional organization of the gender attribution process. *Sociology* 39 (1), 67–87.
Speer, S.A. and Potter, J. (2000) The management of heterosexist talk: Conversational resources and prejudiced claims. *Discourse & Society* 11 (4), 543–572.
Speer, S.A. and Stokoe, E. (2011) An introduction to conversation and gender. In S.A. Speer and E. Stokoe (eds) *Conversation and Gender* (pp. 1–27). Cambridge University Press.
Stivers, T. and Majid, A. (2007) Questioning children: Interactional evidence of implicit bias in medical interviews. *Social Psychology Quarterly* 70 (4), 424–441.
Stokoe, E. (2012) 'You know how men are': Description, categorization and common knowledge in the anatomy of a categorial practice. *Gender & Language* 6 (1), 233–255.
Stokoe, E. (2015) Identifying and responding to possible-isms in institutional encounters: Alignment, impartiality, and the implications for communication training. *Journal of Language and Social Psychology* 34 (4), 427–445.
Stokoe, E.H. and Smithson, J. (2002) Gender and sexuality in talk-in-interaction. In P. McIlvenny (ed.) *Talking Gender and Sexuality* (pp. 79–109). John Benjamins Publishing Company.
Stokoe, E. and Edwards, D. (2007) 'Black this, black that': Racial insults and reported speech in neighbour complaints and police interrogations. *Discourse & Society* 18 (3), 337–372.
Stokoe, E. and Edwards, D. (2012) Mundane morality: Gender, categories and complaints in familial neighbour disputes. *Journal of Applied Linguistics and Professional Practice* 9 (2), 165–192.
Tadic, N. (2019) 'My brain hurts': Incorporating learner interests into the classroom. *Language and Education* 33 (1), 68–84.
Tadic, N. (2023) Preference organization and possible -isms in institutional interaction: The case of adult second language classrooms. *Language in Society*, 1–27.
Tadic, N. (2024) Problematizing possible -isms in adult second language classrooms. *Applied Linguistics*, 1–20.
Tadic, N. and Yu, D. (2020) Constructing the audience in media interviews. In H.Z. Waring and E. Reddington (eds) *Communicating with the Public: Conversation Analytic Studies* (pp. 67–84). Bloomsbury Publishing.
Talmy, S. (2009) Resisting ESL: Categories and sequence in a critically 'motivated' analysis of classroom interaction. In H. Nguyen and G. Kasper (eds) *Talk-in-Interaction: Multilingual Perspectives* (pp. 181–213). University of Hawai'i, National Foreign Language Resource Center.
Talmy, S. (2023) *CA/MCA for DEI: A Case for Motivated Looking.* Paper presented at the 11 Annual Meeting of the Language and Social Interaction Working Group (LANSI), 15 October, New York, NY.

ten Have, P. (2007) *Doing Conversation Analysis* (2nd edn). SAGE.
Tennent, E. and Weatherall, A. (2019) Disclosing violence in calls for help. *Gender and Language* 13 (2), 270–288.
Thornborrow, J. (2001) Questions, control and the organization of talk in calls to a radio phone-in. *Discourse Studies* 3 (1), 119–143.
van de Weerd, P. (2019) 'Those foreigners ruin everything here': Interactional functions of ethnic labelling among pupils in the Netherlands. *Journal of Sociolinguistics* 23 (3), 244–262.
vom Lehn, D. (2014) *Harold Garfinkel: The Creation and Development of Ethnomethodology*. Left Coast Press.
Waring, H.Z. (2011) Learner initiatives and learning opportunities in the language classroom. *Classroom Discourse* 2 (2), 201–218.
Waring, H.Z. (2013) Managing Stacy: A case study of turn-taking in the language classroom. *System* 41 (3), 841–851.
Waring, H.Z. (2014) Managing control and connection in an adult ESL classroom. *Research in the Teaching of English* 52–74.
Waring, H.Z. and Hruska, B.L. (2011) Getting and keeping Nora on board: A novice elementary ESOL student teacher's practices for lesson engagement. *Linguistics and education* 22 (4), 441–455.
Waring, H.Z., Reddington, E. and Tadic, N. (2016) Responding artfully to student-initiated departures in the adult ESL classroom. *Linguistics and Education* 33, 28–39.
Weatherall, A. (2015) Sexism in language and talk-in-interaction. *Journal of Language and Social Psychology* 34 (4), 410–426.
Weiste, E., Voutilainen, L. and Peräkylä, A. (2016) Epistemic asymmetries in psychotherapy interaction: Therapists' practices for displaying access to clients' inner experiences. *Sociology of Health & Illness* 38 (4), 645–661.
West, C. (1979) Against our will: Male interruptions of females in cross-sex conversation. *Annals of the New York Academy of Sciences* 327 (1), 81–96.
West, C. (1995) Women's competence in conversation. *Discourse & Society* 6 (1), 107–131.
West, C. and Zimmerman, D.H. (1977) Women's place in everyday talk: Reflections on parent-child interaction. *Social problems* 24 (5), 521–529.
West, C. and Zimmerman, D.H. (1987) Doing gender. *Gender & Society* 1 (2), 125–151.
West, C. and Garcia, A. (1988) Conversational shift work: A study of topical transitions between women and men. *Social problems* 35 (5), 551–575.
Wetherell, M. (1998) Positioning and interpretative repertoires: Conversation analysis and post-structuralism in dialogue. *Discourse & Society* 9 (3), 387–412.
Whitehead, K.A. (2009) 'Categorizing the categorizer': The management of racial common sense in interaction. *Social Psychology Quarterly* 72 (4), 325–342.
Whitehead, K.A. (2013) Managing self/other relations in complaint sequences: The use of self-deprecating and affiliative racial categorizations. *Research on Language and Social Interaction* 46 (2), 186–203.
Whitehead, K.A. (2015) Everyday antiracism in action: Preference organization in responses to racism. *Journal of Language and Social Psychology* 34 (4), 374–389.
Whitehead, K.A. (2020) The problem of context in the analysis of social action: The case of implicit whiteness in post-apartheid South Africa. *Social Psychology Quarterly* 83 (3), 294–313.
Whitehead, K.A. and Lerner, G.H. (2009) When are persons 'white'?: On some practical asymmetries of racial reference in talk-in-interaction. *Discourse & Society* 20 (5), 613–641.

Whitehead, K.A., Bowman, B. and Raymond, G. (2018) 'Risk factors' in action: The situated constitution of 'risk' in violent interactions. *Psychology of Violence* 8 (3), 329–338.
Wilkes, J. and Speer, S.A. (2021) Reporting microaggressions: Kinship carers' complaints about identity slights. *Journal of Language and Social Psychology* 40 (3), 303–327.
Wilkinson, S. and Kitzinger, C. (2008) Using conversation analysis in feminist and critical research. *Social and Personality Psychology Compass* 2 (2), 555–573.
Wowk, M.T. (2007) Kitzinger's feminist conversation analysis: Critical observations. *Human Studies* 30, 131–155.
Xie, Y. (2023) Talking about the experiences of racism: A study of reporting racism in broadcast interviews. *British Journal of Social Psychology* 62, 1469–1485.
Xie, Y., Kirkwood, S., Laurier, E. and Widdicombe, S. (2021) Racism and misrecognition. *British Journal of Social Psychology* 60 (4), 1177–1195.
Zhang, T. (2023) Contesting reports of racism, contesting the rights to assess. *Social Psychology Quarterly* 86 (2), 130–150.
Zhang, T. and Okazawa, R. (2022) Managing neutrality, rapport, and antiracism in qualitative interviews. *Qualitative Research* 23 (6), 1–25.
Zimmerman, D.H. (1998) Identity, context and interaction. In C. Antaki and S. Widdicombe (eds) *Identities in Talk* (pp. 87–106). Sage.
Zimmermann, D.H. and West, C. (1975) Sex roles, interruptions and silences in conversation. In B. Thorne and N. Henley (eds) *Language and Sex: Difference and Dominance* (pp. 105–129). Newbury House.

# Part 1
# Reproducing Inequality and Injustice

# 2 Investigating Raciolinguistic Ideologies in Interaction

Nadja Tadic, Hansun Zhang Waring and
Elizabeth Reddington

## Introduction

In seeking to illuminate how social inequality and injustice may be transformed or (re)produced, researchers have shown a growing concern with raciolinguistic ideologies – ideologies which construct racialized individuals as linguistically deviant regardless of their objective language production (Flores & Rosa, 2015). Raciolinguistic ideologies are rooted in histories of European colonialism and the co-construction and co-naturalization of language and race (Rosa & Flores, 2017). In pursuit of territorial and epistemological domination, colonizers constructed indigenous populations as racially and linguistically inferior to Europeans; and rather than being a distant, disconnected past, these 'colonial distinctions between Europeanness and non-Europeanness – and, by extension, whiteness and nonwhiteness' (Rosa & Flores, 2017: 622) – continue to be rearticulated and reproduced in current portrayals of racialized communities as linguistically deficient and languageless (Rosa, 2016b).

Expanding on Inoue's (2006) concept of indexical inversion, proponents of the raciolinguistic perspective propose that we consider not how linguistic signs index social categories but instead, 'how language ideologies associated with social categories produce the perception of linguistic signs' (Rosa & Flores, 2017: 628). The raciolinguistic approach thus requires us to shift from examining the practices of racialized speakers to considering the practices of racially hegemonic recipients or 'white listening subjects' (Flores & Rosa, 2015) as they draw on various spoken and non-spoken signs to interpret and categorize their racialized interlocutors. Importantly, 'whiteness functions as a structural position that can be inhabited by whites and nonwhites alike depending on the circumstances' (Rosa & Flores, 2017: 629), with members of historically racialized and previously non-racialized groups potentially occupying the position of white listening subjects and/or of nonwhite, racialized speakers (see also Rosa, 2016b).

A growing body of research has shown how individuals, groups and institutions tacitly reproduce raciolinguistic ideologies (Chaparro, 2019; Cushing & Snell, 2022; Ricklefs, 2021; Rosa, 2016a, 2019; Sung, 2018) and impede racialized speakers' academic and professional development (Briceño *et al.*, 2018; Menard-Warwick, 2022; Mustonen, 2021; Subtirelu, 2017; Thoma, 2020), often despite explicitly stated equity-driven goals and policies (Chávez-Moreno, 2021; Daniels, 2018; Flores *et al.*, 2020; Rosa, 2016b; Swift, 2022). Much of this research is based on ethnographic observations and interviews, with little work analyzing the tacit enactment of raciolinguistic ideologies *in situ* (see Chaparro, 2019; Ricklefs, 2021). To better understand the seen-but-unnoticed ways in which raciolinguistic ideologies emerge in interaction, we use the approach of conversation analysis. Through a nuanced examination of family and institutional talk, we show how raciolinguistic ideologies are (re)produced moment-to-moment as participants, in the course of routine activities, construct non-white English speakers as linguistically deviant and inferior.

## Data and Method

In this study, we examine interaction in both mundane and institutional settings. Data come from a corpus of over 77 hours of video-recorded language-classroom and family-dinner conversations conducted primarily in English in the Northeastern United States. Participants in these conversations represent socioculturally diverse communities: the classroom data involve adult English as a Second Language (ESL) students and their teachers; the dinner data involve a mother, father and their young daughter. Recordings were transcribed in accordance with Jeffersonian (2004) conventions with some adaptations to capture embodied conduct (see Appendix).

Given our broad interest in (re)production of and resistance to unequal power relations, we adopted the lens of critical conversation analysis (see Tadic & Waring, this volume; see also Kitzinger, 2000; Talmy, 2009). We began by collecting instances in which participant conduct appeared to invoke or challenge raciolinguistic ideologies, either explicitly or implicitly. The small number of cases to be presented in this chapter became our collection, which was subjected to closer, turn-by-turn examination in accordance with the principles and techniques of conversation analysis

(CA) (see ten Have, 2007). CA's focus on understanding participant conduct in its local context through turn-by-turn analysis, guided by the question, 'why that now?', offered insight into how emergent contingencies of interaction might bring out (or inhibit) the reproduction of raciolinguistic ideologies. Through such a nuanced examination of interactional practices, conversation analysis is uniquely positioned to uncover the *in situ* reproduction and contestation of raciolinguistic ideologies.

As authors of this chapter coming, respectively, from Serbia, China and the US, we are all fluent speakers of American English either as a second or a first language. We all have multiple years of experience teaching in the adult ESL context, and the second author is the mother in the family data. Our familiarity with or involvement in the study contexts has its obvious advantages, such as clarifying otherwise nebulous contextual details when necessary. The obvious danger, on the other hand, entails becoming distracted or limited by our preconceived notions of what goes on in these settings. In the teaching context, in particular, it took a great deal of discipline not to slip into judgments of good or bad teaching practices. It is a danger we were all very aware of and in our weekly data sessions took great care to minimize by holding each other accountable for grounding our observations in the details of the interactions. In fact, without this disciplined analysis, the second author would not have discovered her own role in reproducing a raciolinguistic ideology. In other words, even as multilingual speakers and educators who wholeheartedly oppose any raciolinguistic ideologies in theory, we are, unfortunately, not immune to perpetuating such ideologies in practice, as made evident by the CA analysis.

## Analysis

In this section, we explore how raciolinguistic ideologies emerge in orientations to English and its speakers during family-dinner and language-classroom interactions. First, we consider participants' treatment of English as a language spoken by 'white' people. We then examine the assessment of (white American) English as a superior language. We end the section by demonstrating how non-white speakers' English is treated as deviant.

### Ascribing English proficiency to whiteness

Participants most clearly reproduced raciolinguistic ideologies by overtly tying assumed English proficiency to (apparent) whiteness. We see this tie in our first extract, which comes from an adult ESL class discussion on communicative strategies. During the discussion, the teacher (T1) recommended that students explicitly state that they are English language learners as a way to preempt any miscommunication with first-language English speakers. The students, however, rejected this suggestion, claiming that their hearable lack of fluency and accuracy is already an evident sign of their language-learner identity (data not shown). We join the class as a student, Katarina (K), reaches the possible completion of this argument against the teacher's suggestion (lines 01–02), and the teacher invokes a raciolinguistic ideology by tying whiteness to (assumed) English competence and pursuing student acceptance of his advice. In the transcript, all participants except for T1 are students.

(1) you actually look American

```
01    K:           yeah but we- you- <of course,> know that-
02                 ↓know that we are not from here.↓ °and [we° ]
03    T1:                                         nods-[yeah.]
04                 yeah. that's [right.]
05    K:                        [ so:: ]
06    T1:  →       .h NO BUT YOU KNOW WHAT, shifts
07                 gaze across Ss-.h BUT a l- A LOT OF YOU
08                 ARE FROM EUROPE, right,=European
09                 countries,=YOU ACTUALLY look (.)
10                 AMERICAN.=right,=unless you start talk↑ing,
11    Ss¹:        hha[   ha  ha  ha  ha  ha  ha    ]
12    T1:            [>>right.=know what I'm saying,<<]
13    K:           hah
14    A:           [.hh ]
15    T1:          [like,] like WE CAN'T ↑TELL. I can't tell
16                 gaze to K-you're from Bra↑zil. right,=you
17                 look, you look American,=right,=unless you
18                 start talking, and then I go ↑oh, there's an
19                 accent.=right,=↑same.
      ((20 lines omitted: J reports intuiting a European classmate's nationality))
20    D:           [but actually you don't know] how much
21                 a p- person kno:w the language. knows the
22                 language.=
23    T1:          =nods-↑yeah.
24    D:           so [you can't] expect that
25    T1:             [but- but-] [yeah.]
26    D:                          [ this ] person
27                 kno:ws very well.=[(                    )]
```

```
28    T1:  →              =[AND MY POINT I:]S,
29                        my point is (.) is uh shifts gaze across Ss-a LOT
30                        of Americans, we assu:me like, even if you
31                        have an accent,=like think of Arnold
32                        Schwarzenegger.
33    D:                  ah.
34    T1:                 right,=
35    D:                  [   nods, smiles   ]
36    T1:                 =HE'S [GOT AN ACCENT] BUT WE- WE
37                        DON'T QUESTION his English at [all.]
38    D:                                              nods-[ m.]
39    T1:                 right,
40    D:                  nods
41    T1:                 so our assumption is >even if you have an<
42                        ↑accent you're gonna <be like> fluent. >you
43                        know what I mean?<
44    Z:                  nods
45    T1:                 that's the as↑sumption, so:: so sometimes
46                        it's oka:y for you to ↑tell us that=
47    D:                  =nods-m.=
```

After acknowledging Katarina's rejection (lines 03–04), the teacher bolsters his advice with a new counterargument in increased volume (from line 06). In this new argument, he references some of the students' European origin (*a lot of you are from Europe,* lines 07–08) and ancestry (*you're from Brazil,* line 16), and claims that these students, despite the features of their speech, might appear American to their interlocutors (*you look American,* lines 09–10 and 17). The teacher thus presupposes that people's countries of origin can be determined based on their physical appearance, and he equates an *American* physical appearance with a *European* one, possibly using the *European* modifier as a stand-in for an arguably more politically charged racial one – 'white'. What's more, considering the larger sequential context in which he is advising his students to make their status as English learners explicit, the teacher here seems to be implying that an individual who appears European (i.e. white) will be seen as American and, therefore, assumed to be proficient in English. While none of the students take issue with the teacher's racial presupposition that Americans look *European* (suggesting its possible naturalization), Diana (D) does challenge the teacher's implied claim that (European) appearance is associated with (English) language proficiency (*you don't know...how much a person knows the language...,* lines 20–22, 24, 26–27).

In countering Diana's challenge, the teacher next formulates a commonly held assumption that Europeans are fluent English speakers (lines 29–31, 41–43), which he attributes to the American category (*a lot of Americans*, lines 29–30). Through repeated pronominal use – *we can't tell* (line 15), *we assume* (line 30) and *we don't question* (lines 36–37), the teacher treats this raciolinguistic assumption as presumably shared among Americans and strengthens it by implicitly invoking his authority on the American category, as its member (*we assume*, line 30) and arguably also as an ESL teacher (i.e. a presumed expert on American language and culture). He further illustrates this newly introduced American assumption with the example of Arnold Schwarzenegger (lines 31–32): a white Hollywood actor and former California governor from a European country, whose language ability was not questioned even though he was hearably a second language English speaker (*he's got an accent*, line 36). With this example, the teacher upgrades his earlier claim, stating not only that looking European leads to the assumption of English competence, but that it does so despite the apparent, hearable limits to such competence (cf. Flores & Rosa, 2015, on the white listening subject). This example is quickly recognized and accepted by Diana (lines 33, 35, 38 and 40) and by Zian (Z) (a student from China) (line 44) and seems to pave the way for the teacher's reissued advice: students should make their language learner status explicit to their interlocutors (from line 45).

In the next extract, we turn from the institutional sphere of the classroom to a family dinner conversation between Mom (M), an Asian American, and Dad (D), a European American, in the presence of their eight-year-old daughter (who is reading at the table and not actively participating). Immediately prior to the extract, Mom has expressed her displeasure with having to remove her shoes at airport security despite her TSA (Transportation Security Administration) precheck status (which should expedite her security screening process by making tasks such as the removal of shoes unnecessary). As the segment starts, the couple comes to the conclusion that it was the type of shoes Mom was wearing (i.e. long boots) that occasioned the need for their removal (lines 01–03). In line 04, immediately upon the completion of Dad's turn-constructional unit, Mom asks whether the same explanation would account for why she was asked if she spoke English. Given the tenuous connection between shoes and English, we can safely assume that Mom's question is designed not to seek information but to express a stance of some sort (also see her smile in line 10) – one that likely problematizes having been asked about her ability to speak English. Our focus, however, is on Dad's response starting in line 09.

(2) you're not white

```
01   D:          that's [why th ]ey made you take 'em off.
02   M:                 [°yeah,°]
03   D:          like regular little sho::es probably not.
04               [°(right.)°]
05   M:          [ is that ]
06               why they asked me (.) [if I speak English?]
07   D:                                [    gaze to M     ]
08               (0.8)-D gazes to M
09   D:    →     ↑no. [ because you don't look like- (.)         ]
10   M:                [gaze down with smile, gaze to D with smile]
11   D:          [you're not white.]
12   M:          [ smiley gaze to D ]
13               (0.8)
14   D:          which is making an assumption
15               [that all white pe-]
16   M:          [in New York lik]e 80 per[cent °of peo-°]
17   D:                                   smiles, gaze to phone-[ I: know.    ]
```

((30 lines omitted: M reports the event in more detail; see also Extract 4))

```
18   D:    →     points to M-I would assu:me if I- if I gra:bbed
19               a white woman [with] (.) u:m
20   M:                        [ hm ]
21   D:          blond hair [and blue eyes.] I would >make
22   M:                     [    nods     ]
23   D:          the assumption that she speaks English<
24               before I make the assumption that a- (.)
25               [which is-] gaze away-I guess gaze to M-wro↓::ng,
26   M:          [ °myeh° ]
27   D:          but that's (.) human ↑nature.=
28               gaze to phone-and I don't know gaze to M
29               (1.0)
30               I don't find it that outrageous. °but-°
31   M:          I don't- like- ↑wh(at) does it matter.
32               it's not like they are interviewing °anybody.°
```

Several features of Dad's response contribute to its hearing as not just reproducing the raciolinguistic ideology that being non-white is tantamount to being a non-English speaker but also explaining how this ideology is a common-sense order. First, while Mom's question conveys a stance that problematizes her being questioned about her linguistic ability, Dad's response does not show clear affiliation with that stance: it is delayed by 0.8 second gap (line 08) and it sidesteps the action of Mom's prior turn (the implicit criticism), attending instead to its format via the disconfirming *no* and an alternative account.

Second, Dad's repair in lines 09 and 11 orients to non-whiteness, as opposed to other categorial alternatives, as a legitimate account for linguistic judgments. Note that he begins with *you don't look like* but replaces it with *you're not white*. By shifting from appearance (where looking like X may be debatable) to a racial/ethnic designation, Dad displays his stance towards *not white* as a superior, more commonsensical explanation (see stress on *white*) for questioning someone's ability to speak English.

Third, this racialized assumption is treated by Dad as natural rather than detrimental. It is only after his explanation is met with Mom's smiling gaze (lines 10 and 12) that Dad is moved to articulate, with an increment, what may be problematic about this explanation (i.e. its basis on an assumption). The apparent concession thereafter (*I know* in line 17), however, is soon replaced by an argument for the naturalness of the assumption (*a white woman with blond hair and blue eyes speaks English* in lines 19 and 21) – one that he would personally make, and make instinctively *before* assuming anything else (e.g. an Asian woman speaks English) (lines 23–24). His acknowledgment of that assumption being *wrong* is mitigated with the epistemic downgrader *I guess*, rendered dubious by the elongated, lowered-pitch delivery of *wrong* and bleached by the pronouncement of the assumption as *human nature*, and by extension, as inevitable and unimpeachable (lines 25 and 27).

It is also interesting to note that although Mom initiates the problematizing of her experience and initially objects to the racialized assumption (line 16), this is not a line of argument that she pursues. In fact, she receives Dad's account with the minimally acknowledging *hm*, nods and a quiet *myeh* without any question or rejection (lines 20, 22 and 26), and her eventual response (lines 31–32) centers on the irrelevance of the TSA agent's question to the task at hand rather than the validity of its raciolinguistic undertone. As such, Mom too may be conceding to the naturalized assumption and thereby be complicit in reproducing this particular raciolinguistic ideology – at least to some extent. Such implicit enactment is further explored in Extract 3.

### Assessing (white American) English as superior

Raciolinguistic ideologies also emerged as participants assessed English in general, and white American English in particular, as superior to other languages and English varieties. In the following extract, we return to the same TSA discussion around the dinner table from the previous section but focus instead on Mom's (M) 'outrage' and how that outrage may implicitly reproduce a hegemonic raciolinguistic ideology despite appearing to resist it. Chronologically, the excerpt is part of the omitted lines in Extract 2 above. It begins with Mom recalling the exact wording of the TSA agent's question, which receives Dad's rather lukewarm response (lines 01–05). Perhaps to pursue clearer affiliation from Dad, Mom proceeds to enact her hypothetical retort to the TSA agent's question (line 06).

(3) what position

```
01    M:           [>she said< do you unders-]
02                 ee- <she either said do you understand
03                 English, [or do you speak English.=
04    D:           [gaze to phone
05                 =°myea:h.°-gaze to M
06    M:    →      I should've said no: I- >I don't understand
07                 a word you're saying.<
08                 (.)
09                 [          hh hh hh           ]
10    D:           [>that's what you should've said.<]-gaze to phone
11    M:           [I don't want to get into trouble. °we'd ( ) -°]
12    D:           [      lifts head, gaze forward          ]
13                 ↑well (.) gaze to M-you have to understand
14                 their position too.
15    M:    →      (2.5)-eats, gaze to D, lightly shakes head
16                 [Wh↑at position.] ehh °hh hh°
17    D:           [   opens mouth ]
18                 rounds lips, lowers head, gaze away-Hh
19                 closes lip, gaze to M
20                 [    (she's-)            ] Alright
21    M:           [blinks, quick head shake]
22    D:           [I understand $what  you're sa(h)ying but-]
23    M:           [h  h  HAHAHAHA heh heh heh heh heh]
```

While the mere recalling of the TSA agent's question (lines 01–03) leaves its problematic nature unarticulated, the enactment of a hypothetical response brings it into relief. The question is, what exactly is being problematized? Mom could have said, 'Why do you ask?' or 'Does it matter?' – a sentiment she expresses later (see end of Extract 2). Instead, her entire response, framed as an ideal one (*should've said*, line 06), entails decimating the agent's doubt with regard to her ability to speak English, as evidenced in her in-English claim of not understanding English. The irony (also see laugh tokens in line 09) is further dramatized via the extreme case formulation (possibly an upgrade of its initial cut-off version) of *don't understand a word* (Pomerantz, 1986), which, in combination with the fast delivery of the entire clause, flaunts her fluency in and command of the English language.

This focus on rejecting the agent's assumption of her English language ability potentially resists the raciolinguistic ideology that non-white speakers do not speak English although that does not appear to be Mom's main concern at the moment. As we noted earlier, her objection to being questioned ends up targeting more its irrelevance than its raciolinguistic undertone, and she essentially acquiesces to the racialized assumption articulated by Dad (see Extract 2, lines 26 and 31–32). What does seem to figure prominently, however, is Mom's orientation to the superiority of English as symbolic capital, which she possesses and would not stand being viewed as without. As shown, even as Dad pushes for Mom to *understand their position* (line 13–14), Mom refuses to relinquish her indignation at the assumption that someone who does not look white might not speak English. During the (2.5) second gap, rather than aligning with Dad's plea to *understand their position*, she remains silent and lightly shakes her head, which prefigures impending disaffiliation (line 15). Indeed, what ensues is an increased-volume, raised-pitch delivery of the rhetorical question *what position* followed by quiet laugh tokens (line 16), which treats any possible position that could have motivated the TSA agent's questioning as outlandish, illegitimate and inexcusable, i.e. Mom's ability of speaking English is not to be questioned under any circumstances. The sentiment is further amplified via her loud laughter in line 23 in response to Dad's struggle of articulating the 'position'. One might argue that Mom's 'outrage' then at least partially contributes to reinforcing the raciolinguistic ideology that installs the superiority of English as its centerpiece.

In the next extract, which is a continuation of the discussion from Extract 1, we witness how not just English, but white American English in particular, is treated as superior by the language teacher and learners. This superior treatment emerges as the participants portray non-white, non-American speakers (specifically Indian speakers of English) as having low English proficiency, thus jointly orienting to English speaker hierarchies. Before the extract, a student, Clare (C), shared her difficulty with talking to technical support representatives due to her unfamiliarity with specialized, tech-related vocabulary. We join the class as Clare contrasts this difficulty with a situation which she experienced as unproblematic: talking to car-rental service representatives. As her contrastive example unfolds, we see Clare invoking raciolinguistic ideologies to construct car-rental service representatives as being of Indian origin and lacking English proficiency. Again, all participants except for the teacher (T1) are students.

(4) Indian accent
```
01    C:           >and so I had to< call and ask.=and every
02                 time I got some on the f- on the- on the
03         →       phone, they had <much> heavier accent than
04         →       me. so I felt [ like ] an American.
05    T1:                         [yeah.]
06                 [yeah.]
07    C:           [ an:d ] then they were like .h (.) u:h like it
08                 was- usually it was- I think it was some call
09                 site in London (>>I just heard something like<<)
10    T1:                              [ yeah,  ]
11    C:           in Indian accent-[oh (hello)] how can I help you?
12                 you know like
13    T1:          YEAH YEAH YEAH,
14    C:           [ind-]
15    T1:          [NO]
16         →       [THAT'S LIKE A REAL PROBLEM. {is uhm]
17                 -gaze to other Ss}
18    C:   →       [    Indian    accent?   and   then       ]
19                 I tried to- to ex↑plain ↑something to him,
20                 like {in Indian accent-I don't under↑stand,
21                 what did you ↑say,} and then I try it
22                 <again,> and then (.) [°eh° °it's° (.) uh yeah that's-]
23    T1:                                [ ha ha ha ha ha ha ha ha     ]
((10 lines omitted: C talks about feeling confident during the reported interaction))
24    C:           [ if] I don't know the ↑words, it's really
25                 like (↓I'm ↓like) ↓oh ↓my ↓god. (.) maybe
26                 it's the wrong ↑wo:rd?
27                 (.)
28    T1:          nods, gaze to C-yeah yeah yeah yeah yeah.
29                 shifts gaze across Ss-okay, so (.) but that is a
30                 rea:l situation,
31    V:           nods
32    T1:          like a lot of our call centers? ar:e
33                 off[shore now.]=
34    A:           [  nods  ]
35    T1:          =they're like in India, or Bangladesh, or
36                 °something like that right,=[so,°]
37    Z:                                       [m::,]
38    T1:  →       so (.) smiles-you actually would have better
39                 English like eh- than a lot of these people
```

40   V:         *smiles*-a:w,
41   T1:        on the call centers.=right,=and so
42              understanding <u>the</u>ir accents, (.) is another
43              additional challenge °that you might
44              face.°=but .h BUT YOU- it SOUNDS like
45              you were very confident, you kne:w what
46              you were saying,

Clare draws on raciolinguistic ideologies as she ascribes consistent (*every time,* lines 01–02) language-related issues to (what turns out to be) the category of Indian call-center representatives. She assesses category members' accent as hearably non-standard and non-American – *much heavier* than her own (line 03) and noticeably foreign-sounding (*I felt like an American,* line 04) – thus positioning herself as (comparatively) proficient and treating American English as superior to other possible English varieties. As Clare continues her telling, she voices one representative's speech (lines 11–12), formulates their accent as *Indian* (line 18), and then complains about their repeated comprehension issues (lines 19–22). Clare's very voicing of the Indian accent could be heard as mocking invoked category members, given that she is not an (aspiring) incumbent of this category; and her overall category work could be heard as derogatory, given that she portrays Indian call-service representatives as generally inferior to English speakers. Nevertheless, the teacher treats Clare's derogatory category work as unproblematic, aligning and affiliating with her through claims of understanding (line 13), an affiliative assessment (*that's a real problem,* line 16), and appreciative laughter at Clare's construction of category members' frustratingly low English proficiency (line 23).

Upon concluding her telling (omitted lines), Clare returns to her original issue – struggling to communicate clearly when she lacks specialized vocabulary (lines 24–26) – and thus makes advice for managing her communicative trouble relevant next. Although, in accordance with the contiguity principle (Sacks, 1987), the teacher seemingly initiates a response to Clare's re-stated trouble (repeated acknowledgements followed by *okay so,* lines 28–29), he soon abandons this trajectory and instead comments on Clare's contrastive example, treating interactions with Indian call-service representatives as relevant and worthy of highlighting for the entire class. In his commentary, the teacher validates Clare's categorization as factual or *real* (line 30) and expands on it with a three-part list (lines 35–36). Although he does ultimately attribute Clare's reported interactional trouble with Indian call-service representatives to variation in pronunciation (*understanding their accents,* line 42), he nevertheless reinforces Clare's claim that these representatives' English language abilities are lacking compared to those of the present ESL learners, whose proficiency he compliments (*you actually would have better English,* lines 38–39). The teacher's stress on *you* and his use of *actually* in this compliment do appear to frame his contrast between the students and the invoked category as somewhat unexpected, possibly due to the fact that the representatives have been hired to provide assistance in English and should, by implication, be more proficient than English language learners. Regardless, however, *that* Indian call-center representatives' English is inferior is left unchallenged, and the very fact that it is unchallenged seems to suggest the participants' orientation to it as acceptable or, at the very least, recognizable.

### Responding to non-white english as deviant

In this final section we examine how non-white, non-American speakers' English is more implicitly treated as deviant, specifically in repair sequences. Importantly, the non-white, non-American speakers in question are students in ESL classrooms, where various factors might contribute to their English being targeted for repair: (1) their hearably 'non-target-like' English use due to their still-developing English competence; (2) their presumed (if not hearable) lack of English competence due to their omni-relevant English learner role; and/or (3) raciolinguistic ideologies which 'prime' their white-listening subjects to treat their English as deficient. Recognizing that interactants *could* orient to raciolinguistic ideologies as (partly) shaping repair sequences in ESL classrooms, we consider how treating learners' familiar words as unfamiliar through repair might implicitly reinforce the raciolinguistic connection between being non-white/non-American and being a deficient English speaker.

In Extract 5, an Asian student refers to a famous American – Helen Keller – in a class discussion. The white American instructor (T2), however, does not initially recognize the name, leading to repair pursuit and (playful) correction. The episode occurs in a lower-intermediate ESL class following a small group activity in which students discussed reading biographies. As the extract begins, Sakiko (S), a Japanese student, shares the name of the person whose biography she was interested in. All participants except for T2 are students.

(5) Helen Keller
01   S:         °uh when I::-° when I was a child?
02   T2:        *nods*-m::.
03   S:         *gaze down*-I'm very interested i:n *gaze to T2*-Helen

```
04                   (Kirrah)?
05                   (0.3)
06   T2:    →        furrows brow, clasps hands behind head-who?
07                   mouth open
08   S:              gaze to student to her right-↑u::m (0.2) gaze to T2,
09                   brows raised-Helen (Kirrah)?
10   T2:    →        tilts chin down
11   S:              covers mouth with open palm-u::m
12                   gaze to Ss on left-(uh)
13   J:              gaze to S, leans forward-ah [Helen Kell(ah).
14   T2:                                        [gaze to J
15   S:              [gaze to J, nods, smiles-Helen (Kirrah).
16   T2:             [gaze to S
17   J:              [   gaze to T2-(Helen.)    ]
18   S:              [gaze to T2, frowns, gaze to J] opens mouth
19                   gaze to T2-Helen- Hele:n (Kirrah).
20                   (0.2)
21   T2:    →        gaze up-explain. (.) gaze to S-yourself. please.
22                   smiles
23   S:              u::m, (0.8) u:h this is a- #u:(m)-# she is a
24                   gi::RL?
((6 lines omitted: S explains that Keller had meningitis))
25   T2:    →        {nods-okay,} >oh.< {shakes head-.TCH} .hh
26                   (0.2) sighs, drops hands to book in lap-HHHHH
27                   gaze to desk, smiles, rolls chair back-↓Sakiko:.
28   Ss:             la[ughter
29   S:                [smiles, gaze to Ss
30   T2:                [puts book on desk, picks up marker, smiles, stands
31          →        walks to whiteboard, turns to board-are you talking
32                   about- writes ['Helen Keller'
33   S:                             [smiling-°yeah.° y↑(HH)eah yeah. .h
34   T2:             turns to Ss, smiling
35   S:              Helen (Kirrah). [shakes head-(no:?)
36   M:                              [hh smiles-pf::
37                   hh hh hh gaze to S-I: [did not get (°what you
38   S:                                    [gaze to M, smiling
39   M:              [gaze ahead-said.°)
40   S:              [gaze ahead-hhh
41   M:              laughter
42   T2:    →        smiling, shakes head-Saki↓ko:- [#I mea:n come
43                   o::n.#
44   S:                                             [smiles-hhhh
45   T2:    →        turns to whiteboard->(th- th- th- th-)< this is
46                   underlines 'l'-a l::, underlines 'll'-this is a l:,=
```

```
47                      underlines 'r'- =[this is an turns to Ss-r:,
48      S:                              [smiling-oh closes eyes,
49                      covers mouth-r↑eally?
50      T2:     →       #right? <I mean raises arms at sides, palms
51                      down-c'mon.# walks to chair, repeatedly points
52                      index fingers to S-°these are-° these are
53                      different ↑SOU:nds.
54      S:              smiling-.hh (this o::ne, very) d↑iffere::nt,
```

Note that Sakiko produces 'Helen Keller' without explanation (lines 03–04), treating the famous figure as familiar to her audience. While the rising intonation at the end of the name could be heard as inviting a display of recognition, the teacher has trouble recognizing the reference, perhaps due to the student's pronunciation. As represented in the transcript, the pronunciation of the *l* and vowel sounds, as well as the stress placement in 'Keller', are hearable as different from standard American pronunciation. There is a (0.3) second gap, and the teacher initiates repair, targeting the name as the trouble source: *who?* (line 06).

After turning briefly to her partner, Sakiko shifts her gaze to the teacher and repeats the name with eyebrows raised (lines 08–09), displaying surprise at the teacher's non-comprehension. Again, however, the teacher does not display recognition (line 10), and Sakiko gazes to other students, perhaps seeking recognition from them instead (lines 11–12). The name is comprehensible to at least one: a Korean student, Jia (J), leans forward, gazes to Sakiko, and produces a change-of-state- token (*ah*) (Heritage, 1984) before 'Helen Keller', displaying (sudden) recognition (line 13). Although the teacher briefly gazes to Jia (line 14), he does not signal recognition of her production. Sakiko repeats 'Helen Keller' again (line 19), but after a short gap, the teacher continues the repair pursuit: he produces a short directive, *explain*, to which he adds *yourself* (line 21). Here, the teacher frames his lack of understanding as a problem with Sakiko's contribution, one that she is still responsible for correcting via explanation, and not as a problem on his part – i.e. of his own hearing or understanding. Although mitigated with a *please* and a smile (lines 21–22), the teacher's approach positions Sakiko as a non-fluent speaker of English.

In response, Sakiko references Keller's bout with meningitis (omitted lines), after which the teacher produces a change-of-state token, *oh* (line 25), finally displaying his recognition of Sakiko's reference to Hellen Keller. Rather than confirming his understanding and moving the discussion forward, however, the teacher playfully 'reprimands' Sakiko for creating the confusion. He shakes his head, sighs, exhales loudly and says *Sakiko* with a smile and exaggerated prosody, including a pitch drop (lines 25–27) – as if to say, 'Sakiko, you should have known better' – eliciting laughter from the students and a smile from Sakiko. The teacher then walks to the whiteboard and writes 'Helen Keller' as he asks Sakiko to confirm (lines 30–32).

At this point, Maria (M), a Georgian student, smiles, laughs and says that she *did not get* the name either (lines 36–37 and 39), and the teacher continues to, playfully, 'reprimand' Sakiko (lines 42–43). He provides teasing instruction in pronunciation, highlighting her pronunciation of the *l* and *r* sounds as the cause of difficulty (lines 45–47). Pointing to Sakiko, he states that *these are different sounds* (lines 51–53). Notably, he does not specify that they are different sounds in English (the distinction does not exist in Japanese), but instead implicitly treats this feature of the English language as a more general and obvious rule. Throughout, Sakiko has smiled but also displayed new recognition of her pronunciation 'problems' (*oh really*, lines 48–49, and *different*, lines 54). The teacher finally shifts back to on-task talk by asking Sakiko a follow-up question about her interest in Keller's biography (data not shown).

The extended teasing by the teacher keeps the focus on Sakiko's pronunciation and underscores that the responsibility for his non-comprehension lies with her non-fluent speech. The teacher's failure to recognize the familiar name 'Helen Keller' when produced by two Asian speakers (Sakiko and Jia) is not framed, for instance, as a hearing difficulty, or as a result of his lack of familiarity with the speech of English speakers of particular backgrounds. The teacher's problematizing of Sakiko's contribution and the teasing that follows can be seen as implicitly reinforcing the connection between non-white/non-American users of English and deficient speech. It would warrant further research to determine whether the misunderstanding may also be a result of the pervasiveness of such ideology: whether a white, American teacher might anticipate problematic, non-fluent speech from non-white, non-American speakers of English in an ESL class, leading him to find the familiar unfamiliar.

In the final extract, we similarly see raciolinguistic ideologies potentially at work as another ESL teacher (T3) responds quite differently to a Caucasian student's and an Asian student's communication troubles. The teacher has asked students to share personality traits that are important for success (data not shown). After the first candidate response (*goals*, line 01) is accepted (line 03), Irina (I), a Russian student, and Yunsuki (Y), a Japanese student, offer further responses, which engender some troubles in speaking, hearing and understanding. All participants except for T3 are students.

(6) stick with

```
01   I:         m:: (0.4) well- goals,
02              (0.2)
03   T3:        [ nods ]
04   I:         [and uh-] (0.3) m:: (1.5) be strange,
05   T3:   →    gaze to I
06              (0.4)
07   T3:   →    [ gaze to I,  tilts head ]
08   G:         [   hard   work.     ]
09   T3:        hard wo[rk. ↑yeah.    ]-gaze to I, nods
10   I:                [<hard work,>]
11   T3:        >yeah yeah yeah,< gaze to G
12              (0.3)
13   T3:        okay,-gaze to I, then to N, smiles
14              (0.2)
15   Y:         stick with °some thing.°-gaze to T3, moves right
16              arm to the right side and then back to middle
17   T3:   →    wha[t?]-leans in, gaze to Y
18   Y:            [s-] stick with °some thing.°-moves right arm to right
19   T3:        to- (.)
20   Y:         stick. °stick° with. (.) stick.
21   T3:        smiles
22              (0.2)
23   Y:         smiles-<°stick with.°>
24              (0.2)
25   T3:        m:[::: ]-gaze to side, then to Y
26   Y:           [sti]ck. {°°°stick.°°°-gaze to Ss, moves right
27              arm to middle of desk, holds pen}
28   G:         stick?
29   T3:        [gaze to G, then back to Y
30   Y:         [stick.-gaze to G
31   T3:        <stake?>
32   Y:         stick.-gaze to T3
33   T3:        stick- lifts torso slightly-{opens eyes wide-O::::h}
34              to stick with somethi:ng.
35   Y:         stick with.
36   T3:        nods, gaze across Ss->stick with something oh
37              v-< [ very ] good yeh-=
38   Y:             [(stick.)]
39   T3:        =gaze to N and H->to stick with
40              something?<=mea:ns that like .hh you keep
41              going. so even when it's hard,=you don't
42              give up.=you just [li:ke  ] nods-continue.=
43   ( ):                         [mhm.]
44   I:         =[aha, ]
```

```
45    T3:    =gaze to Y->[stick] [with something.<=
46    Y:                  [nods
47    T3:    =[↑yeah good.]-gaze to handout, nods
48    I:                =[stick with. ]
49    T3:    that's: very good. .h (.) yeah.
50           (0.2)
51    T3:    gaze to Ss, smiles slightly
52           (0.6)
53    T3:    anything gaze to handout-else?
```

Irina follows up her initial response to the teacher's question (line 01) with another candidate answer interlaced with intra-turn pauses and delivered in semi-rising intonation: *be strange* (lines 04). Since the teacher elicited traits that can foster success, *strange[ness]*, with its potential negative connotations, might appear as somewhat inapposite; and we see that it is in fact not met with acceptance. Instead of acknowledging or accepting Irina's answer, the teacher merely gazes at her for 0.4 seconds (lines 05–06), possibly creating a space for Irina to initiate a self-repair and clarify her response (cf. Schegloff *et al.*, 1977, on a preference for self- over other-correction). As no self-repair occurs, the teacher, still gazing at Irina, merely tilts her head (line 07), as if non-verbally hinting at (or prefacing) a repair initiation (Seo & Koshik, 2010). However, in overlap with this head tilt, another student, Giorgi (G), proffers another response to the teacher's question *(hard work,* line 08), which the teacher immediately accepts (line 09), abandoning the incipient repair sequence that could have addressed the trouble around Irina's inapposite turn. Interestingly, once Yunsuki's response similarly causes interactional trouble, the repair sequence proceeds quite differently.

In line 15, Yunsuki proffers the verb phrase *stick with some thing [sic]*, with the verb slightly emphasized and the object delivered in a *sotto voce* as two separate words. This time, the teacher initiates repair immediately, with an emphasized open-class repair initiator in rising intonation *(what?,* line 17). Unlike her embodied response to Irina's inapposite answer, the teacher's response to Yunsuki does not leave space for the preferred self-initiated self-repair (Schegloff *et al.*, 1977), and it targets Yunsuki's entire turn as somehow, unidentifiably problematic – in terms of hearing, speaking and/or understanding. Apparently treating the teacher's repair initiation as targeting a problem of hearing and speaking (specifically stress), Yunsuki repeats his turn, shifting his emphasis from the verb to the preposition (line 18). His repair is met with yet another repair initiation: a cut-off *to* (line 19), which projects an infinitive form and thus treats Yunsuki's verb choice as a trouble source. Yunsuki completes this repair by repeatedly providing the elicited verb, now without the object: he delivers the verb with and without the preposition (line 20), with added stress (line 20) and in a slower pace (line 23), but all to no avail. The teacher responds to these various repair solutions with a mitigative smile (line 21), a non-lexical 'thinking' vocalization (line 25) and, after Giorgi (G) offers a candidate hearing in rising intonation (line 28), with her own (incorrect) candidate hearing (*stake*, line 31). Once Yunsuki yet again repeats his verb immediately after the teacher's candidate repair solution, the teacher takes up his pronunciation and finally displays a correct(ed) hearing through an elongated change-of-state token (line 33) (Heritage, 1984) and multiple repeats of Yunsuki's verb phrase (lines 34, 36, 39–40 and 45). She further highlights the phrase by explaining its meaning to the whole class (lines 39–42) and repeatedly positively assesses Yunsuki's response (lines 37, 47 and 49), thus possibly also 'compensating' for her earlier inability to hear and/or understand his contribution.

These observably different ways in which the teacher addresses interactional problems with Irina and Yunsuki could be interpreted, by analysts and participants alike, as grounded in raciolinguistic ideologies. The teacher allows Irina – a Caucasian student from Russia – the space to voluntarily initiate and complete a repair of her own inapposite response, but she does not allow the same space to Yunsuki – an Asian student from Japan. This is not to say that raciolinguistic ideologies alone are in fact at work here, or that they are at work at all. Namely, it is possible that sequential organization and the nature of the interactional trouble contributed to the teacher's differential treatment. Irina had already secured the teacher's recipiency with a turn-initial *and* before introducing her response. In this way, Irina might have 'helped' the teacher hear (and understand) her response more clearly, even if the nuances of that response (i.e. negative connotation) were problematic. Additionally, although the teacher might have further pursued Irina's trouble source, any such pursuit was derailed once another student offered an alternative response, initiating a new sequence. Yunsuki's response, on the other hand, was delivered without already-secured teacher recipiency and with a decrease in volume, which might have rendered it more difficult to hear. It is therefore possible that the teacher was simply treating the problem of not hearing a student as more 'serious' and in need of repair than a problem of a student clearly, though inexactly, expressing herself. While we cannot settle the question of whether this interaction was ultimately shaped by raciolinguistic ideologies and/or by sequence and repair organization, it is important to acknowledge that it could have been experienced as shaped by either (or both) by the participants themselves. In fact, that Yunsuki kept repeating rather than rephrasing his trouble source might suggest his own orientation to and resistance of raciolinguistic ideologies in the interaction. By sticking with his initial response, Yunsuki placed the responsibility for the lack of understanding on the teacher's, i.e. the white listening subject's, hearing ability rather than on his own speaking ability.

## Discussion and Conclusion

In this chapter, we have shown how participants may, implicitly and explicitly, (re)produce raciolinguistic ideologies in both mundane and institutional interaction. These ideologies emerged as participants ascribed English proficiency to whiteness, treated (white American) English as superior, and responded to non-white English as deviant; and through CA's detail-oriented, sequential analysis, we identified specific vehicles for this (tacit) ideological work *in situ*, including embedded presuppositions, category references, proterms, assessments, agreements and repair practices. As such, we hope to have offered a fine-grained glimpse into inequality and exclusion in the intersectionality between race and language. Notably, such exclusionary treatment is not the main business of these exchanges but is 'effortlessly' embedded in a range of routine activities such as accounts, complaints and repairs. It is also exercised and left unchallenged by not only white but also non-white participants. Both observations speak to the potentially alarming extent to which raciolinguistic ideologies are naturalized and sedimented into our collective consciousness. One might argue that it is the unique tool of CA that has allowed us to look in these unlikely places and find surprising evidence for the often-covert reproduction of such ideologies. In that sense then, our findings contribute to the literature on raciolinguistic ideology by increasing both the scope in which and the depth at which such ideology may be exposed and examined. Importantly, given the limited number of instances upon which our analysis is based, we are merely unveiling what methods of instantiating racial ideologies are possible, rather than what is generalizable in the sense of 'the traditional "distributional" understanding of generalizability' (Perakyla, 2004: 296–297). As Pomerantz (1990: 233) writes, the value of CA is that 'we have identified a method ... and subsequent research can establish patterns of occurrences'.

Still, given how deeply tacit or hidden in plain sight the practices detailed in this chapter are, we hope that our findings will bring a wake-up call to the most well-intentioned teachers and parents who would never have otherwise construed their own conduct as perpetuating prejudices. For the teachers featured here, they are simply doing the best they can to perform the most routine work of informing, steering and responding. And for the parents, they are merely engaging in the most mundane activity of mealtime chitchat. Although the child is otherwise preoccupied at the time, the TSA conversation nevertheless constitutes the environment of socialization for the child and is potentially consequential for her developing ideology, even if not in that particular instance at that particular time. Without the forensic probe of CA, however, it may seem unfathomable that it is precisely in the routine and the mundane that certain raciolinguistic ideologies safely find their habitat. And for that matter, it is precisely in the routine and the mundane that we, as teachers and parents, should look – and look first – for any negative ideological traces and imprints that we may have inadvertently left – and can strive to eliminate – in our future encounters.

## Note

(1) 'Ss' stands for multiple students.

## Appendix: Transcription symbols for embodied actions

*nods*         font in italics marks embodied behavior
{*nods*-words}  dash marks co-occurrence of embodied behavior and verbal elements; curly brackets mark the beginning and ending of such co-occurrence when necessary

## References

Briceño, A., Rodriguez-Mojica, C. and Muñoz-Muñoz, E. (2018) From English learner to Spanish learner: Raciolinguistic beliefs that influence heritage Spanish speaking teacher candidates. *Language and Education* 32 (3), 212–226.

Chaparro, S.E. (2019) 'But mom! I'm not a Spanish boy': Raciolinguistic socialization in a two-way immersion bilingual program. *Linguistics and Education* 50, 1–12.

Chávez-Moreno, L.C. (2021) Racist and raciolinguistic teacher ideologies: When bilingual education is 'inherently culturally relevant' for latinxs. *The Urban Review* 54, 554–575.

Cushing, I. and Snell, J. (2022) The (white) ears of Ofsted: A raciolinguistic perspective on the listening practices of the schools inspectorate. *Language in Society* 52 (3).

Daniels, J.R. (2018) 'There's no way this isn't racist': White women teachers and the raciolinguistic ideologies of teaching code-switching. *Journal of Linguistic Anthropology* 28 (2), 156–174.

Flores, N. and Rosa, J. (2015) Undoing appropriateness: Raciolinguistic ideologies and language diversity in education. *Harvard Educational Review* 85 (2), 149–171.

Flores, N., Phuong, J.J. and Venegas, K.M. (2020) 'Technically an EL': The production of raciolinguistic categories in a dual language school. *Tesol Quarterly* 54 (3), 629–651.
Heritage, J. (1984) A change-of-state token and aspects of its sequential placement. In J. M. Atkinson and J. Heritage (eds) *Structures of Social Action: Studies in Conversation Analysis* (pp. 299–345). Cambridge University Press.
Inoue, M. (2006) *Vicarious Language: Gender and Linguistic Modernity in Japan*. University of California Press.
Menard-Warwick, J. (2022) Raciolinguistic ideologies and second language Spanish: Case study of an interracial couple. *Applied Linguistics* 43 (1), 45–64.
Mustonen, S. (2021) 'I'll always have black hair'–challenging raciolinguistic ideologies in Finnish schools. *Nordic Journal of Studies in Educational Policy* 7 (3), 159–168.
Perakyla, A. (2004) Reliability and validity in research based on naturally occurring social interaction. In D. Silverman (ed.) *Qualitative Research: Theory, Method, and Practice* (2nd edn, pp. 283–304). Sage.
Pomerantz, A. (1986) Extreme case formulations: A way of legitimizing claims. *Human Studies* 9 (2), 219–229.
Pomerantz, A. (1990) On the validity and generalizability of conversation analytic methods: Conversation analytic claims. *Communication Monographs* 57 (3), 231–235.
Ricklefs, M.A. (2021) Functions of language use and raciolinguistic ideologies in students' interactions. *Bilingual Research Journal* 44 (1), 90–107.
Rosa, J. (2016a) Racializing language, regimenting Latinas/os: Chronotope, social tense, and American raciolinguistic futures. *Language & Communication* 46, 106–117.
Rosa, J. (2016b) Standardization, racialization, languagelessness: Raciolinguistic ideologies across communicative contexts. *Journal of Linguistic Anthropology* 26 (2), 162–183.
Rosa, J. (2019) *Looking Like a Language, Sounding Like a Race: Inequality and Ingenuity in the Learning of Latina/o Identities*. Oxford University Press.
Rosa, J. and Flores, N. (2017) Unsettling race and language: Toward a raciolinguistic perspective. *Language in Society* 46 (5), 621–647.
Sacks, H. (1987) On the preferences for agreement and contiguity in sequences in conversation. In G. Button and J.R.E. Lee (eds) *Talk and Social Organization* (pp. 54–69). Multilingual Matters.
Schegloff, E.A., Jefferson, G. and Sacks, H. (1977) The preference for self-correction in the organization of repair in conversation. *Language* 53 (2), 361–382.
Seo, M.S. and Koshik, I. (2010) A conversation analytic study of gestures that engender repair in ESL conversational tutoring. *Journal of Pragmatics* 42 (8), 2219–2239.
Subtirelu, N.C. (2017) Raciolinguistic ideology and Spanish-English bilingualism on the US labor market: An analysis of online job advertisements. *Language in Society* 46 (4), 477–505.
Sung, K.K. (2018) Raciolinguistic ideology of antiblackness: Bilingual education, tracking, and the multiracial imaginary in urban schools. *International Journal of Qualitative Studies in Education* 31 (8), 667–683.
Swift, K. (2022) 'The good English': The ideological construction of the target language in adult ESOL. *Language in Society* 51 (2), 309–331.
Thoma, N. (2020) 'I don't want to be pushed into an Islamic school': Biography and raciolinguistic ideologies in education. *Race Ethnicity and Education*. https://doi.org/10.1080/13613324.2020.1798390

# 3 Racist Renditions: Mock Language in Interaction

Elliott M. Hoey and Chase Wesley Raymond

## Introduction

In her seminal article 'Language, Race, and White Public Space', Jane Hill (1998) focuses on the discursive practices that constitute Whiteness as an unquestioned, unmarked, normalized order within US society. Hill writes that 'White public space' is constructed through:

(i) intense monitoring of the speech of racialized populations such as Chicanos, Latinos and African Americans for signs of linguistic disorder, and
(ii) the invisibility of almost identical signs in the speech of Whites, where language mixing, required for the expression of a highly valued type of colloquial persona, takes several forms (1998: 680).

Hill (1993, *et seq.*) offers what she calls 'Mock Spanish' as a case-in-point, describing several indexical strategies recurrently used in producing this mock variety:

(i) Semantic pejoration of Spanish words – the use of positive or neutral Spanish words in humorous or negative contexts (e.g., *nada* to mean 'less than nothing', *peso* to convey 'cheap')
(ii) Mock Spanish euphemism – the use of obscene or scatological Spanish words in place of English equivalents (e.g., the use of *cojones*)
(iii) The use of Spanish grammatical elements – the addition of the 'Spanish' suffix +*o* to nouns and the use of the definite article *el* (e.g., *el cheapo*)

(iv) Hyperanglicization – parodic pronunciations and orthographic representations that reflect an exaggerated English phonology (e.g., *Fleas Navidad* on a Christmas card).
(summarized in Barrett, 2006: 164; Schwartz, 2011: 653–4)

Notwithstanding the direct indexicality of Mock Spanish, 'which includes dimensions such as an easygoing and relaxed attitude, a sense of humor, cosmopolitanism, and regional authenticity', Hill (2005) argues there is also an indirect indexical relationship at work in that 'a "deep background", a fully naturalized set of understandings of persons in Spanish-speaking populations' is necessary for participants to appreciate the 'humor' of Mock Spanish in the first place (2005: 114). That is, for such formulations to make sense, participants must tap into 'racist stereotypes of Spanish speakers, and more broadly, of all members of historically Spanish-speaking populations as lazy, dirty, unintelligent, sexually loose, and politically corrupt, as persons who speak a language that is not only disorderly and somewhat primitive but also "easy" and well suited to insincerity and to talk suited to sloth, filth, licentiousness, and the like' (Hill, 2005: 114; see also Barrett, 2006; Hill, 1993, 1998, 2008; Rosa, 2016; Schwartz, 2011).

Hill's work on Mock Spanish has inspired explorations of different dimensions of 'mock' languages, including 'Mock Chinese' (Nassenstein, 2020), 'Mock Taiwanese-Accented Mandarin' (Su, 2004), 'Mock Filipino' (Hiramoto, 2011) and 'Mock ESL' (Talmy, 2010). Such scholars have interrogated the design and the semiotics of mock language, underscoring the racial and cultural ideologies and stereotypes linked to their use and interpretation. This is all the more evident in researchers' invocation of racial categories as part of their analytic terminology – e.g. 'Mock Asian' (Chun, 2004) and 'Mock White Girl' (Slobe, 2018) (see also Mason Carris, 2011, on '*la voz gringa*' and Schwartz, 2008, on '*Gringoism*'). In addition to the different languages and sociocultural contexts represented in this literature, we find a diversity of interactional settings and data types examined. These range from spoken practices used in everyday conversations (e.g. Chun, 2009), to those used in on-stage performances, movies, YouTube and television (e.g. Chun, 2004; Hiramoto, 2011; Slobe, 2018), to written practices observed in online contexts (e.g. Ronkin & Karn, 1999; Su, 2004), and in advertisements, greeting cards, t-shirts and the like (e.g. Callahan, 2010; Potowski, 2011). Ethnographic and experimental research in this area routinely and explicitly draws upon a mix of these materials as sources of data (e.g. Barrett, 1996; Callahan, 2010, 2014; Hill, 1993, 1998, 2008; Nassenstein, 2020; Roth-Gordon, 2011).

In an adjacent body of work, researchers interested in social actions in interactive contexts have investigated various forms of what can be conceptualized as 'imitation' – e.g. self- and other-repetition; partial, full, modified and expanded verbal repeats – and considered their import by reference to their sequential environments. Early work on next-turn repair initiation, for instance, showed how other-repetition may be taken as prefatory to disagreement (Schegloff et al., 1977). Subsequent studies on the recycling of others' talk began to explicate the precise operation of other disaffiliative practices, with a range of researchers illustrating how imitation can be used to comment on or display some stance towards the source and/or animator of the imitated talk. Couper-Kuhlen (1996), for example, demonstrated how English-speaking participants prosodically distinguish acts of quotation from mockery via relative or absolute register matching, respectively (see also Culpeper, 2005). Similarly, studies of children's argumentation (Goodwin & Goodwin, 1987) and classroom interactions (Tainio, 2012a, 2012b) have shown the more biting edge of imitation, where participants use the practice for criticism and disaffiliation.

The present study brings together these interdisciplinary lines of inquiry by considering mock language *as an interactional practice* – that is, as produced and understood in the service of action. Drawing upon a corpus of racist/racialized altercations (see next section), we use conversation analysis (CA) to uncover how mock-language practices can emerge within, and be fitted to, the particulars of their interactional environments. We discuss what these practices accomplish within the immediacy of heated exchanges and how such actions work to maintain 'White public space'.[1]

## Data and Method

Data for this study are from the open-access Corpus of Language Discrimination in Interaction (CLDI) (Raymond et al., in prep.-a). The interactions in the CLDI, composed of videos drawn primarily from institutional security cameras and private citizens' smartphones, show concrete instances of language policing and discrimination. Specifically, they involve one party – the Aggressor – harassing another party – the Target – for the language they are speaking or otherwise endorsing in public (e.g. restaurants, parks, parking lots).[2]

The CLDI offers an opportunity to examine mock language 'in action'. Because we have audio-visual data of real-time, authentic interactions, we can ask what mock language accomplishes within interaction – that is, we can consider mock language *as an interactional practice*. In addition, we attend to the use of mock language in demonstrably disaffiliative, argumentative, racist/racialized encounters among strangers. In these exchanges, unvarnished racist sentiments regularly reach the interactional surface in far more explicit ways than in other sorts of data, where the 'covertness' and 'indirectness' (see especially Schwartz, 2011: 653–660) of mock-language practices are often at the core of their pervasiveness and oppressive power. By contrast, in our cases, overt mocking is a primary and identifiable feature of the turns in question.

In what follows, we describe the operation of what we are calling 'racist renditions' based on a collection of 27 cases identified in the CLDI. These are verbal actions produced during an ongoing altercation, typically in responsive position, whereby the speaker (i.e. Aggressor) conspicuously adopts in a hearably mocking manner one or more features of the recipient's (i.e. Target) language variety. In our data, Aggressors use what would be called 'standard' US English, and Targets use Spanish, Mandarin or, as we will see, some variety of English. Regarding our terminology, these are 'renditions' in that they are not strict repetitions, but instead interpretations or performances of the recipient's language variety. We take this to be 'racist' in that the recipients and their languages are racialized through acts of abuse and domination, which analysts are able to bear concrete witness to at both the immediate (i.e. local, sequential) level as well as across the exchanges more broadly.

We examine these data using CA, which aims to uncover the practices, and normative organizations of practice, through which participants constitute and make sense of action in interaction (for an overview, see Clift, 2016). Candidate practices of action are considered both singularly and across collections (see e.g. Clift & Raymond, 2018; Hoey & Kendrick, 2017). We take a critical perspective in our analysis, highlighting not only how racist renditions are designed and what they achieve *in situ*, but also how those designs and functions are predicated on racist ideological foundations and serve to maintain 'White public space'. A critical CA approach reveals that racist renditions put racist ideology into action, enacting a form of linguistic abuse that is identifiable as such through the particulars of their sequential deployment. We undertake this study from particular positions with respect to the research topic and data. Both authors are US-born scholars of language and social interaction whose first and main language is US English. In addition to these national and professional identities, what is brought to bear on particular analyses is the first author's self-identification as Chinese-American, and the second author's expertise in Spanish linguistics.

## Analysis

We show two devices used in the production of racist renditions. In the first case, a Target's usage of a non-English language is subsequently mocked through a turn made of context-specific nonsense syllables.[3] We then turn to cases where Targets' English-language usage is mocked in next turn through a scrupulous emphasis of its 'non-native' features. With these responsively-positioned devices, Aggressors operate on the *design* of the prior speaker's turn and notably do not deal with its content or action implications. As such, racist renditions cast Targets' speech not only as unintelligible, but as unworthy of comprehension. Sequentially, this unilaterally pushes for sequence termination in that it constrains possibilities for next actions. The responsive options by the Target become limited to either silence – which is what the Aggressor aims for, we argue – or some defense or counterattack – which, as we will show, risks furnishing the Aggressor with fresh content for further language-based attack. We argue that this practice is thus a particularly salient sequential-interactional tool in the policing of 'White public space' and maintenance of English dominance in the US.

### Racist renditions of Target's non-English language usage

In several cases, we have the following sequence:

Target: turn in a non-English language
 (*addressed to someone other than the Aggressor*)
Aggressor: rendition of the prior turn using nonsense syllables
 (*addressed to the Target*)

Amidst an ongoing altercation, the Target produces some talk in a non-English language. This is usually addressed to the Target's companion, who understands what was said, but is also audible to the Aggressor.[4] Although the Aggressor was not addressed, they nevertheless self-select to interject (Lerner, 2019) this racist rendition device. The Aggressor's 'response' to the Target's turn is built with nonsense syllables that approximate linguistic features of the non-English language; that is, the Aggressor works to prosodically-phonetically 'format tie' (Goodwin, 1990: 177–185) their utterance to the Target's prior through a mocking imitation of the particulars of that prior turn. Interactionally, though, this action by the Aggressor is not linked to the Target's prior turn through any sort of conditional relevance (Schegloff & Sacks, 1973); indeed, the content and action implication of the Target's turn are likely opaque to the Aggressor, which underlies the operation of the practice as accomplishing sequential obstruction. Whatever the Target was pursuing with their initial turn is treated not merely as unintelligible (which might warrant repair; Schegloff *et al.*, 1977) but as undeserving of comprehension. The Aggressor's purposefully nonsensical rendition serves to obstruct the Target's line of action by disattending whatever action was done prior and constraining what can be done next. As the case below shows, the aimed-for sequential outcome is for the Target to be silenced. In this respect, the practice pushes for sequence termination by offering what potentially stands as the 'final word' of the exchange.

Consider case (1) below, which shows an ongoing altercation in a parking lot right as the Target begins recording video on her smartphone.[5] The inciting event appears to have involved the (non)use of a vehicle turn signal, which the Aggressor links explicitly to the Target's racial identity.[6] The Aggressor has subsequently parked her car so that the Target and her Companion cannot leave their parking space. The focal sequence appears near the end of this transcript; however, we include much of the preceding action to show how the racist rendition is not the sole instance of hostility, but rather is situated in a stream of verbal and physical abuse by the Aggressor.

Orienting to camera (Laurier & Philo, 2006), the Aggressor raises her middle fingers, advances towards the Target and gives an ironic performance, singing a little melody and an *I love you too* (line 07). The Aggressor then suddenly escalates the situation: she strikes at the Target's smartphone camera, calls her a *fucking bitch*, and shoves her into the side of her car while demanding she *get out of here* (lines 08–09). The Aggressor then shouts about the Target starting the conflict due to her alleged non-use of a turn signal. As she does so, she approaches the Target, who reacts by taking a step backward and directing a kick toward the Aggressor (though doesn't make contact). After things come to an apparent impasse, the Aggressor instructs the person seated in her car to *Get my phone* so she can call the police to have the Target charged *for kicking me* (lines 39–42). As the Aggressor is visibly occupied with her phone, the Target likewise instructs her Companion (in Mandarin) to call the police (lines 43, 46).

(1) CLDI_047
```
    01      AGG:    Wha:t?
    02              (.)
    03      AGG:    If you fuckin do: that, you fuckin chi:nk(h).
    04              Δ(0.5)
            agg     Δwalks twd COM->
```

```
05      COM:    ~Can we pl(h)e(h)ase just .hh- (go now)~
06              Δ(1.3)
     agg        ->Δgives middle fingers to TAR's camera,
                advances towards TAR->
07      AGG:    ↑ahla*lalala:, ↑lalalalala:, I ↑love you ↑too:.
08              Δ(0.8)Δ (yeah) you fuckin bitch,
     agg        Δstrikes cameraΔ
09              Δget out of here ma:n,Δ oka:y?
     agg        Δshoves TAR into carΔ
```

((29 lines removed. The Aggressor claims that Target initiated the conflict because of her non-use of signal lights. As she does so, she advances towards the Target, who kicks in her direction, though doesn't make contact. The Aggressor then issues several threats in response, and resolves to call the police to report Target for the kick.))

```
39      AGG:    I:'m calling nine one one, and >I'm gonna
40              have you< charged.
41              (0.5)
42      AGG:    for [kicking me.
43      TAR:        [Ta yijing da [chi le. Kuaidian da.
                    She called the police late. Call them now..
44      AGG:                      [You ↑just kicked me right
45              here.
46      TAR:    Kuaidian [da. Xianzai jui da.
                Call them now. Just call now.
47      AGG             [<YOU JU:ST KICKED ME
48              RIGHT HERE, BI:TCH.>
49              (.)
50      TAR:    Dǎ- wǒ dǎ tā le ma? ((to COM))
                Hi- did I hit her?
51              (0.3)
52      AGG:    ahr rye >nyow=nyow=nyow<. Kay:, shut up.
                [ʔɑʲ ɹaɪ njaʊ njaʊ njaʊ njaʊ]
53              (1.3)
54      COM:    Can we please [just     ] chi:ll.
55      AGG:                  [↑Nope.]
56                      (0.5)
57      AGG:    Tell her to ch ((video ends))
```

Overlapping with the Target's Mandarin-language turn, the Aggressor redelivers her account for calling the police (lines 43–45). Then again, she recycles her account in overlap with the Target's Mandarin-language turn, modifying it with elevated intensity and a turn-final derogatory address term BI:TCH (lines 46–48). The Target does not respond to this, but instead directs another turn in Mandarin to her Companion, *Dǎ- wǒ dǎ tā le ma?* 'Hi- did I hit her?' (line 50). It is this usage of a non-English language that gets targeted by the Aggressor in next turn.

Though this turn was addressed to the Target's Companion, the Aggressor self-selects to speak next, thereby intruding upon the (Mandarin-language) exchange of which she was not a ratified participant. The Aggressor's racist rendition features nonsense syllables, several of which are reduplicated, which approximate Mandarin morphophonology. Specifically, we see a heavy reliance on nasal velars and vocalic codas, and a hearable 'choppiness' where each syllable receives roughly the same prosodic emphasis (see Chun, 2004; Nassenstein, 2020). Additionally, the rendition copies other aspects of the Target's turn in more or less 'absolute' terms (see Couper-Kuhlen, 1996): Both turns are six syllables long, stressed on the second syllable, and nearly identical in duration (Target's 750ms and Aggressor's 800ms).

What this racist rendition accomplishes is more than mocking the sounds of another language. It is predicated on the opacity of the non-English language to the Aggressor and thereby highlights the linguistic distinction between these parties. But rather than being a marker of the Aggressor's ignorance of Mandarin or an occasion to seek greater understanding of the other, this difference is used to shut down further talk. In the same way that the designedly nonsensical turn offers no substantive response to the Target's initial turn, it also implicates no particular next action. The apparent interactional goal is to immobilize the continued use of Mandarin by making it near impossible to produce a relevant next action. Additional evidence that this device is meant to unilaterally terminate the sequence is found in the Aggressor's turn-extension, *Kay: shut up* (line 52). Moreover, when the Target's Companion asks *Can we please…*, the Aggressor issues ↑*Nope.* interjacently (Sacks, *et al.*, 1974), before the verb of the request is even delivered, and with a labial closure that declines expansion.

This case demonstrates how a Target's use of a non-English language may be used as an occasion for the Aggressor to intervene in that trajectory of action. In this sequential environment, Aggressors find themselves excluded linguistically, through the Target's use of a language they cannot understand, and interactionally, due to not having been allocated a turn. Despite their lack of linguistic resources to engage with the prior non-English turn, however, Aggressors may nonetheless work to reassert agency from responsive position by interjecting a mock-language turn. With this racist rendition device, Aggressors produce a wholesale replacement of a non-English turn with nonsense syllables that approximate the sounds of that language, thereby trivializing and overriding the actions being done in the non-English language, and unilaterally pushing to terminate that line of action.

### Racist renditions of Target's English-language usage

In another set of cases, we have the following sequence:

Target: turn in English
(*addressed to the Aggressor*)
Aggressor: rendition of some feature(s) of the prior turn as 'non-native'
(*addressed to the Target*)

In an ongoing altercation, the Target addresses an English-language turn to the Aggressor. Then, the Aggressor responds in a way that exaggerates some 'non-native' ('accented', 'non-standard', etc.) pronunciational and/ or grammatical form(s), which are attributed to the Target's prior turn or to their general linguistic repertoire.[7] Compared to the racialized nonsense syllables examined in the previous section, this device for producing a racist rendition is more focused in its operation. Rather than wholly supplanting the Target's turn with a nonsensical one, the Aggressor selectively substitutes their own 'native' features with the Target's 'non-native' ones.

This shift in the Aggressor's speech is notable for at least two reasons. First, their speech prior to our turns of interest does not incorporate mock-language features, and thus we can ask why they are produced at these moments. And second, the specific 'non-native' features that are now being treated as interactionally problematic have not been treated as such until this moment. Prior to this point, the Target's English, including the pronunciational/grammatical variants in question, were treated as intelligible. This suggests that Aggressors are *able* to respond to the content, action(s) and implication(s) of the turn in question, but *elect* not to do so. Instead of producing a relevant next action, the Aggressor questions the intelligibility of the Target's speech. This works to topicalize non-nativeness such that, as with the device analyzed in the prior section, the Target's trajectory of action becomes derailed.

Consider case (2), which shows two separate instances of this sequence. Here, the Target is a driver for Lyft, a rideshare service coordinated via smartphone, and the Aggressor is his passenger in the backseat of the car. Prior to this, the participants were arguing over wearing a facemask in the car, to which the Aggressor objected, despite it being required by Lyft at

58   Part 1: Reproducing Inequality and Injustice

the time in accordance with COVID-19 pandemic regulations. This escalated until the Target stopped the car and asked the Aggressor to leave. The extract below begins as the passenger objects to this. Not only does it mean that he would need to find another way to his destination, but the Target's decision to *finish* (rather than *cancel*) the trip means that he would still need to pay for this prematurely completed ride.

(2) CLDI_025

```
178   AGG:    <How can you sa:y you finished the tri:p>
179            (0.8) when (.) I want to [go: (.) over THERE.
180   TAR:                              [I did finish the trip.
181            I finished the trip.
182            (2.0)
183   AGG:    You didn't cancel the trip [though.
184   TAR:                               [I di:d- No I
185            didn't cancel I finished the trip. (.)
187            [It's different.
188   AGG:    [Okay so I'll >just have to< call Lyft and then
189            complain about [you.
190   TAR:                   [GO AHEAD,
191   AGG:    Okay, that's what I'll do then.=
192   TAR:    =Go ahead. I have bideo,
                                 ['biðio]
193            (1.5)
194   AGG:    Yeah you got *bideo.=
                            ['bɪdio]
                          *gazes at TAR through rearview->
195   TAR:    =↑Yeah.=
196   AGG:    =You got bideo?=
197   TAR:    =∆↑Yeah.=
              ∆gazes at AGG through rearview->>
198   AGG:    =Hey you got *bideo?*
                           *with intensified/widened gaze*
199            (.)
200   TAR:    ↑Yeah.
201   AGG:    Hey you ever take English class, you got bideo?
202            (1.3)
203   AGG:    You got bideo?
204            ≈(3.0)≈
              both    ≈mutual gaze through rearview≈
205   AGG:    [*You little b-]
              *begins opening car door to exit->
206   TAR:    [Do- do you ] take *a morals: (0.3) class?
                                            ['morɑlz]
```

```
                  agg                *suspends opening door->>
207     AGG:      Do I take what?
208     TAR:      Morals.
                  ['morɑlz]
209               (1.0)
210     AGG:      What's m- What's mohdahls.=
                  ['morʊɫz]
211     TAR:      =You don't even- you don't- you don't even
212               speak [Eng:lish.
213     AGG:              [No I: I don't- I don't kno:,
214               .hh cuz I speak English:.
215               (.)
216     TAR:      Yeah, (.) you think you'd speak
217               [E- you'd speak English, [but you don't.
218     AGG:      [Where you from   (.)    [bo::y?8
219     TAR:      I'm from here.
220               (.)
221     AGG:      .tch No you're not.=
222     TAR:      =Ye:s I am.
223     AGG:      You're a fuckin wetback9.
```

When the Aggressor's repeated objections prove unsuccessful in changing the Target's decision, the Aggressor threatens to *call Lyft and then complain about [the Target]* (lines 178–189). The Target responds by emphatically welcoming the threat with *GO AHEAD*, after which he informs the Aggressor that he has a video-recording of the ride (lines 190–192) – i.e. a basis for dismissing the threat. In producing the word 'video', the Target uses a bilabial stop [b] (in line with Spanish phonotactic norms) rather than a labiodental fricative [v] (in line with 'standard' English pronunciation).[10] This pronunciation is then targeted and introduced in the Aggressor's next several turns using the word *bideo* (lines 194, 196, 198, 201, 203).

The Aggressor's renditions of *bideo* require some contextualization. The Target had used a bilabial articulation (rather than labiodental) at least five times in this encounter (and indeed, two of these were the word 'video'; data not shown), and this pronunciation was not problematized in any way. This indicates that the Aggressor had no issue with understanding the Target's talk in general, and no problem with understanding this pronunciation in particular. Additionally, prior to this point the Aggressor had not substituted [v] for [b] in his own talk, and so the introduction of that substitution in *bideo* (line 194, *et seq.*) was apparently done for cause. Through this selective substitution, the Aggressor problematizes the Target's English proficiency and topicalizes 'non-nativeness'.

In this case, the racist rendition is done while issuing a declaratively formatted request for confirmation, *you got bideo* (line 194). The Target treats this as a request for confirmation by responding with a plain *yeah*, evidently not hearing or choosing not to orient to the intended mocking action. This occasions two additional pursuits by the Aggressor, who heightens subsequent productions of *you got bideo* with the addition of rising prosody (line 196), the attention-shifter *hey*, and widened/intensified eyes (line 198). The Target again responds to these with *yeah* (lines 197, 200). In light of the Target's lack of orientation to the mock *bideo* pronunciation, the Aggressor more explicitly topicalizes the matter of non-nativeness by asking *Hey you ever take English class*, followed by two additional renditions of *you got bideo*? (lines 201–203). Together, these treat the Target's responses as insufficiently orienting to the hostile mockery of the Aggressor.

Three seconds of silence then elapse during which there is sustained eye contact between Aggressor and Target via the rearview mirror (line 204). This lapse in turn-by-turn talk (Hoey, 2020) indicates that the Aggressor awaits some response to his topicalization of non-nativeness. Part of how the device operates as a racist practice inheres in such moments. Like responding to the nonsense deformations examined above, the Aggressor's aimed-for response is silent submission. We see some orientation to this in how the Aggressor ends the lapse (Hoey, 2018): while starting to exit the car, he 'gets in the last word' with *You little b-* (line 206), presumably on his way to calling the Target 'bitch'.

For the Target, this lapse also points to a difficulty in formulating a response. Recipients of such verbal abuse find themselves in a bind because the sequential environment pushes for a response (to counterattack, defend themselves, etc.), yet their speech is what furnishes the materials for ridicule. Indeed, this is what happens next. Countering the Aggressor's *you ever take English class*, the Target poses a question in kind, *do you take a morals: (0.3) class?* (line 206). His pronunciation of *morals* includes an 'accented' alveolar tap [ɾ] rather than a 'standard' postalveolar approximant [ɹ]. This occasions repair initiation by the Aggressor (*Do I take what?*), followed by the incorporation of the alveolar tap in another racist rendition *What's m- What's mohdahls* (line 210).

This example illustrates how a Target's English-language usage may serve as a resource for verbal abuse. With this device, Aggressors claim misunderstanding and attribute that misunderstanding to the 'non-nativeness' of some feature(s) of the Target's speech. Importantly, these are not naïve or innocent misunderstandings on the part of Aggressors (cf. genuine other-initiations of repair; Schegloff et al., 1977), but rather performed misunderstandings, produced so as to hijack the trajectory of action underway by topicalizing 'nativeness' vs. 'non-nativeness' as relevant categories.

## The ideological basis of racist renditions

Before proceeding on to our Discussion, let us consider one final case in (3). In this interaction, the Aggressor employs both of the devices examined above, and in a way that reveals the ideological foundations of racist renditions. The Target in this recording uses only 'standard' US English, and so he supplies no 'non-native' speech to mock. However, the Target is visibly East Asian, and this categorization supplies what is needed for the Aggressor's racist renditions. This case therefore profoundly illustrates that racist renditions are fundamentally based on raciolinguistic ideologies about what sorts of sounds racialized others might produce.

In case (3), we join a dispute in a parking lot involving participants whose cars are parked side by side.[11] While the precise substance of the dispute is unclear, the video prior to the transcript below showed the Aggressor making racist comments (e.g. *go home*) and threats (*I play games where you get fucked to death*). The Target began recording, soon moving out of his car to document the Aggressor's license plate and narrate for the camera what had transpired (lines 27, 29–30). This is treated as an escalation, as the Aggressor threatens to call the police who will take him to *rea:l jai:l* (lines 28, 32). For the remainder of the exchange, he is positioned in front of her car, recording, while she stands next to the opened driver's side door of her car.

(3) CLDI_029
```
    27    TAR:    *So this lady,*
                  *pans camera to license plate*
    28    AGG:    I:'m calling [the police on you.]
    29    TAR:                 [JU::st    made a:] (.) racist
    30            comment.=I can't ↑believe thi:s.
    31            Δ*(1.5)
          agg     Δmoves to, stands near driver's side door->>
          tar     *stands in front of AGG's car, facing her->>
    32    AGG:    You:: are gonna go to <rea:l jai:l no:w.>
    33            (0.5)
    34    TAR:    We[ll great, you are-
    35    AGG:      [↑You undastan me Tschi:na:ma:n?↑=
                   [ʌndʌstæn]   [tsʰaɪnəmæːn]
```

```
36   TAR:         =I think you're go[ing
37   AGG:                       [↑y'undastan me
38                Tschinama:n?↑
39                (0.8)
40   AGG:         ↑You undastan me Tschinama:n↑≤.
41   TAR:         <Re::spect>=
42   AGG:         =rethp#e[:ct
                  [ɹiθpɛːˈkt]
43   TAR:                 [<Re:spect peo[ple>,
44   AGG:                               [rethp#ect,
45   TAR:         [la:dy.
46   AGG:         [↑I can' undastan you language e-
47                [Tschinama:n.↑
48   TAR:         [<Re::s:pect> <lady.>
49   AGG:         ↑Rethp#ect?↑ Then you move your car.
50                (1.5)
51   TAR:         [There you go.
52   AGG:         [You are WAY too clo:se. Get away from me=
53   TAR:         =There you go:.
54   AGG:         yehpuhbleuhyuh? [(     )
                  [ˈjɛpəblə'jʌ]
55   TAR:                         [*<You don't even kno:w,>
                                  *pans camera to show space
                                  on both sides of AGG's car->
56   AGG:         [yehpuhbleuhyuh?
57   TAR:         [<how to park the ca:r.>*
                                       ------------------>*
58   AGG:         ↑you thpeak Engle:sh?↑
59   TAR:         [<You don't even know.>
60   AGG:         [↑Do you know who my family ↑is?=
61   TAR:         =There you go=
62   AGG:         =↑Do you know who my family is? Do you
63                know who your family is? Go home to
64                your fam-uh-ly.↑
```

After the Aggressor's threat (*You:: are gonna go to <rea:l jai:l no:w.>*, line 32), she gazes to the Target in expectation of a response. However, there is no immediate uptake, but a 0.5-second silence (line 33). This gap provides for turn-continuation by the Aggressor (Sacks *et al.*, 1974), who treats the Target's silence as indicating problems in comprehension. She repeatedly asks ↑*You undastan me Tschi:na:ma:n?*↑ (lines 35, 37–38, 40). She designs these renditions in an approximation of Mandarin phonology, including syllable-timed rhythm (a 'choppiness' with roughly equal prosodic weight for each syllable), weakened syllabic codas (r-deletion and d-deletion in *undastan*), and substitution of the palato-alveolar affricate [tʃ] with a heavily aspirated dental affricate [t̪s̪ʰ] at the beginning of the pejorative 'Chinaman'. Notably, these pronunciational features are totally absent from the Target's English, which is describable as hearably 'standard'. What's more, there is no evidence that the Target has problems understanding the Aggressor's speech. His 'problem' in understanding, then, is wholly attributed to him by the Aggressor, on the basis of her (repeated) racialized categorization of him as 'Chinaman'. That is, the Aggressor uses her racialization of the Target alone as a foundation for introducing mock-language features, irrespective of the Target's actual speech (cf. Culpeper, 2005), and she then uses this virtual misunderstanding as a basis for racist abuse.

As their interaction proceeds, the Aggressor moves further from the actual details of the interaction and deeper into the raciolinguistic ideologies that underpin the practice. Responding to the Aggressor's provocations, the Target tells her <Re::spect> (line 41), which he expands in subsequent self-repeats as <Re:spect people>, la:dy. and <Re::s:pect> <lady.> (lines 43, 45, 48). Though he produces these with a 'standard' alveolar [s] and modal voicing, the Aggressor selects these features for substitution – replacing [s] with an interdental [θ] 'th'-sound and modal voicing with harsh laryngealization in *rethpe#ct* [ɹiθpɛːˈkt] (lines 42, 44, 49).

These substitutions might be curious at first, since they have no obvious analogues in Mandarin. We might explain them as drawing upon Western discourses of Asian masculinity to index weakness or femininity (Shek, 2007), an interpretation that is consistent with the Aggressor's continued usage of high pitch throughout her renditions and her closing reference to the Target's *little boyfriend* (data not shown). At the same time, there is data-internal evidence to see these substitutions as her *ad hoc* efforts at producing 'deformed' English. Embedded among her renditions we see ↑*I can' undastan you language eh- Tschinama:n.*↑ (lines 46–47) – an explicit (though obviously nonserious) claim of non-understanding. Additionally, in this claim she substitutes the possessive 'your' with *you*, which gives her caricature a 'Tarzan'-like simplicity. The evident aim of the Aggressor, then, is to impute to the Target – despite all experiential evidence to the contrary – an unintelligibility that renders him, his talk, his actions and his language as inconsequential for the progression of the interaction. Additional evidence that the Aggressor is not actually working in pursuit of genuine shared understanding can be found in her continued interjacent overlap throughout the exchange (Drew, 2009; Sacks *et al.*, 1974; Schegloff, 2000b).

The final aspect which we would like to draw attention to is the Aggressor's use of nonsense syllables *yehpuhbluehyeh?* (line 54 and repeated in line 56). This is produced as a nonsense deformation of the Target's prior *English*-language turn *There you go* (line 53). Her turn thus combines both of the devices described above. It follows on from an English-language turn, and is therefore like our second example; but it also is formatted as a wholesale replacement of that turn using nonsense syllables, and is therefore akin to our first case. We take this blending of devices as an indication that they are the same kind of thing for participants rather than wholly distinct practices. Both are aimed at browbeating the Target into silence, and both do so through the deployment of raciolinguistic ideologies about intelligibility and relative worth.

In sum, this case demonstrates that, to produce a racist rendition, Aggressors need no actual materials from the interaction on which to operate. It suffices that a racialized Target is present, whose categorization as such furnishes all that is needed for this form of verbal abuse.

## Discussion and Conclusion

In this chapter, we have offered an interactional take on mock language, thereby contributing to research in this area on two foundational fronts. First, we brought a novel sort of data into the discussion of mock language and what it is used to do. Whereas prior work has focused on relatively covert or seemingly benign forms of mock language, here we have captured a dimension of the phenomenon in its vibrant hostility. Within the CLDI, mock-language practices like racist renditions are regularly situated within streams of racist, homophobic and other forms of abuse. That we routinely find such practices working together within confrontational contexts offers additional evidence that mock-language practices find their foundations in racist ideologies, as argued in prior work (e.g. Chun, 2009; Hill, 1993, *et seq.*; Hiramoto, 2011; Nassenstein, 2020; Schwartz, 2011).[12] We thus contribute to research in this arena by further illustrating how language can be used as a sort of 'proxy' for the on-the-ground accomplishment of racism and other forms of discrimination in social life (see e.g. Alim *et al.*, 2016; Lippi-Green, 2012; Rosa & Flores, 2017).

Second, by using CA, we have expanded the theoretical and methodological toolkit for examining mock language. Specifically, we have considered the phenomenon as an interactional practice – as concrete means for participants to *get things done* within real-time interaction. With this perspective, we asked: What are particular sorts of 'linguistic disorder'

(Hill, 1998: 680) being mobilized for in these contentious interactions, and how do they achieve those actions in context? A CA approach allowed us to both expand the definition of mock language and zero in on a particular mock-language practice.

With racist renditions, speakers work to cast Targets' speech as nonstandard, incomprehensible and unworthy of comprehension. At the level of action, Aggressors intercede in the trajectory of action initiated by the Target and endeavor to supplant or derail it. As we have shown, racist renditions can be fitted to their sequential contexts in terms of the particulars of their design – e.g. matching the number of syllables in a prior turn. This demonstrates how the precise form and action implications of such turns cannot be understood apart from their sequential environments. Moreover, while a nonsense turn like *yehpuhbleuhyuh?* (Example 3) may not closely pattern the specific features of Mock Asian described by Chun (2004), it nonetheless recognizably performs 'Mock Asian' in the sequential context where it occurs. Our interactional approach to mock language thus highlights not only that certain features are recurrently used to index certain raciolinguistic groups, but also that such features *can be reflexively constituted as such in interaction*. The ideological 'set' of linguistic features used to mock a particular language or group is thus importantly revealed to be one with fuzzy boundaries as opposed to a finite listing.

In a similar vein, we have focused less on the fact that Mock Asian and Mock Spanish (for example) are enacted by *different* linguistic features and are used to target *different* groups of speakers, and more on what those features are deployed to accomplish *in situ*. In doing so, we have uncovered interactional commonalities *across* mock varieties and targeted groups. We have argued that racist renditions are used to reassert agency and push for termination of the trajectory of action underway. And so while 'Mock X' and 'Mock Y' may be constituted by ideologically distinct sets of features, as prior research has shown, and while 'Mock X' may be deemed relevant with one recipient but 'Mock Y' with another, we nonetheless see an *interactional* commonality with regard to what such ideologically informed features are mobilized to accomplish in these antagonistic encounters.

As practices, racist renditions are part of participants' broader racist and other discriminatory repertoires. It is thus unsurprising that many cases in the CLDI that feature mock language likewise feature explicit epithets and slurs, be they racist, homophobic, etc. (e.g. *chink* [1], *boy*, *wetback* [2], and *chinaman* [3]). Indeed, like epithets (see e.g. Bustamonte, 1972; Croom, 2014, 2018; Embrick & Henricks, 2013), racist renditions can be trotted out in conflictual interaction as necessary.[13] This distributional commonality with epithets points to their shared 'lowest common denominator' quality, in that Aggressors appear to draw on such resources when in conflict with a racialized other at points when other rhetorical wells have seemingly run dry. In Extract 2, for instance, the Target's cheeky dismissal of the Aggressor's threat (with *I got video*) does not receive a response fitted to that action, but a racist rendition of the Target's pronunciation of 'video'. It is a matter for future research to investigate more systematically the ways in which the racially focused interactional practices examined here intersect with those targeting other social categories and features of identity (e.g. gender, sexuality, physicality).[14]

Here we note an interesting family resemblance with the sequential organization of repair. Repair is considered a 'priority activity' (Schegloff *et al.*, 1977: 720) in that '[i]ts actions can supersede other actions, in the sense that they can replace or defer whatever else was due next ... It is the *only* action type that we know of now which has this property' (Schegloff, 2000a: 208, original emphasis). Whatever is said, a next speaker can always say 'Pardon?', for example, thereby initiating repair and halting – albeit momentarily – the trajectory of action in progress. It is therefore a powerful interactional move. Racist renditions, we suggest, resemble other-initiated repair in both its action context non-specificity, as well as in the sequence-/action-halting power it wields.

We take racist renditions to constitute a concrete method through which individuals of color are 'visibly constrained by rigid norms of linguistic purity, but white linguistic disorder goes unchallenged' (Zentella, 2003: 53). While the practice is seemingly usable 'anywhere', as we just argued, part of its power as a tool of domination is that it is not usable by 'anyone' (cf. 'true' other-initiated repair). Rather, it is asymmetrically available to members of the relational pair dominant language speaker– subordinate(d) language speaker. In our data, it is properly used by speakers of 'standard' US English against those who are raciolinguistically categorized as e.g. Spanish(-speaking) and Chinese(-speaking) – members who are unable to deploy the same devices in return. Indeed, a racialized categorization alone can provide for their proper use, as shown by Extract 3. The ideological basis for this recalls Sacks' (1992: 394) description of certain membership categories as 'protected against induction', such that evidence to the contrary (i.e. Target's use of 'standard' English) does not foreclose the usability of a (raciolinguistic) category.[15]

The asymmetric availability of racist renditions provides for what the practice gets used for: to obstruct and terminate a course of action undertaken by a racialized other. What we have described in this chapter, then, is the sequential organization of one mechanism by which White public space is patrolled and maintained, and one means by which raciolinguistic ideology is translated into action.

## Notes

(1) Readers should be aware that the transcripts below include explicitly racist, homophobic and other derogatory speech. We occasionally cite these in the text as well.
(2) While our interest in this chapter remains on the focal linguistic practice, data from the CLDI also provide for studies of video practices (e.g. Broth *et al.*, 2014). Indeed, we see in some of the extracts in this chapter how a participant's status as videographer is oriented to in the unfolding interaction. In [1] and [3], the cameraphone's roving and recording status constitutes the material object itself as a relevant resource for interaction. And in [2] we see how the dashboard camera's operation is explicitly thematized for talk. For more discussion, see Raymond *et al.* (in prep.-b).
(3) Our usage of 'non-English language' is meant to foreground the relevance of that categorization for the members themselves. Indeed, the 'foreignness' of non-English talk (to the Aggressor) provides in part for the recognizability of the practice as racist.
(4) We can imagine a case where the Target addresses the Aggressor using a non-English language, but we do not find this in our collection.
(5) Transcripts follow Jefferson (2004) for audible conduct, and Mondada (2018) for visible conduct (indicated in gray). For the focal practice, some additional conventions were adopted. The targeted speech appears in a box and the racist rendition in **boldface**, as in the schematic above. Additionally, for analytic purposes we rendered some speech in Jeffersonian 'eye dialect' and have provided phonetic transcriptions using the International Phonetic Alphabet underneath.
(6) Within US culture, a stereotype of (East) Asians is that they are bad drivers. This background context may inform the tenor of the exchange. Note also the earlier epithet *chi:nk* (line 3) (on which see Croom, 2018).
(7) Our use of scare quotes around 'standard', 'accented' and other such qualifiers underscores that these are not objective or absolute categorizations, but rather ideological and racialized ones (see e.g. Alim *et al.*, 2016; Lippi-Green, 2012; Rosa & Flores, 2017). See also next section.
(8) On the racist implications of the vocative *boy*, see Bennett-Alexander (2010).
(9) With regard to the origins and significance of this particular slur, Bustamonte (1972) writes that migrants who move from Mexico to the US illegally were derogatorily called *wetbacks* '…because they cross[ed] the Rio Grande [river] without the benefit of a bridge' (1972: 706). As Croom (2014) reports, however, the slur has now broadened to include any Latin American immigrant living in the US without documentation, no matter their specific country of origin or their mode of transport/arrival to the US (see also Embrick & Henricks, 2013: 204–205).
(10) The Target self-identifies as bilingual in English and Spanish. In contrast to English, most dialects of Spanish do not have a bilabial /b/ vs. labiodental /v/ phonemic distinction, instead using solely bilabials [b] and [β]. Moreover, word-initially only the plosive [b] is used (e.g. Spanish *video* is pronounced [bi'ðeo]).
(11) In many cases from the CLDI, recording starts during an ongoing altercation, and so what occasioned the dispute is often lost and can only be inferred. For this case, the Aggressor was documented in other public places harassing Asian people simply for

going about their business in public view. We assume a similar thing happened in this case.
(12) While not the focus of the present analysis, it is worthwhile to highlight the public nature of these contentious and often violent interactions – i.e. that they are witnessed and witnessable by others, who may or may not intervene but nonetheless experience the confrontation and may be affected by it.
(13) Prior researchers have noted this 'flexibility' of mock language in less antagonistic interactions as well, with Barrett (2006: 166) stating plainly, of Mock Spanish, that 'its context-of-occurrence is largely unrestricted'.
(14) The Aggressor in Extract 2, for example, in data not shown here, refers to the Target's 'faggoty white glasses' (on *fag[got]*, see Pascoe, 2012: especially 55–59), in addition to claiming to be able to physically harm him.
(15) Hill (1998: 681) similarly observes that 'it is well-known that Whites will hear 'accent' even when, objectively, none is present, if they can detect any other signs of a racialized identity'.

## References

Alim, H.S., Rickford, J.R. and Ball, A.F. (2016) *Raciolinguistics: How Language Shapes our Ideas About Race*. Oxford University Press.
Barrett, R. (2006) Language ideology and racial inequality: Competing functions of Spanish in an Anglo-owned Mexican Restaurant. *Language in Society* 35, 163–204.
Bennett-Alexander, D.D. (2010) The use of the term 'boy' as evidence of race discrimination: Apparently, the 11th Circuit didn't get the memo? Paper presented at the Southeastern Academy of Legal Studies in Business. Available online: https://ssrn.com/abstract=1785095.
Broth, M., Laurier, E. and Mondada, L. (eds) (2014) *Studies of Video Practices: Video at Work*. Routledge.
Bustamante, J.A. (1972) The 'wetback' as deviant: An application of labeling theory. *American Journal of Sociology* 77 (4), 706–18.
Callahan, L. (2010) Speaking with (dis)respect: A study of reactions to Mock Spanish. *Language and Intercultural Communication* 10 (4), 299–317.
Callahan, L. (2014) The importance of being earnest: Mock Spanish, mass media, and the implications for language learners. *Spanish in Context* 11 (2), 202–220.
Chun, E.W. (2004) Ideologies of legitimate mockery: Margaret Cho's revoicings of Mock Asian. *Pragmatics* 14 (2–3), 263–289.
Chun, E.W. (2009) Speaking like Asian immigrants: Intersections of accommodation and mocking at a U.S. high school. *Pragmatics* 19 (1), 17–38.
Clift, R. (2016) *Conversation Analysis*. Cambridge University Press.
Clift, R. and Raymond, C.W. (2018) Actions in practice: On details in collections. *Discourse Studies* 20 (1), 90–119.
Couper-Kuhlen, E. (1996) The prosody of repetition: on quoting and mimicry. In E. Couper-Kuhlen and M. Selting (eds) *Prosody in Conversation* (pp. 266–405). Cambridge University Press.
Croom, A.M. (2014) Spanish slurs and stereotypes for Mexican-Americans in the USA: A context-sensitive account of derogation and appropriation. *Pragmática Sociocultural/Sociocultural Pragmatics* 2 (2), 145–179.
Croom, A. M. (2018) Asian slurs and stereotypes in the USA: A context-sensitive account of derogation and appropriation. *Pragmatics and Society* 9 (4), 495–517

Culpeper, J. (2005) Impoliteness and entertainment in the television quiz show: The Weakest Link. *Journal of Politeness Research* 1, 35–72.
Drew, P. (2009) 'Quit talking while I'm interrupting:' (A comparison between) positions of overlap onset in conversation. In M. Haakana, M. Laakso and J. Lindström (eds) *Talk in Interaction: Comparative Dimensions* (pp. 70–93). Finnish Literature Society.
Embrick, D.G. and Henricks, K. (2013) Discursive colorlines at work: How epithets and stereotypes are racially unequal. *Symbolic Interaction* 36 (2), 197–215.
Goodwin, M.H. (1990) *He-Said-She-Said: Talk as Social Organziation among Black Children*. Indiana University Press.
Goodwin, M.H. and Goodwin, C. (1987) Children's arguing. In S. Philips, S. Steele and C. Tanz (eds) *Language, Gender and Sex in Comparative Perspective* (pp. 200–248). Cambridge University Press.
Hill, J.H. (1993) Hasta la vista, baby: Anglo Spanish in the American Southwest. *Critique of Anthropology* 13 (2), 145–76.
Hill, J.H. (1998) Language, race and White public space. *American Anthropologist* 100 (3), 680–89.
Hill, J.H. (2005) Intertextuality as source and evidence for indirect indexical meanings. *Journal of Linguistic Anthropology* 15 (1), 113–24.
Hill, J.H. (2008) *The Everyday Language of White Racism*. Wiley-Blackwell.
Hiramoto, M. (2011) Is dat dog you're eating?: Mock Filipino, Hawai'i Creole, and local elitism. *Pragmatics* 21 (3), 341–71.
Hoey, E.M. (2018) How speakers continue with talk after a lapse in conversation. *Research on Language and Social Interaction* 51 (3), 329–46.
Hoey, E.M. (2020) *When Conversation Lapses: The Public Accountability of Silent Copresence*. Oxford University Press.
Hoey, E.M. and Kendrick, K.H. (2017) Conversation analysis. In A.M.B. De Groot and Peter Hagoort (eds) *Research Methods in Psycholinguistics and the Neurobiology of Language* (pp. 151–173). Wiley-Blackwell.
Jefferson, G. (2004) Glossary of Transcript Symbols with an Introduction. In G.H. Lerner (ed.) *Conversation Analysis: Studies from the First Generation* (pp. 13–31). John Benjamins.
Laurier, E. and Philo, C. (2006) Natural problems of naturalistic video data. In H. Knoblauch, J. Raab, H.-G Soeffner and B. Schnettler (eds) *Video-Analysis Methodology and Methods, Qualitative Audiovisual Data Analysis in Sociology* (pp. 183–192). Peter Lang.
Lerner, G.H. (2019) When someone other than the addressed recipient speaks next: Three kinds of intervening action after the selection of next speaker. *Research on Language and Social Interaction* 52 (4), 388–405.
Lippi-Green, R. (2012) *English with an Accent: Language, Ideology, and Discrimination in the United States*. Routledge.
Mason Carris, L. (2011) La voz gringa: Latino stylization of linguistic (in)authenticity as social critique. *Discourse & Society* 22 (4), 474–490.
Mondada, L. (2018) Multiple temporalities of language and body in interaction: Challenges for transcribing multimodality. *Research on Language and Social Interaction* 51 (1), 85–106.
Nassenstein, N. (2020) Mock Chinese in Kinshasa: On Lingala speakers' offensive language use and verbal hostility. In N. Nassenstein and A. Storch (eds) *Swearing and Cursing: Contexts and Practices in a Critical Linguistic Perspective* (pp. 185–208). De Gruyter.

Pascoe, C.J. (2012) *Dude, You're a Fag*. University of California Press.
Potowski, K. (2011) Linguistic and cultural authenticity of 'Spanglish' greeting cards. *International Journal of Multilingualism* 8 (4), 324–344.
Raymond, C.W., Albert, S., Hoey, E.M., Grothues, N., Henry, J., Marrese, O., Pielke, M., Reynolds, E. and Tom, R.G. (in prep.-a) The corpus of language discrimination interaction *(CLDI)*. Manuscript, University of Colorado, Boulder.
Raymond, C.W., Albert, S., Hoey, E.M., Grothues, N., Henry, J., Marrese, O., Pielke, M., Reynolds, E. and Tom, R.G. (in prep.-b). *De facto* language policy in practice: Ideologies in action in everyday public life. Manuscript, University of Colorado, Boulder.
Ronkin, M. and Karn, H.E. (1999) Mock Ebonics: Linguistic racism in parodies of Ebonics on the internet. *Journal of Sociolinguistics* 3 (3), 360–380.
Rosa, J. (2016) From mock Spanish to inverted Spanglish. In H.S. Alim, J.R. Rickford and A.F. Ball (eds) *Raciolinguistics: How Language Shapes our Ideas About Race* (pp. 65–80). Oxford University Press.
Rosa, J. and Flores, N. (2017) Unsettling race and language: Toward a raciolinguistic perspective. *Language in Society* 46 (5), 621–647.
Sacks, H. (1992) *Lectures on Conversation (vol. 1 & vol. 2)*. Blackwell.
Sacks, H., Schegloff, E.A. and Jefferson, G. (1974) A simplest systematics for the organization of turn-taking for conversation. *Language* 50, 696–735.
Schegloff, E.A. (2000a) When 'others' initiate repair. *Applied Linguistics* 21 (2), 205–243.
Schegloff, E.A. (2000b) Overlapping talk and the organization of turn-taking for conversation. *Language in Society* 29 (1), 1–63.
Schegloff, E.A. and Sacks, H. (1973) Opening Up Closings. *Semiotica* 8 (4), 289–327.
Schwartz, A. (2008) Their language, our Spanish: Introducing public discourses of 'Gringoism' as racializing linguistic and cultural reappropriation. *Spanish in Context* 5 (2), 224–245.
Schwartz, A. (2011) Mockery and appropriation of Spanish in White spaces: Perceptions of Latinos in the United States. In M. Díaz-Campos (ed.) *The Handbook of Hispanic Sociolinguistics* (pp. 646–63). Blackwell.
Shek, Y.L. (2007) Asian American masculinity: A review of the literature. *The Journal of Men's Studies* 14 (3), 379–391.
Slobe, T. (2018) Style, stance, and social meaning in mock white girl. *Language in Society* 47 (4), 541–567.
Su, H.Y. (2004) Mock Taiwanese-accented Mandarin in the internet community in Taiwan: The interaction between technology, linguistic practice, and language ideologies. In P. LeVine and R. Scollon (eds) *Discourse and Technology: Multimodal Discourse Analysis* (pp. 59–70). Georgetown University Press.
Tainio, L. (2012a) Prosodic imitation as a means of receiving and displaying a critical stance in classroom interaction. *Text & Talk* 32 (4), 547–568.
Tainio, L. (2012b) Prosodic imitation in classroom interaction: A gendered practice of empowerment? *Gender & Language* 6 (1), 197–232.
Talmy, S. (2010) Achieving distinction through Mock ESL: A critical pragmatics analysis of classroom talk in a high school. *Pragmatics and Language Learning* 12 (1), 215–54.
Zentella, A.C. (2003) 'José, can you see?': Latin@ responses to racist discourse. In D. Sommer (ed.) *Bilingual Games* (pp. 51–66). Palgrave-Macmillan.

# 4 Talk in Local News Broadcasts: Reinforcing Negative Views towards the Hawaiian Language

Scott Saft

**Introduction**

This chapter applies some of the basic analytic tools provided by conversation analysis (CA), particularly, its focus on the sequential organization of social interaction and its elucidation of member practices such as categories, formulations and reported speech, to develop an analysis that is critical of news broadcasts. More specifically, the analysis describes how the sequencing of talk on news reports on local television broadcasts in Hawai'i contributes to the continued suppression of the Hawaiian language, a language that is endangered but was declared in 1978 to be one of two official languages (together with English) of the state. The analysis shows that talk in the reports problematizes the usage of Hawaiian in public contexts and also works to deter wider discussion of Hawaiian's role in society.

Within CA, the news broadcast is considered a form of institutional talk in which the institutional context imposes interactional organizations that differ from everyday conversation (Clayman, 1992; Greatbatch, 1992; Heritage & Clayman, 2010). Previous CA research on talk in the news has focused primarily on exchanges of interaction, particularly 'news interviews, campaign debates, radio call-in shows, and talk shows of various stripes' (Heritage & Clayman, 2010: 1). Such a focus has allowed analysts, through what has been termed a 'next-turn proof procedure' (Hutchby & Wooffitt, 1998), to pay close attention to how the participants themselves understand prior turns of talk and to describe how participants construct turn-taking practices that orient not only to institutional identities, such as interviewer and interviewee, but also to the fact that the talk is produced for a viewing audience typically not 'at the site of production' (Hutchby, 2003: 437).

This chapter departs from prior CA research in that it does not center on exchanges of interaction. Instead, the focus is on the way the news reports are pieced together sequentially with various voices, including voice-overs from news reporters and video and audio clips of interviews with key participants. By paying attention to the local practices employed in the reports, particularly the usage in voice-overs of strategically placed categories, formulations and reported speech, the analysis builds on prior CA research underscoring that neutrality, considered foundational to quality journalism, is achieved (or not) through talk in news broadcasts. After demonstrating how the news reports produce non-neutral portrayals of attempts to speak Hawaiian, the chapter concludes by briefly considering the critical potential of CA to reveal how the organization of talk in an institutional context such as a news broadcast may reinforce already existing power asymmetries present in society.

To set the context concerning power asymmetries in Hawaiian society, we can note that although the Hawaiian language thrived throughout most of the 1800s, increased American influence eventually resulted in a coup d'état in 1893 by a group of American businessmen who overthrew the Hawaiian monarchy and installed a provisionary American-based government that worked to facilitate a rapid language shift to English. English was made the official language of education in 1896 and, faced with punishment in school for using their native tongue, many Native Hawaiians were forced to make the agonizing decision to stop speaking Hawaiian with their children. Language endangerment continued to the extent that it was estimated in the early 1980s that there were less than 50 children growing up with Hawaiian as one of their primary languages (Wilson & Kamanā, 2001).

Nonetheless, soon after Hawai'i was declared an official US state in 1959, many people of Native Hawaiian ancestry adopted a renewed interest in Hawaiian practices, such as navigation, canoeing, lei-making and dance, and also began activism to fight for Hawaiian lands, access to water and Hawaiian sovereignty. Activism during this period led to an official declaration in 1978 at a state convention of Hawaiian as one of two official languages of the state. This declaration helped empower a group of language activists to establish the non-profit organization 'Aha Pūnana Leo in 1983, which was modeled after a similar organization in New Zealand for the Māori language and which led to the establishment of first Hawaiian immersion preschool in 1984 in Kekaha on the island of

Kauaʻi. The number of preschools subsequently grew, and educational structures through Hawaiian expanded to the elementary, junior high and high school levels (Wilson & Kamanā, 2001; Wilson & Kawaiʻaeʻa, 2007). Moreover, it is now possible to earn a BA, MA and PhD in Hawaiʻi through programs of study conducted primarily with Hawaiian as the language of instruction (Silva, 2017).

Still, despite the advances made in education, the Hawaiian language faces challenges in terms of acceptance in daily life in Hawaiʻi. The language is heard frequently in public in local stores as it is used by families of speakers, but as Wilson and Kamanā (2013) note, there are few neighborhoods that currently use Hawaiian as their dominant language. Furthermore, despite the creation of Hawaiian language pathways in education, the language struggles to be recognized in other public domains of society, such as government, law, business and the media. In terms of media, there are initiatives like ʻŌiwi TV that provides content in the Hawaiian language on the internet, social media and cable television. In addition, a local television station maintained for several years a short early morning Hawaiian language segment. Still, local mainstream television is just one of many public domains into which the Hawaiian language has struggled to gain strong footing. The unwritten assumption is that televised news programming occurs through the medium of English. As the analysis in this chapter suggests, this lack of access is reinforced through news reports that, despite treating the Hawaiian language as a newsworthy topic, are often organized in a way that portrays the usage of Hawaiian in public domains in a negative light and more generally works to discourage serious consideration of Hawaiian as a language on equal footing with English.

### Data and Method

The analysis is based on four short news reports occurring between 2013 and 2018 on two of the local television networks in Hawaiʻi, KITV4 and KHON2, which deliver prime time local news across the islands. The four reports are available on YouTube as stand-alone video clips at the following addresses.

News Report 1 (from KITV4): 4 August 2013
https://www.youtube.com/watch?v=leH8SD3j48Q&t=50s
News Report 2 (from KHON2): 25 January 2018
https://www.youtube.com/watch?v=vg2Yu6Uhukg
News Report 3: (from KITV4): 5 March 2014
https://www.youtube.com/watch?v=AOw3LWDLYPU&t=3s

News Report 4: (from KHON2): 24 January 2018
https://www.youtube.com/watch?v=STOHm2hB4J4

The excerpts of data employ the same transcription symbols as the other chapters with the addition of double parentheses to indicate commentary supplied by the author to help readers follow the flow of the news reports. In addition, spates of talk in Hawaiian are represented in italics in the transcripts. Given that the focus of the analysis is on the way the talk is pieced together across the different voices of the participants, some prosodic and visual details have been omitted from the transcripts in order to facilitate understanding of the sequential flow of the talk.

Following the CA perspective, discussion of the data proceeds predominantly on a turn-by-turn basis with a particular emphasis on the elucidation of member practices such as formulations and reported speech. In addition, the analysis employs ideas from membership categorization analysis (MCA) as a part of paying close attention to the verbal categories employed by the participants within the sequential flow of the interaction.

While the analysis is based on the sequentiality of the talk and thus employs the CA 'next-turn proof procedure' as much as possible, the analyst also recognizes his reliance on his own knowledge, understanding and interpretation of the data. This includes his understanding of the English language, the primary language of the data, but it also features his interpretations based on his work in Hawaiʻi as an educator and supporter of the movement to revitalize the Hawaiian language. Through this work, the analyst has developed a strong sense of the unequal relationship between English and Hawaiian in Hawaiian society, which has served as a motivation to produce the current critical analysis to elucidate how the media often perpetuates and reinforces inequalities between the two official languages of the state.

## Analysis

### Introduction of the news reports by the anchors

The analysis to follow is divided into two parts; the initial part focuses on the introduction by the news anchors of the topics of the four reports listed above, and the second part concentrates specifically on the details of two of the reports, one that centers on an attempt to use Hawaiian on the floor of the State House of Representatives and another that concerns a man who tried to employ Hawaiian in court. The first four excerpts presented below show that the news reports all begin in a similar way.

(1) From News Report 1: KITV4 NEWS
```
01      PY:     A Native Hawaiian claims the state is putting
02              up roadblocks to Hawai'i's native language,
03              he says effort to communicate in Hawaiian
04              actually landed him in court. KITV's Paul
05              Drewes explains
```

(2) From News Report 2: KHON 2
```
01      JM:     Egregious and disturbing (.) that's what the Native Hawaiian
02              Legal Corporation is calling a judge's decision to issue a Maui
03              man's arrest after he refused to speak English in court. ((begins
04              showing a clip in the background without sound of the Maui man
05              in court- he and the judge are visible)) The warrant for Sam Ka'eo
06              was recalled this morning but what happened is raising questions
07              about the acceptance and use of the Hawaiian language in court
08              and whether it should have been handled differently. Jenn Boneza
09              joins us with more, Jenn
```

(3) From News Report 3: KITV4 NEWS
```
01      YD:     Representative Faye Hanohano causes another big stir at the
02              state capitol and this time it isn't what she said but how she
03              said it. Good evening, I am Yunji De Nies.
04      PA:     Thank you so much for joining us. I am Paula Akana.
05              Hanohano spoke Hawaiian and Hawaiian only during one
06              comment on the house floor (.) that caused a ruckus. The
07              representative has already been accused of being rude and
08              possibly racist. Now some wondered if she is within her right
09              to speak Hawaiian without translating. KITV 4's Andrew
10              Perreira joins us with that answer.
```

(4) From News Report 4: KHON 2
```
01      HD:     Good evening everybody and thank you for joining us.
02              Tonight a UH- Maui assistant professor of Hawaiian Studies
03              has a warrant out for his arrest after refusing to speak English
04              in a court appearance today.
05      MY:     Samuel Ka'eo told us he is fighting for his right to speak
06              his native language. Our Alexander Zannes spoke with him
07              tonight on what he plans to do now.
```

Unlike Excerpts (1) and (2), which feature a single anchor, Excerpts (3) and (4) begin with two anchors introducing the topic of the report, but they all adopt a similar structure as the anchors first introduce a topic related to the usage of the Hawaiian language in public and then designate a news reporter to present the details of the story. The anchor PY in Excerpt (1) informs viewers of a Native Hawaiian who ended up in court for attempting to use Hawaiian and subsequently calls on the reporter Paul Drewes in lines 04–05 to explain. The anchor JM in Excerpt (2) refers to a man who was arrested after refusing to speak English in court and then turns the report over in line 08–09 to Jenn Boneza. Two anchors in Excerpt (3), YD and PA, refer to a member of the Hawaiian House of Representatives who spoke Hawaiian on the house floor and then call on Andrew Perreira in lines 09–10 to join them, and Excerpt (4) shows two anchors, HD and MY, describing an arrest warrant for a Maui professor who refused to speak English (the same person referred to in Excerpt (2)) before bringing in Alexander Zannes in lines 05–06. Excerpts (3) and (4) specifically invoke the term *rights*, thus suggesting that the news report to follow will have a focus on Hawaiian language speaking rights in public domains. Excerpts (1) and (2) do not specifically employ the terms *rights*, but it is clear from these topic introductions that the report centers on the usage of Hawaiian in public.

Given that the anchors represent the viewing audience's first chance to hear the topic of the story, it is important to take a closer look at the language employed by the anchors to introduce the topics. In particular, the choice of descriptive terms by the anchors reveals certain stances toward the topic and the people involved. One example is the anchor JM's usage of the descriptive terms *egregious* and *disturbing* in line 01 in Excerpt (2) in reference to the judge's decision to issue an arrest warrant. These terms come with a very negative evaluation of the decision, but the anchor also uses reported speech through the verb *is calling* to attribute these terms to the Native Hawaiian Legal Corporation. Accordingly, the anchor can seemingly employ these terms and still maintain a stance of neutrality as he is merely reporting what some other entity said. However, the same anchor also describes the man's action by saying in line 03 that he *refused to speak English in court*. Here, it is notable that the verbal category *refuse* brings with it a sense of defiance that may differ considerably from another verbal description that could have been chosen, for instance, 'spoke Hawaiian in court' or 'spoke only Hawaiian in court'. The descriptive term *refuse*, thus, provides viewers with a negative articulation of the man's action before the details of the report are presented.

Through the strand of CA known as MCA, analysts have had a significant interest in the verbal categories employed in talk to describe people and have placed a specific focus on describing the inferential processes participants use to deploy person category terms, such as 'baby', 'mother' or 'adult' (Schegloff, 2007). Yet, as Schegloff notes, MCA derived from Harvey Sacks' general interest in word selection, that is, 'how speakers come to use the words they do' (Schegloff, 2007: 463). Hence, even though 'refuse' refers directly to an action, the selection of this verbal category also says something about the person doing the refusing, namely, that they are defiant. Furthermore, we can suggest that the image of the person being described would vary if a different verbal category had been chosen, for instance if he had been characterized as 'speaking in Hawaiian'. It is therefore important to also point out a possible pattern in these verbal categories given that a different anchor from the same channel in Excerpt (4) employs the same phrase *refusing to speak English* in line 03 to refer to the same action of speaking Hawaiian by the same man. Likewise, we may further consider what these verbal categories are saying about speakers of Hawaiian when we note that the first anchor of Excerpt (3) employs the description *another big stir* in line 01 to refer to the action of Representative Hanohano. This characterization seems to inform viewers from the outset that Hanohano is the type of person to cause big stirs, with her usage of Hawaiian being one example. This description is reinforced in line 06 by the second anchor who specifically describes Hanohano's usage of Hawaiian as causing a *ruckus*. Like *big stir*, *ruckus* is a negative way of presenting the usage of Hawaiian to viewers. Verbal categories, as Edwards (1997: 224) states, 'are not just reflections of how they [the speakers] see things, or the way things are'. Instead, they are 'resources with which speakers perform discursive actions' (Edwards, 1997: 224). In these introductions, then, the viewers are not merely introduced in a neutral way to usages of Hawaiian in public; rather, viewers are presented, before the actual news report begins, with verbal categories that frame the users and the usage of Hawaiian in a negative light.

In emphasizing how talk in news broadcasts sometimes diverges from stances of neutrality, prior CA research has described turn construction practices used by news interviewers that perform adversarial acts and thus encourage antagonistic interaction (Clayman, 1992; Heritage & Clayman, 2010). As the first four excerpts suggest, verbal categories employed by anchors may also be a practice through which news is presented in a way that is far from neutral. Indeed, the remainder of the analysis demonstrates that the news reports in two of the broadcasts shown in excerpts (1) – (4) employed sequential resources, including further verbal categories, that build on the negative portrayals of the usage of Hawaiian in public initiated by the anchors.

### The news report

In all four excerpts just discussed, the named reporters went on to present the report immediately after being designated by the anchors.

78  Part 1: Reproducing Inequality and Injustice

Excerpt (5), which continues from Excerpt (3), shows how Andrew Perreira (AP) starts reporting Representative Hanohano's usage of Hawaiian on the floor of the Hawaiian House of Representatives. Here, it should be recalled that the anchor PA, in designating AP to make the report, noted in lines 08–09 that *now some wondered if she is within her right to speak Hawaiian without translating.* As shown below, AP's initial action in the report is to provide an answer.

(5) Continuation from Excerpt (3)

```
11    AP:   Paula, yes, Hawaiʻi is the only state in the union with two
12          official languages. (.) Representative Hanohano was using
13          one of them.
14          ((Cuts to a clip of the scene of the floor of the House of
15          Representatives but without sound))
16    AP:   Like most legislative bodies the House of Representatives
17          has its own rules regarding conduct.
18          ((Cuts to a clip of an interview with Representative Gene
19          Ward))
20    GW:   They should be proud of the way that we speak, the way that
21          we dress, and the way that we behave. ((Returns to the House floor
22          and shows Hanohano with the microphone))
23    AP:   So when embattled representative Faye Hanohano of Puna
24          spoke in her native language
25          ((Shows the Vice Speaker of the House, John Mizuno))
26    JM:   Representative Hanohano
27    FH:   Mahalo hoʻomalu ʻōlelo kākoʻo loa makemake au i ka
28          haʻiʻōlelo o ka luna makaʻāinana mai Kapolei mai e komo
29          i loko o ka puke hale no ka makaʻāinana.
30    AP:   It touched off a mini firestorm as Vice Speaker John
31          Mizuno presided over the chamber.
32    JM:   Representative Hanohano (.) could you please translate for
33          the members?
34          (1.5)
35    FH:   ʻAʻole au e makemake e unuhi mai I don't wanna translate.
36          Mahalo.
37    AP:   This exchange prompted a clearly frustrated Mizuno to bang
38          the gavel.
39    JM:   Recess subject to th- the call of the chair, recess. ((Bangs
40          gavel))
```

AP first of all offers in line 11 the answer *yes* and explains through line 13 that Representative Hanohano was within her rights to speak Hawaiian without translating because she was using one of the two official languages of the state. However, rather than pursue the topic of Hawaiian language speaking rights, AP proceeds in lines 16–17 by mentioning the existence of rules regarding conduct in the House of Representatives. This then serves as a segue into a clip in lines 20–21 of an interview with Gene Ward, a member of the House of Representatives who was present for that particular session, who employs the pronoun *they* in line 20 in an apparent reference to the constituents served by the representatives and who states through line 21 that *they should be proud of the way we speak, the way we dress, the way that we behave*. The report then moves in line 23 to a voice-over from AP that leads with *so*, a term indicating that the talk to follow is not only connected to the previous talk but also, as Raymond (2004: 186) notes, prefaces a turn that is to provide the 'upshot of prior talk'. In other words, by leading with *so*, AP displays a direct link between the just-mentioned rules of conduct and Hanohano's action of speaking Hawaiian that is about to be presented from line 23. Moreover, in connecting rules of conduct to Hanohano's Hawaiian speech, AP employs the descriptive category *embattled* to describe Hanohano, thus reinforcing the image of Hanohano already initiated by the two anchors in Excerpt (3) with categories such as *another big stir* and *ruckus*. Here it is relevant that the two anchors in Excerpt (3) had also described Hanohano herself as *racist* and *rude*. Thus, even before introducing Hanohano's actual Hawaiian speech, AP has already done work in this report through lines 23–24 to suggest to the viewers that there may be a problem with Hanohano and her conduct.

Following the initial *so* in line 23, AP constructs what Lerner (1991) describes as a 'compound turn-constructional unit' with his utterance *when embattled representative Faye Hanohano of Puna spoke in her native language*. As Lerner (1991) notes, compound units can provide co-participants the opportunity to complete the latter half of the turn. Here, though, instead of a next participant, AP uses this segment initiated by *when* in line 23 to insert a clip of Hanohano's speech in Hawaiian. The clip begins in line 26 with Vice Speaker John Mizuno calling on Hanohano to speak, which leads to her statement in Hawaiian in lines 27–29. Next, AP uses a voice-over in line 30 to produce the second segment of the compound turn-constructional unit he himself initiated in lines 23–24, and he employs this segment to formulate for the viewing audience what they are witnessing, namely, an action that *touched off a firestorm*.

The notion of formulation has occupied an important place in the CA perspective in that formulations are one common practice through which participants demonstrate how they understand the unfolding interaction. As Garfinkel and Sacks (1970: 351) note in their seminal paper, it is through formulations that participants do the action of 'saying-in-so-many-words-what-we-are-doing (or what we are talking about, or who is talking, or who we are, or where we are)'. Although not part of a direct interactional exchange, the formulation by AP in line 30 performs an important role given that talk in the institutional context of a news report is produced for a viewing audience. With the formulation *a mini firestorm*, the reporter is providing the audience with a specific interpretation of Hanohano's usage of Hawaiian, namely, that it should be seen as controversial. It should, in short, be viewed as an action that could set of a *mini firestorm*. Furthermore, this formulation also offers the viewers a frame for understanding that the information to follow in the report should be seen in terms of this *mini firestorm*. Indeed, following AP's voice-over in lines 30–31, the clip showing the interaction between Mizuno and Hanohano on the House floor continues as Mizuno in line 32–33 asks Hanohano to translate and as Hanohano, after a 1.5-second pause, responds again in Hawaiian in line 35 before switching to English to state that she does not want to translate (which is in fact a translation of her Hawaiian utterance in this line). Then the report inserts another voice-over from AP in line 37–38 that serves as a formulation that provides viewers with an interpretation of Mizuno's subsequent action. AP describes Mizuno as *clearly frustrated* and suggests that this frustration led him to bang the gavel. The report then plays in lines 39–40 Mizuno's actual words as he calls for recess and does indeed bang the gavel. Regardless of Mizuno's actual internal state at that particular time, this formulation of him as *clearly frustrated* encourages the audience to view Hanohano's action of speaking Hawaiian without translation as incendiary since it is the source of Mizuno's frustration.

It should be stressed that it is the sequential organization of this news report that makes it possible for AP to formulate Hanohano's usage of Hawaiian as controversial. It is the strategic sequential placement of the formulations that allow the news report, first of all, to present the event that occurred using actual video clips and, at the same time, to insert commentary to assist viewers to see the event as controversial. Additionally, the sequential organization has effectively moved the report away from the topic of Hawaiian speaking rights that was raised by one of the anchors and responded to briefly by AP in lines 11–12. Largely through these formulations, the topic of the news report has shifted through line 40 from Hawaiian speaking rights to a portrayal of Hanohano's attempt to speak in only Hawaiian as controversial.

Although this work is done largely through AP's formulations, there is important category work involved as well. In particular, it is notable that in the initial segment of AP's compound turn-constructional unit in lines 23–24, he refers to Hanohano as speaking in *her native language*, a word choice that frames Hanohano not as speaking an official language of the state but rather as speaking a language specific to her. This move to use a category that personalizes her language selection comes shortly after AP characterized Hawaiian in lines 11–13 as an official language of the state. To be sure, it is undoubtedly easy for viewers to make the connection between Hanohano's native language and the official language mentioned in lines 11–13, but this subtle change in category work by AP is just one move contributing to a larger shift away from the subject of Hawaiian speaking rights to the problems caused by Hanohano's usage of Hawaiian. She was not speaking an official language of the state but rather engaging in a much more personal act of using her native language. The continuation of this news report, shown below in Excerpt (6), provides further examples of resources that were used to shift the focus of this particular report.

(6) Continuation from Excerpt (5)

| | | |
|---|---|---|
| 41 | AP: | After a short interval, Mizuno came back with this. |
| 42 | JM: | Rule 60.1 provides (.) members should conduct themselves |
| 43 | | in a respectful manner. |
| 44 | AP: | Quickly, Representative Gene Ward stood up and said |
| 45 | | there is precedent here. |
| 46 | GW: | Well, according to the constitution there are two official |
| 47 | | languages, English and Hawaiian therefore no translation is |
| 48 | | needed, that was the prevailing legal authority two or three years |
| 49 | | ago. So Mr. Speaker I think you've sort of varied a little off |
| 50 | | course from that. |
| 51 | AP: | Mizuno agreed there is no issue with the language Hanohano |
| 52 | | spoke. |
| 53 | FH: | *Kākoʻo loa, makemake au i ka haʻiʻōlelo o=* |
| 54 | | ((Her Hawaiian speech is still heard continuing in the |
| 55 | | background)) |
| 56 | AP: | =KITV4 has a translation of what she actually said. |
| 57 | | ((Shows the translation on the screen and reads it)) |
| 58 | | Thank you Mr. Speaker of the House. I would like the speech |
| 59 | | of the representative from Kapolei to be entered into the |
| 60 | | House of Representatives log. Hanohano had simply stated |
| 61 | | that she echoed the words of Representative Sharon Har of |
| 62 | | Kapolei and wanted them to be entered into the official journal |
| 63 | | as hers. Ward points out that he was not coming to Hanohano's |
| 64 | | defense across the board. she still faces possible penalties for |
| 65 | | allegedly berating HPU student Aaron Jacobs during a hearing |
| 66 | | and lashing out at DNLR staff with remarks described as abusive, |
| 67 | | racially discriminatory, and inappropriate. |
| 68 | GW: | I wasn't defending what she was saying or some of the things |

82  Part 1: Reproducing Inequality and Injustice

```
69              she has said in the past because they were pretty reprehensible
70              things.
71              ((News report goes back to AP behind a desk with a picture of
72              a gavel, both a Hawaiian and a United States flag with the words
73              'Hanohano Language Controversy' on the screen))
74     AP:     Today Mizuno said the exchange with Hanohano brings up an
75              interesting point whether the House should pay for a Hawaiian
76              interpreter during floor and committee sessions. House Speaker
77              Joe Suki will make that final call. Yunji back to you.
```

After AP announces in line 41 that Mizuno came back after a short interval with a statement, a clip is shown in lines 42–43 of Vice Speaker Mizuno referencing a specific rule that *members should conduct themselves in a respectful manner*. Even though neither Hanohano nor the Hawaiian language is specifically named by Mizuno, the news report is structured sequentially in a way that suggests that Mizuno was indeed referring to Hanohano's usage of Hawaiian. This is recognizable through AP's announcement in lines 44–45 that Representative Gene Ward *quickly* responded, and, via a clip of Ward speaking on the House floor, Ward explains in lines 46–49 to Mizuno that no translation is necessary because Hawaiian and English are both official languages according to the constitution. In the same clip, Ward suggests in lines 49–50 that Mizuno, by questioning Hanohano's conduct, has *varied a little off course from that*. Through a voice-over in lines 51–52, AP explains that Mizuno agreed that there is no issue with the language, and, as the news report begins to repeat Hanohano's Hawaiian speech from the beginning in line 53, AP states in line 56 that they have a translation, which is projected on the screen. He then reads the translation just the way it is presented on the screen, and he continues in lines 60–63 with a formulation that tells viewers that *Hanohano had simply stated that she echoed the words of Representative Sharon Har of Kapolei and wanted them to be entered into the official journal as hers*.

Through the beginning of line 63, the focus of the news report has seemingly shifted back to rights to use the Hawaiian language in an official venue such as the floor of the House of Representatives. AP's formulation of Hanohano's Hawaiian speech as *simply* stating her support for another representative's words seemingly contrasts with the previous formulation of her action as setting off a *mini firestorm*. However, AP begins in the latter part of line 63 to move once again away from Hawaiian language rights in order to refocus on Hanohano's conduct. After stating in line 63 that *Ward points out that he was not coming to Hanohano's defense across the board*, AP provides the information in lines 64–67 that

Hanohano still faces *penalties* for disparaging a university student with words *described as abusive, racially discriminatory, and inappropriate*. The news report then offers a clip from an interview with Gene Ward, the same representative who had defended the usage of Hawaiian on the House floor, in which he explicitly states in lines 68–70 that he was not *defending what she was saying or some of the things she has said in the past* since *they were pretty reprehensible things*. The news report then switches to show AP behind a desk with the words *Hanohano Language Controversy* behind him as he brings the news report to a close lines 74–77 by noting first that the exchange with Hanohano *brings up an interesting point* about whether to pay or not for Hawaiian language interpretation and second that this decision will be made by the House Speaker. No further mention is made of the issues of rights to speak Hawaiian as the reporter gives the floor back in line 77 to one of the anchors, signaling the end of the report.

As was the case with some of the categories chosen earlier in the report to describe Hanohano and her behavior, some of the verbal categories in Excerpt (6) are strikingly negative. This includes AP's usage of the descriptor *berating* to describe Hanohano's action toward a HPU student, and it also includes the phrase *abusive, racially discriminatory, and inappropriate* to refer to some of her previous remarks. Even though the report ends with a mention of the possibility of a Hawaiian language interpreter, the reporter has used these verbal categories to maintain the focus specifically on Hanohano's behavior and depict it in a negative way. These descriptors are used to refer to Hanohano's prior behavior, but the connection to her most recent action of speaking Hawaiian on the House floor is made clear by the projection at the end of the words *Hanohano language controversy* on the screen, which functions as one final formulation for viewers to emphasize that the usage of Hawaiian by Hanohano shown in the report is to be viewed as problematic. Despite the mention of Hawaiian as an official language of the state and despite the usage of the term *rights* on a couple of occasions, the news report has, via resources such as categories and formulations, created a sequential organization that moves the focus of the report away from Hawaiian speaking rights to construct Hanohano's attempt to speak Hawaiian without translation as a problem.

In their research, critical discourse analysts have sometimes expressed concern about a tendency in news discourse to engage in the process of generalization, that is, to use individual events to make general, sweeping assumptions about people and/or groups of people that may reinforce stereotypes about that group (Teo, 2000; van Dijk, 1993). The organization of the news report in Excerpts (5) and (6) suggests, however, a type of opposite process whereby the news report uses sequential resources to avoid moving to and staying at the more general level of Hawaiian speaking rights. Even AP's concluding move in lines 52–55, which brings in the possibility of Hawaiian language interpreters on the House floor, does not directly address the right to employ Hawaiian on the house floor but instead refers to a still-to-be made decision by a person in authority, House Speaker Joe Suki. The invocation of the title and name of the authority figure suggests that it is not a decision open to discussion but rather to be decided by one specific individual. The next excerpt, which focuses on the man described in Excerpt (4) as an *assistant professor of Hawaiian Studies* and also as *fighting for his right to speak his native language*, reveals a similarly organized report that works to avoid general discussion of Hawaiian language speaking rights. Excerpt (7) below shows the continuation after the anchors had turned the story over in lines 06–07 of Excerpt (4) to the reporter Alexander Zannes (AZ). Before AZ's voice is heard, the report shows a clip of the interactional exchange between the judge and Sam Kaʻeo (SK) in the courtroom that led to the arrest warrant.

(7) Continuation from Excerpt (4)

| | | | |
|---|---|---|---|
| 08 | Judge: | | I am going to give you another opportunity Mr. Kaʻeo just to |
| 09 | | | identify yourself just so the record is clear I am going to ask you |
| 10 | | | one last time is your name Samuel Kaʻeo. |
| 11 | SK: | | *Eia au ke kū nei ma mua ou ʻo ia ke kanaka āu i kāhea mai* |
| 12 | | | *nei ke kū nei ma mua ou e ka lunakānāwai*= |
| 13 | AZ: | | =It was this exchange that ultimately led to a warrant being |
| 14 | | | issued for Samuel Kaʻeo's arrest. Kaʻeo who speaks Hawaiian |
| 15 | | | and English fluently chose to address the judge in Hawaiian. |
| 16 | | | Judge Blaine Kobayashi said the court was unable to determine |
| 17 | | | if Kaʻeo was present. |
| 18 | | | ((Switches to a clip of Kaʻeo speaking in English after the court |
| 19 | | | hearing in response to a video interview with AZ)) |
| 20 | SK: | | Uhm and so I was quite surprised at the very beginning he made |
| 21 | | | an issue of somehow my responses because it was in Hawaiian. Uh |
| 22 | | | he had a huge issue with that and uhm you know he pretended |
| 23 | | | somehow that I really wasn't there today, somehow was invisible. |
| 24 | AZ: | | Kaʻeo faces charges in connection with a protest last August. He |
| 25 | | | had requested a Hawaiian language interpreter but one was not |
| 26 | | | available. So the court granted the state's motion to have the trial |
| 27 | | | continue in English. Kaʻeo says he should be able to defend |
| 28 | | | himself in Hawaiian saying he believes he and others have |
| 29 | | | the right to do so. |
| 30 | SK: | | I think I gotta put this in context you know here I am as a |

```
31                Hawaiian person representing myself in a criminal issue due to
32                uhm fighting on the behalf of the Hawaiian people and using
33                Hawaiian language is the best way to express that this is a
34                Hawaiian issue uhm and that being taken away from me.
35                ((Switches to a video of the courtroom showing supporters of
36                Kaʻeo in the audience))
37      ??:       hewa
38      ??:       he[wa
39      ??:       [hewa
40      ??:       hewa
```

As shown in the excerpt, the judge states in lines 08–09 that he will offer Kaʻeo *another opportunity* to identify himself as Samuel Kaʻeo, thus indicating that it is not the judge's first attempt to get Kaʻeo to respond in English. This time as well, though, Kaʻeo answers in Hawaiian. Then, through a voice-over in lines 13–14, AK produces a formulation as he explains to the viewers what they just saw, namely, that this was the exchange that resulted in the arrest warrant. In making this formulation in this particular sequential location, AZ directly suggests to the viewers that Kaʻeo's usage of Hawaiian is the cause of the arrest warrant. AZ builds on this point in lines 14–15 by first noting that Kaʻeo speaks both Hawaiian and English fluently and by then utilizing the verbal category *chose* to formulate Kaʻeo's action of speaking Hawaiian as a choice, thereby indicating that Kaʻeo could have spoken in English. This category of *chose* also builds on the characterization of Kaʻeo in the introduction of the report in Excerpt (4) as *refusing to speak English in a court appearance*. AZ ends this voice-over in lines 16–17 by engaging in the practice of reported speech to state that *Judge Blaine Kobayashi said the court was unable to determine if Kaʻeo was present*. In doing so, AZ employs the title and full name of Kobayashi, category work that points to the official sense of the interaction as well as the decision to issue the arrest warrant.

Following AZ's formulations and categories in lines 13–17 that frame the choice of Hawaiian as the cause of arrest, the report presents an excerpt from an interview with Kaʻeo in lines 20–23 in which he directly expresses his view that the judge had an issue with his usage of Hawaiian. The report then provides another voice-over from AZ in lines 24–29 that explains the reason why Kaʻeo was in court and also that he had requested a Hawaiian language interpreter. AZ concludes this voice-over in lines 27–29 by using reported speech to state Kaʻeo's belief that people should have the right to defend themselves in court in Hawaiian. This is followed by more speech from Kaʻeo in lines 30–34 in which he gives an account for why Hawaiian should be allowed in the courtroom; he is speaking as a Hawaiian person representing the Hawaiian people and hence Hawaiian is the best way to speak to a Hawaiian issue. This excerpt concludes with another clip from the courtroom showing several members of the audience shouting the Hawaiian word *hewa* 'wrong' in response to the judge's unwillingness to recognize Ka'eo and his usage of Hawaiian.

Even though AK makes it clear through formulations and categories that Ka'eo's choice of Hawaiian (and refusal to speak English) in court has led to the warrant for his arrest, it is notable that the report allows Ka'eo to voice his side of the story. In particular, the second interview clip in lines 30–34 seemingly moves the report toward the topic of the right to use Hawaiian in a courtroom context, especially when the issue at hand is a *Hawaiian issue*. Yet, as shown below in Excerpt (8), despite an additional clip from Ka'eo, AZ continues to employ categories and reported speech that prevent the report from fully considering the right to speak Hawaiian.

Excerpt (8): Continuation from Excerpt (7)
```
41    AZ:    A spokesperson for judiciary told us there is no legal
42           requirement to provide Hawaiian language interpreters to
43           court participants who speak English but prefer to speak in
44           Hawaiian.
45           ((Moves back to showing Ka'eo as he responds to a previously
46           recorded interview))
47    SK:    We'll continue to demand through my words that I be
48           recognized as a human being, that we as Hawaiians have a right.
49           It is just a human right that we have to speak our own language.
50           ((Moves to showing the reporter AZ at the studio with a picture
51           of the words 'language battle' above a courtroom gavel in the
52           background))
53    AZ:    A spokesperson for the judiciary says Ka'eo is not being singled
54           out. Ka'eo told me he himself plans to turn himself into
55           authorities. He plans to continue speaking Hawaiian in future
56           court hearings. Howard.
```

Instead of building on Ka'eo's suggestion in lines 33–34 that *Hawaiian language is the best way to express that this is a Hawaiian issue*, AZ employs the category of *a spokesperson for judiciary* to invoke another official position in line 41 in order to note that there is no legal requirement to provide Hawaiian language interpreters. In doing so, his usage of the verbal category *prefer* in the phrase *prefer to speak in Hawaiian*, much like the verb form *chose* in line 15, emphasizes that speaking Hawaiian in court is an individual preference and not a right to speak an official language. In this sense, then, AZ's reported speech and categories in lines 41–44 indicate an official stance that opposes Kaʻeo's call to use Hawaiian in court to speak to Hawaiian issues. Still, though, the report produces in lines 47–49 another clip from the interview with Kaʻeo that presents an arguably even stronger statement concerning Hawaiian speaking rights. Kaʻeo employs the pronoun *we* three times and the possessive form *our* once to refer to the collective group of Native Hawaiians as he emphasizes that it is *just a human right that we have to speak our language*. His usage of plural first person pronouns display that Kaʻeo is framing this not as his individual right but as a right for all Native Hawaiians.

Nonetheless, despite Kaʻeo's attempt to frame this as a group right, AZ concludes the story in lines 53–56 without any reference to the speaking rights of Native Hawaiians. As the screen shows AZ standing by himself in the studio with the phrase *language battle* behind him, AZ first invokes more reported speech from the *spokesperson for the judiciary* to state that Kaʻeo *is not being singled out*. Although *singled out* implies the existence of others, AZ does not elaborate in a way that might consider the possibility that there exists a group who wants to use Hawaiian in court. In fact, AZ refocuses on Kaʻeo as an individual actor as he offers reported speech from Kaʻeo in lines 54–56 to note that Kaʻeo *plans to continue speaking Hawaiian in future court hearings*. In doing so, AZ twice employs the singular pronoun *he* to concentrate on Kaʻeo as one individual, a practice which contrasts with Kaʻeo's usage of the plural pronoun *we* in lines 47–49 to attempt to move the discussion to the larger issue of group rights.

In this sense, then, the phrase *language battles* on the screen serves as a formulation in at least two ways. It first of all further encourages viewers, through the term *battle*, to see Kaʻeo's usage of Hawaiian in court as controversial. Such a depiction of Hawaiian as controversial builds on AZ's first formulation of Hawaiian as the reason for the arrest warrant in lines 13–17 of Excerpt (7) and also on the usage of verbal categories such as *chose* and *prefer*, emphasizing that Hawaiian speakers are capable of employing English in court. Second of all, *language battles* also works as a fitting synopsis of the juxtaposition created by the sequential organization of the news report. Although each of the three clips from the interview with Kaʻeo shows attempts to speak to the general issue of Hawaiian language speaking rights, next turns are occupied by voice-overs from AZ who, through categorical terms such as *chose* and *prefer*, reported speech from official positions like the *spokesperson for the judiciary*, and the singular pronoun *he*, keeps the focus on Kaʻeo's actions and avoids taking up the larger issue of rights to speak Hawaiian in court.

The news report shown in Excerpts (7) and (8) shares similarities with the report presented in Excerpts (5) and (6). Both consist of a sequential organization that allows for practices such as categories, formulations and reported speech to portray the usage of Hawaiian in public as controversial and to prevent a sustained concentration on the rights of Hawaiian language speakers to use one of the official languages of the state. In particular, it is strategically placed voice-overs from the reporters that allow the reports to construct individual acts of speaking Hawaiian as controversial. In Excerpts (5) and (6), the reporter AP employs especially formulations and categories to ensure that the report frames Hanohano's usage of Hawaiian in the House of Representatives as problematic, and in Excerpts (7) and (8), it is AZ's use of reported speech in addition to formulations and categories that portray Kaʻeo's attempt to speak Hawaiian in court as a *battle*. The final section below considers the potential of a microanalysis of speaking practices to underscore how unequal power relations can be constructed and reinforced in an institutional context such as a news broadcast.

## Discussion and Conclusion

In an analysis of confrontations on talk radio, Hutchby (1996) describes how the turn-taking system of the program, particularly the fact that the host has the priority to speak first and thus lead with confrontational questions, allows the host to control the organization as well as the content of the talk. This system of turn-taking, a defining feature of the talk radio institutional context, serves as the basis of constructing power asymmetries realized through the host's ability to utilize turns to challenge callers and create an adversarial environment. Although the news reports considered in this chapter do not center on exchanges of interaction, there is a parallel with talk radio in that the sequential organization of the reports derives directly from the fact that representatives of the institution, anchors, reporters, producers, etc. possess the institutional power to control how the reports are organized. It is this institutional power that allows the creators of the reports to arrange information sequentially as they desire, including the strategic insertion of voice-overs with practices such as categories, formulations and reported speech that construct content that reinforces power asymmetries in society. As shown in the analysis, it is through the deployment of categories, formulations and reported speech that the reports construct negative images of attempts to use Hawaiian in public and also pit governmental voices against the individual voices of 'controversial' Hawaiian speakers. As evidenced from the analysis, there are a growing number of Hawaiian speakers such as Representative Hanohano and Samuel Kaʻeo who attempt to challenge existing power asymmetries by employing Hawaiian in public contexts, but they are frequently branded as controversial and treated as renegades attempting to deviate from the norm. Moreover, by keeping the news reports centered on the individual usages of Hawaiian by controversial figures, the reports, while raising the question of the right to speak Hawaiian in public, avoid having to maintain a focus on the greater issue that is actually behind these attempts to speak Hawaiian in venues such as the floor of the House or Representatives and in court. The analysis has elucidated practices such as categories, formulations and reported speech that make it possible to portray attempts to speak Hawaiian as problematic and to avoid devoting significant time and space to consideration of rights. These practices, in sum, help to reinforce the current asymmetrical relationship between Hawaiian and English.

Herein lies the value of employing CA in an analysis intended to be critical of language used in an institutional setting such as a news broadcast. With its focus on the organization of talk, CA has the potential to enlighten our understanding of some of the practices at the micro-level of talk that contribute to the maintenance of power asymmetries in society. While many Hawaiian speakers are surely aware of the existing asymmetries at the level of government policy that make it difficult to make in-roads in Hawaiian speaking rights, a CA analysis helps elucidate how certain practices in talk in news broadcasts do not produce mere neutral representations of events but in fact produce them in ways that function to reinforce power asymmetries concerning the limited role of Hawaiian in society. A CA analysis holds, in other words, the power to expose how these practices work in the news broadcast and also the potential to inform and educate people, in this case supporters of the Hawaiian language, about practices used in local mainstream news broadcasts that may function to impede the progress of Hawaiian in society. This analysis focused on categories, formulations and reported speech in a small sample of news reports on local news programs in Hawaiʻi, and it is hoped that additional critically-minded microanalyses of talk in the future continue to explicate in more detail how these and other practices contribute to power asymmetries concerning issues not only in Hawaiʻi but also throughout the world.

## References

Clayman, S. (1992) Footing in the achievement of neutrality: The case of news interview discourse. In P. Drew and J. Heritage (eds) *Talk at Work: Interaction in Institutional Settings* (pp. 268–301). Cambridge University Press.
Edwards, D. (1997) *Discourse and Cognition*. Sage.
Garfinkel, H. and Sacks, H. (1970) On formal structures of practical action. In J.C. McKinney and E. Tiryakian (eds) *Theoretical Sociology: Perspectives and Developments* (pp. 338–366). Appleton-Century Crofts.
Greatbatch, D. (1992) On the management of disagreement between news interviewers. In P. Drew and J. Heritage (eds) *Talk at Work: Interaction in Institutional Settings* (pp. 163–198). Cambridge University Press.
Heritage, J. and Clayman, S. (2010) *Talk in Action: Interactions, Identities, and Institutions*. Wiley-Blackwell.
Hutchby, I. (1996) *Confrontation Talk: Arguments, Asymmetries, and Power on Talk Radio*. Routledge.
Hutchby, I. (2003) Conversation analysis and the study of broadcast talk. In R. Sanders and K. Fitch (eds) *Handbook of Language and Social Interaction* (pp. 437–460). Lawrence Erlbaum.
Hutchby, I. and Wooffitt, R. (1998) *Conversation Analysis: Principles, Practices and Applications*. Polity Press.
Lerner, G. (1991) On the syntax of sentences-in-progress. *Language in Society* 20, 441–458.
Raymond, G. (2004) The stand-alone 'so' in ordinary conversation. *Research on Language and Social Interaction* 37 (2), 185–218.
Schegloff, E. (2007) A tutorial on membership categorization. *Journal of Pragmatics* 39 (3), 462–482.
Silva, N. (2017) *The Power of the Steel-tipped Pen: Reconstructing Native Hawaiian Intellectual History*. Duke University Press.
Teo, P. (2000) Racism in the news: A critical discourse analysis of news reporting in two Australian newspapers. *Discourse & Society* 11 (1), 7–49.
Van Dijk, T. (1993) Principles of critical discourse analysis. *Discourse & Society* 4 (2), 249–283.
Wilson, W. and Kamanā, K. (2001) Mai loko mai o ka 'i'ini: Proceeding from a dream, the 'Aha Pūnana Leo connection in Hawaiian language revitalization. In L. Hinton and K. Hale (eds) *The Greenbook of Language Revitalization in Practice* (pp. 147–176). Academic Press.
Wilson, W. and Kawaeʻaeʻa, K. (2007) I kumu lālā: Let there be sources; let there be branches: Teacher education in the College of Hawaiian Language. *Journal of American Indian Education* 46 (3), 37–53.
Wilson, W. and Kamanā, K. (2013) E paepae hou 'ia ka pōhaku: Reset the stones of the Hawaiian house platform. In L. Hinton (ed.) *Bringing our Languages Home: Language Revitalization for Families* (pp. 101–117). Heyday Books.

# 5 Inequality in Action: Granting Emergency Service Requests in a Highly Resource-Constrained Context

Catherine L. Tam, Kevin A. Whitehead and
Geoffrey Raymond

## Introduction

Calling an emergency service line implies a need for an emergency service (Drew & Walker, 2010; Heritage & Clayman, 2010; Zimmerman, 1984, 1992), displays the caller's entitlement to receive the service (Curl & Drew, 2008; M.R. Whalen & Zimmerman, 1990), and positions them as a (potential) beneficiary of a service, with call-takers serving as gatekeepers to the service and thus as (potential) benefactors (Clayman & Heritage, 2014; Drew & Walker, 2010; Heritage & Clayman, 2010; Raymond & Zimmerman, 2007, 2016). Conversely, a call-taker's granting of the request for service and the caller's tacit acceptance of the granting by moving to the call's closing conveys the participants' mutual understanding that a service will be dispatched that is appropriately calibrated and timed in light of the nature and severity of the emergency at hand. In Garfinkel's (1963, 1967) terms, participants act in accordance with 'the natural attitude of daily life' (also see Schütz, 1953: 5), displaying 'trust' that the emergency service institution will function as expected as a background condition for the accomplishment of the actions of requesting and providing services (cf. Garcia & Parmer, 1999; Heritage, 1984; Watson, 2009). In this respect, a caller's willingness to end the call and await the arrival of the service reflects their trust that institutional actors will fulfill the obligations entailed by the call-taker's granting of the service. Where participants may have grounds to anticipate that the fulfillment of this 'social contract' may be so substantially delayed as to call into question its status as an *emergency* service, they may deploy practices to prospectively manage the trouble that might otherwise ensue from such failures. These practices may be understood as being designed to shore up trust in the institution's ability to meet its obligations in the face of circumstances that may give rise to doubt or concern in this regard.

Precisely because trust is foundational to institutional realities, participants must routinely manage conduct, events and outcomes that may undermine it. For example, callers may contend with a call-taker's skepticism regarding their claims (Garcia & Parmer, 1999) or even the project that occasioned their call (Raymond & Zimmerman, 2016). Conversely, callers doubting whether service providers will respond in a timely manner to putative emergencies may attempt to 'game the system' by formulating circumstances in ways designed to secure a highest-priority dispatch (see Moskos, 2008: 89–110). The import of these routine 'seen but unnoticed' (Garfinkel, 1967: 37) ways in which participants contend with trust that has been diminished or otherwise frayed are cast into stark relief by circumstances where communities lose trust altogether. For example, Desmond, Papachristos and Kirk (2016) document a substantial decline in 911 calls by Milwaukee residents following a highly publicized, racially motivated beating of a Black civilian by white officers. In the aftermath of the beating and the city's failure to take action against its perpetrators, Desmond *et al.* (2016: 870) observed a 'large and durable' decline in 911 calls (approximately 22,000 fewer calls in one year) from Black communities in the year following the beating, making the 'cit[y] as a whole, and the Black community in particular, less safe'. Relatedly, Bell (2017: 2054) uses the concept of 'legal estrangement' to describe the chronic and pervasive loss of trust associated with 'the intuition among many people in poor communities of color that the law operates to exclude them from society'.

Cases such as those documented by Desmond *et al.* (2016) and Bell (2017) thus show that either specific events or exclusionary practices used over long periods can be associated with communities losing trust in public institutions. Similarly to the cases described by Desmond *et al.* (2016) and Bell (2017), inequalities in the provision of emergency services in South Africa are directly connected to histories of racial oppression and exclusion. Specifically, the South African healthcare system consists of public and private sector service providers, with the public sector's emergency services being managed at a provincial government level. Although almost 65% of the South African population rely on public sector services, ongoing legacies of the apartheid system, along with subsequent mismanagement and corruption, have contributed to public healthcare being substantially under-resourced and overburdened relative to the private sector (see e.g. Coovadia et al., 2009; Horwitz, 2009).

In this report, we examine calls to an emergency service call center in South Africa, showing how participants' orientations to these material circumstances – and the issues of trust that may arise from the ways that emergency services are constrained by them – become evident in their conduct in the calls. Specifically, we consider some practices deployed by call-takers in the turns in which they grant service requests and examine how calls are brought to closing thereafter. Crucially, the practices we describe have not been reported as routine components of grantings and closings in previous studies of emergency service calls.

Conversation analytic research on emergency calls across a range of countries has examined how the benefactor and beneficiary positions are produced in and through the call's structure, which is built around a service request/response adjacency pair sequence (Zimmerman, 1984), along with pre- and insert expansions of this sequence yielding an overall structure consisting of five distinct phases: (i) opening/identification, (ii) request, (iii) interrogative series, (iv) response and (v) closing (Heritage & Clayman, 2010; Kevoe-Feldman, 2019; Zimmerman, 1984, 1992). Routine grantings of service request and call closing (cf. Raymond & Zimmerman, 2016: 722) in previous CA literature are shown in Excerpts 1 and 2 (for further instances, see Raymond & Zimmerman, 2007: 37; J. Whalen et al., 1988: 344; Zimmerman, 1984: 214, 1992: 37):

(1) [Heritage & Clayman, 2010: 90]
```
01    CT:         We'll get somebody there right away.=
02    C:          =o:kay thank yo[u
03    CT:                        [<mm bye>
```

(2) [Raymond & Zimmerman, 2016: 723]
```
01    CT:         Okay we'll get somebody over there.
02    C:          Tha::nk you.
03    CT:         Mmhm b[ye.
04    C:                [°Buh bye
```

As these cases demonstrate, the turn in which the granting of the request is produced may (or may not) include a turn-initial *okay* (as in Excerpt 2, line 01), which displays the call-taker's receipt and acceptance of the information the caller has given, and marks the transition from the interrogative series to the call-taker's granting of the service request (Heritage & Clayman, 2010; Raymond & Zimmerman, 2007, 2016; Zimmerman, 1984). The granting itself recurrently consists of a single component in the form of a service announcement, which in some cases includes an indication of the immediacy of the dispatch of the service (as in Excerpt 1, line 01), while in other cases leaves this unspecified (as in Excerpt 2, line 01). The caller then recurrently responds to the granting with a 'service receipt' (Raymond & Zimmerman, 2016) in the form of a token such as *okay* (as in Excerpt 1, line 02) and, where relevant, appreciations such as *thank you* (as in line 02 of both excerpts). These may in turn be ratified by the call-taker's production of a receipt token such as *mm* (as seen in line 03 of both excerpts). Finally, the call-taker moves to bring the call to a close by producing a terminal particle such as *bye* (as in line 03 of both excerpts), to which the caller may respond with a reciprocal terminal particle before the call is terminated.

Our review of the literature revealed only one case, reported by Drew and Walker (2010: 109), and shown in Excerpt 3, in which the granting turn included additional components beyond those shown in Excerpts 1 and 2. As Drew and Walker (2010: 108–109) note, a key feature of this case is the question of whether the caller's complaint (a nosebleed resulting from being punched 'by a taxi driver') is serious enough to warrant provision of the requested service, although the call-taker does eventually grant the request and dispatch the police to the incident.

(3) [Drew & Walker, 2010: 109]
```
01    CT:         =Alr:ght we'll get police back down
02                to you as soon as we can sir.=Okay?=
03    C:          =Okay.
04    CT:         Bye bye.
05    CT:         ((makes a loud snoring sound))
```

In addition to the turn-initial *Alr:ght* and the service announcement (*we'll get the police back down to you*), the granting in this case includes two additional components not present in the routine cases shown in Excerpts 1–2. The first of these is an indication of contingency (*as soon as we can*) that implicates a possible delay, and the second is a tag question (*okay?*) that invites the caller's acceptance of this possibility. While Drew and Walker's (2010: 107–110) analysis of this case does not focus on these details of the call-taker's granting and the caller's response, our analysis is nevertheless consistent with their observations about the high-entitlement form used in the request ('I need the police, right now'). Specifically, the two components used to expand the call taker's service announcement apparently address, and seek the caller's acceptance of, a possible discrepancy between what the caller has sought and what the call-taker can or will provide – that is, services will be dispatched, but as a matter of lower priority than the caller evidently expects. In this way, the expansion of the service announcement seeks to preemptively manage the possible mistrust that might otherwise emerge by reference to the delay the call-taker is evidently anticipating. Note then, while the caller produces the service receipt *Okay* (line 03), he does not produce an appreciation of the granting of the sort seen in Excerpts 1–2.[1]

These observations are further elucidated by Raymond and Zimmerman's (2016) more recent analysis of two types of trouble that may occasion expansions of closings in emergency calls. The first of these is what Raymond and Zimmerman (2016) call 'routine troubles', which involve cases in which the aligned projects of the participants (seeking and providing help) give rise to contingencies related to achieving their possible completion, such as call taker verifying information provided by the caller and caller providing additional information relevant for the dispatch of help. The expansions occasioned by such cases are thus designed to bring these articulated projects to completion and sustain the alignment of the identities of the call-taker and caller as benefactor and beneficiary respectively. In contrast, in '*non*-routine troubles, one or both of these features (alignment and completion) are at issue' (Raymond & Zimmerman, 2016: 727; emphasis in original). This includes cases where (as in Excerpt 3) callers' responses to the call-taker's indication of service provision 'simply acknowledge it with "okay" while declining to accept it as a resolution to the project they have pursued up to that point' (Raymond & Zimmerman, 2016: 729). Returning to Excerpt 2, we can now note that the caller's acknowledgement of the call-taker's contingent granting of the service without appreciating it treats the promise of service as departing from or falling short of what he had sought, thereby displaying that he and the call-taker have not fully accomplished alignment as help-seeker and help-provider (Raymond & Zimmerman, 2016).

A further, unequivocal, indication of the misalignment between the caller and call-taker in Excerpt 3 is then provided by the call-taker's production of a loud snoring sound after terminating the call (line 05), which, as Drew and Walker (2010: 109) note, displays his assessment of the call as 'a waste of police time'. The additional, non-routine, components of the granting in this case – as in the cases Raymond and Zimmerman (2016) examine – thus appear to be occasioned by, and reflect the call-taker's orientation to, the questionable legitimacy of the service request and therefore the non-routine nature of the call (also see Garcia & Parmer, 1999; J. Whalen et al., 1988; M.R. Whalen & Zimmerman, 1990). In contrast, in our data call-takers' routine uses of these additional components in granting the service, callers' uptake of them, and the additional complexities of subsequent moves to closing of calls together indicate that they are designed to manage issues of trust arising from participants' orientations to structural limits on the capacity of the institution to provide a timely service, rather than from call takers' assessment of the legitimacy of the caller's emergency.[2] Our analyses of these practices thus show how participants in settings characterized by high levels of material inequality and associated resource constraints may work to manage the gap between what may be expected and what can be provided by the service institution, and thereby mitigate the potential issues of trust that may arise from this gap. We thereby demonstrate the value of a critical CA approach for investigating how social problems with origins outside of particular forms of institutional interaction can become observable in participants' orientations and conduct in the interactions.

## Data and Method

We utilize a critical CA approach to examine a collection (see Schegloff, 1996) consisting of the grantings and subsequent movement to closing in 63 recorded calls to a government-operated emergency medical call center in the Western Cape province of South Africa. While the call center from which our data are drawn was reportedly relatively high-performing compared to call centers operated by other provincial governments at the time of recording, it nonetheless operated under highly resource-constrained conditions; receiving an average of approximately 1800 calls every 24 hours, while having only 65 ambulances available to dispatch for emergency responses. Consequently, wait times for the arrival of an ambulance can vary widely, from as short as a few minutes to as long as several hours. Thus, while it is a routine feature of emergency dispatch worldwide that call-takers cannot reliably estimate or inform callers how long the wait for an ambulance may be, the scope of this uncertainty is of a different order of magnitude for call-takers – and, by extension, callers – in our data than it is for emergency services in better-resourced contexts.

Although South Africa had 11 official languages at the time, the majority of residents of the region served by the call center speak Afrikaans or English as a first language, with a sizable minority of isiXhosa speakers and small minorities of speakers of other languages also resident in the region. As is the case for other government institutions in South Africa, the official language of the call center was English, but call-takers were typically bilingual in English and Afrikaans. As fluent speakers of both English and Afrikaans, we were able to include calls conducted in both of these languages in our analysis, but we excluded a small number of calls conducted in isiXhosa due to our lack of fluency in this language.

The data extracts included in the analysis that follows were selected so as to illustrate the range of components present in grantings across the data set, and the range of variations in their production by call-takers and uptake by callers. In cases where calls were partly or entirely conducted in Afrikaans, English translations are provided in italics on the lines below the corresponding Afrikaans talk. Participants' names have been replaced with pseudonyms, and all other identifying information revealed in the calls has been altered in the transcripts.

As is unavoidably the case in undertaking any sociological analysis, we necessarily used our own and others' members' knowledge in order to recognize the members' knowledge being used by the participants in our data (cf. Garfinkel, 1967). In addition to providing the descriptions of the setting and data, we have worked throughout our analysis, on a case-by-case basis, to render our recognition and use of such members' knowledge as explicitly as possible, especially when analyzing details that may be opaque for readers who are unfamiliar with features of the setting and other relevant contextual matters to which participants appeared to be oriented.[3]

## Analysis

We begin our analysis by examining the practices participants routinely use to manage potential service delays – and the associated issues of trust in the institution described above – in cases where the call-taker grants the caller's request prospectively, i.e. by indicating that an ambulance will be dispatched at some point in the future. We then consider how participants may manage these issues of trust even in cases where the call-taker indicates that an ambulance has already been dispatched. Finally, we examine a deviant case in which trouble arises in relation to the call-taker's use of these practices for managing trust, with the caller treating them as implicating the call-taker's assessment of the seriousness of the emergency, as opposed to the capacity of the institution to provide services in a timely manner.

## Managing trust in cases of pending dispatch

In addition to the service announcement component systematically produced by call-takers in the calls reported in the literature (as shown in Excerpts 1–2 above), call-takers in both English and Afrikaans language calls in our data recurrently and routinely produced contingency and tag question components similar to those produced by the call-taker in the deviant case shown in Excerpt 3. This is illustrated by Excerpt 4, in which the caller is a 29-week pregnant woman who has reported labor pains and vaginal bleeding.

```
(4) Routine granting [22510543]
    01    CT:    Mevrou, ons >stuur die< ambulaans
                 Madam we'll send the ambulance
    02           >uit daarso< so gou as moontlik, ↑hoor?
                 out there as soon as possible, hear?
    03           (0.6)
    04    C:     Baie dank↑ie.
                 Thank you very much.
    05    CT:    Plesi::er:.
                 Pleasure.
    06           (.)
    07    CT:    Buh=by:e:
    08    C:     By:e.
```

The granting turn begins with a service announcement (*madam we'll send the ambulance out there*; lines 01–02), followed by an indication of contingency (*as soon as possible*; line 02), and a tag question (*hear?*; line 02). Crucially, in contrast to the case shown in Excerpt 3, there is no evidence in Excerpt 4 (nor in other cases throughout our data in which these additional components are produced) of their production as conveying skepticism on the part of the call-taker with respect to the legitimacy of the request for service, and thus as reflecting a 'non-routine trouble' of the type described by Raymond and Zimmerman (2016) in the call. Instead, in our data these components appear to display call-takers' orientation to, and serve as practices for managing, 'routine troubles' of a different nature from those identified by Raymond and Zimmerman (2016) – namely, troubles arising routinely from the resource-related contingencies that characterize the context in which the call center operates, and the potential consequences of these contingencies for participants' trust in the institution's capacity to provide immediate service.

Specifically, the second component (the indication of contingency) is oriented to what callers in this context are likely to know, or perhaps not know, about the potential wait times for the service they have requested. That is, it effectively acknowledges that a service-seeker may experience what they could deem to be a significant wait time, while simultaneously being designed to reassure them that the wait time will be as short as possible. As such, while the contingency component in Excerpt 3 evidently arises from the individual agency or judgment of the call-taker in relation to a particular, potentially questionable, request for service, call-takers' routine production of this component in our data seems to be a practice for pre-emptively managing systematic uncertainties implicating (mis)trust in the institution's capacity to provide timely services even in cases of entirely legitimate emergencies.

This routine uncertainty, in turn, gives rise to a systematic uncertainty as to whether the (contingent) granting of the service request adequately meets the caller's service provision expectations, and thus whether (in Raymond and Zimmerman's [2016] terms) the alignment of the caller and call-taker as help-seeker and help-provider has been adequately accomplished and the interaction can be brought to a close. The third component, the tag question, invites the caller to acknowledge the contingent terms of the granting, and thereby displays the call-taker's orientation to establishing an intersubjective understanding and acceptance of this uncertainty (cf. Hepburn & Potter, 2010; Heritage, 2002; Sacks et al., 1974).[4]

Moreover, in contrast to the dissatisfaction displayed by the Excerpt 3 caller in response to the contingent granting of the service request, the caller in Excerpt 4 (and recurrently in other calls in our data, as in Excerpts 1–2) aligns with the granting: following a brief silence[5] (line 03), the caller displays appreciation. In this way, the caller aligns with the call-taker's treatment of the contingent service granting as arising from potential mistrust in the institution's capacity to provide a timely service, rather than (as in Excerpt 3) as casting doubt on the legitimacy of the emergency. As such, the caller and call-taker accomplish alignment as help-seeker and help-provider, and (similarly to the routine cases shown in Excerpts 1–2), the call moves thereafter to closing within a few turns (lines 05 to 08).

Further evidence for the systematic use of these practices can be seen in cases, such as Excerpt 5 below, in which the granting is produced twice as a result of a re-opening of the interrogative phase by the call-taker, with the second iteration of the granting including the same components as the first. In this case, the patient is an insulin-dependent diabetic who is reportedly confused and intermittently losing consciousness.

(5) Repeated granting [10224]
```
01   CT:    O:kay. .h U::m: we're gonna ↑send out an
02          ambulance <as ↓soon as possible,> ↓hey,
03          <and he did take his medication,
04          <i[s he on ↑insulin?
05   C:      [°Yes.°
06          (1.5)
07   C:     Yes, he's on insulin.
08   CT:    Is Thomas on insulin?
09          (0.8)
10   CT:    In:su[lin: depen:dent. ((typing noises))
11   C:          [Yes.
12   CT:    An' he did eat, you said ↑ey?
13          (1.5)
14   C:     >°Het hy geëet al?°< ((speaking off phone))
            Did he eat?
15          (2.0) ((inaudible talk by person off phone))
16   C:     Yes, he ate already.
17          (0.4)
18   CT:    O:kay ma'am.
19          (.)
20   CT:    We're >gonna send out the ambulance<
21          as soon as we can, ↑hey?
22          (1.3)
23   C:     Thank you ma'am.
24   CT:    ↑Alri:g[ht the:n, ba ↑by:e:?
25   C:           [(°Okay, thank you.°)
26   C:     (°Bye°.)
27          (0.8)
28   C:     (°Bye°.)
```

In lines 01–02, the call-taker grants the request for service, with the granting including similar components to those seen in Excerpt 4 – a service announcement, an indication of contingency, and a tag question. However, before the caller responds to the granting, the call-taker quickly initiates a further series of questions about the patient, which the caller answers (lines 03–16) – with this expansion of the call being an instance of what Raymond and Zimmerman (2016), as noted above, describe as a routine trouble. After registering receipt and acceptance of the caller's responses (line 18), the call-taker re-issues the granting, which again includes the service announcement (line 20) as well as the contingency component and the tag question (line 21). As Schegloff (2004) notes, repeats of prior utterances may omit elements that the speaker thereby treats as 'dispensable', and the call-taker's inclusion of all of these components in the second iterations of grantings in cases such as this thereby treats them as 'indispensable' elements of the action produced through this turn. As in Excerpt 4, following an initial silence (line 22), the caller displays appreciation for the granting (line 23), and the call is brought to a close shortly thereafter.

Excerpt 6 illustrates an alternative form of the contingency component that call-takers in some cases in our data – both in English and Afrikaans calls – utilized. In this case, an ambulance has been requested on behalf of an 18-year-old full-term pregnant patient who is reportedly in labor, but whose water has not yet broken.

(6) Alternative granting [IR 10198]
```
01      CT:     [>°Okay, ons gaan° vir julle ↑eerste<
                we're going to for you first
02              beskikbaar ambulaans >uitstuur, (net)
                available ambulance send out, (just)
03              uitkyk vir die< ambulaans, ↑hoer?
                look out for the ambulance, hear?
04              (0.5)
05      C:      pt=O:kay.=
06      CT:     =Dankie:, ↓by:e[:.
                Thank you, bye.
07      C:               [Okay, by::e.
```

As in Excerpts 4 and 5, the call-taker produces a service announcement followed by a contingency component, but in this case the contingency component is produced in the form *the first available ambulance* (lines 01–02). While more explicitly (compared to the *as soon as possible* form of the contingency component used in Excerpts 4 and 5) indicating to the caller that an ambulance may not be immediately available, this form of the component also more explicitly informs the caller that the patient will be 'first in line' for an ambulance once one is available, and thus that the legitimacy of the emergency is not in question. The granting in this case also includes an additional instruction to the caller to *just look out for the ambulance* (lines 02–03), which is evidently designed to manage an additional resource-related difficulty that ambulance drivers reported recurrently encountering in locating patients in areas with inadequate street signage and/or numbering, especially when (as in this case) callers do not have a landline or mobile phone number where they can be reached in the event of such locational difficulties.

Also, as in Excerpts 4 and 5, the granting ends with a tag question, although it appears after the additional instruction rather than after the contingency component. The tag question here nonetheless appears to serve a similar function to those produced in the prior excerpts, prompting the caller to align with the instruction the call-taker has issued and, by extension, with the contingent service the call-taker has granted. In response, the caller acknowledges the call-taker's turn (line 06) but does not produce a display of appreciation of the sort produced by the callers in Excerpts 4 and 5. There is thus evidence of misalignment of the caller and call-taker as help-seeker and help provider, which the call-taker manages by thanking the caller (line 06), thereby implementing a reversal of the default alignment of caller and call-taker as beneficiary and benefactor by treating the caller's actions as benefitting the call-taker, rather than vice versa (cf. Raymond & Zimmerman, 2016; also see Clayman & Heritage, 2014). This is facilitated in part by the caller's status as someone seeking help on behalf of a patient rather than on her own behalf (see Raymond & Zimmerman, 2016), and by the call-taker having just issued an instruction that recruits the caller to assist the institution in carrying out its work.

The call-taker then immediately moves to close the call by producing the terminal particle *bye* (line 06), and the caller responds (slightly in overlap with the end of the call-taker's turn) by aligning with both the reversal of the benefactor-beneficiary identities with *Okay* and with the move to close the call with a reciprocal terminal particle (line 07). The misalignment in this case is thus swiftly resolved without further expansion of the closing phase of the call.

## Managing trust in cases of immediate dispatch

The systematic issues of trust managed using the practices described in the prior section can be further appreciated in cases where the ambulance is dispatched immediately, but the service granting is nonetheless treated as a matter of uncertainty. This can be seen in cases in our data in which call-takers indicate (in the turn ordinarily occupied by the granting) that an ambulance has already been dispatched. That is, rather than merely granting the request for service, the call-taker may report that the request has *already* been granted and the ambulance is *en route*, as in Excerpt 7, which involves a full-term pregnant patient in labor.

(7) Immediate dispatch [301023]
    01    CT:        O<u>k</u>ay, ons s- (.) ambul<u>aa</u>ns is op
                     *Okay, we s- (.) ambulance is on*

```
02                pad, ↑hoer?
                  the way, hear?
03                (0.2)
04       C:       .h Okay, baie dankie meneer.=
                  Okay, thank you very much sir.
05       CT:      =°Danki:e, ba ↑by[e.°
                  Thank you, ba bye.
06       C:                      [Okay, ↑by:e:.
```

Here, the call-taker initially appears to be headed toward a granting similar to those seen in previous excerpts, before initiating repair (Schegloff, 2013; Schegloff *et al.*, 1977) to instead formulate the service as having already been dispatched: the call-taker cuts off after saying *ons s-* – apparently headed toward a granting of the form *ons sal...* (*we will...*) – and informs the caller that the *ambulaans is op pad* (*ambulance is on the way* – lines 01–02). While this self-initiated repair does not reveal whether the call-taker was headed toward the production of a simple granting similar to those seen in Excerpts 1–2, or a granting including the contingency component seen in Excerpts 3–6, it does display the call-taker's orientation to the immediate dispatch of an ambulance as an alternative to the original (and thereby 'default') trajectory of the granting, suggesting that call-takers can adapt their granting practices to prevailing conditions on a case-by-case basis.

Also noteworthy in this case is the call-taker's production of a tag question in the granting turn, thereby prompting the caller to align with the granting of the service even in the absence of the contingency components seen in Excerpts 4–6 (also see Schegloff, 2004). This demonstrates that even when an ambulance is available immediately, call-takers may nonetheless work to pre-emptively manage potential troubles with respect to their alignment with callers as help-provider and help-seeker, thereby displaying an orientation to pervasive uncertainty about the timely delivery of the service even though it has been announced as having already been dispatched.

A particularly telling orientation of this nature on the part of a caller can be seen in Excerpt 8. Here, a non-contingent granting is followed by an expansion of the closing sequence in which the caller asks about the likely wait time for the ambulance, with the call-taker then indicating that it has already been dispatched. In this case, the patient is a 60-year-old man who is experiencing chest pains and has a history of hypertension.

```
(8) Non-contingent granting [10646]
       01      CT:       .h >Okay, ↑thank you ma'am we're
       02                gonna send a <ambulance out, ↑hey:?
```

```
03                    You must just [(       )
04      C:                     [Okay, th↑a:nk you my dear.
05                    <To twentix Queen Mary Street in
06                    Ruy:terwa:cht?
07      CT:           Yes, [we've got it [(    )
08      C:                  [.hhh      [Okay- Um:: they w-
09                    they w↑on't be too long, ↓he:y?
10      CT:           No, dey on their way now.
11      C:            O:kay thank >yo[u my< dear:, ↑bye[::.
12      CT:                          [Okay.                [Bye.
```

The granting the call-taker initially produces in this case (lines 01–02) resembles those shown in Excerpts 1–2 by lacking the contingency component seen in Excerpts 3–6, and thereby implying the immediate dispatch of the ambulance without explicitly (as in Excerpt 7) indicating that it has already been dispatched. However, it does include the tag question (*hey?*) similar to those observed in Excerpts 3–7, and the call-taker also begins to formulate an additional instruction component (*You must just*), as seen in Excerpt 6, before aborting it as the caller begins to respond in overlap (lines 03–04). While the caller initially responds by aligning with and appreciating the granting (line 04; cf. Excerpts 1, 2, 4, 5 and 7), she then initiates an expansion of the granting sequence, requesting confirmation that the call-taker has the address at which the patient is located (lines 05–06).[6] Following the call-taker's confirmation (line 07), the caller produces an aligning *Okay* (line 08) before cutting off to initiate a further sequence expansion with a query regarding the potential wait time for the ambulance (lines 08–09). This query serves as evidence that in the absence of either the type of assurance provided by the contingency component (as in Excerpts 4–6), or the production of an explicit indication by the call-taker that the ambulance is *en route* already (as in Excerpt 7), callers may treat as inadequate the type of service announcement that, in calls such as those shown in Excerpts 1–2, is treated as indicative of immediate dispatch. That is, if a granting includes a service announcement in the prospective *we're gonna...* form without also including a contingency component, callers may treat the contingency component as relevantly absent from the granting, thereby treating the precise nature of the granting as uncertain.

It is noteworthy, however, that the polarity of the caller's query projects a *no* answer (Raymond, 2003), and thus treats the granting the call-taker has provided as most likely, albeit not unequivocally, indicating the immediate or imminent dispatch of an ambulance. The call-taker aligns with this producing (as projected by the question) a turn-initial *No* before reporting, similarly to the call-taker in Excerpt 7, that the ambulance team is *on their way now* (line 10). The caller and call-taker thus collaboratively treat the contingency-free service announcement the call-taker initially produces as effectively equivalent (or at least near-equivalent) to the 'en route', form of the granting she subsequently provides. The caller then produces alignment and appreciation tokens, and the call quickly moves to closing. The expansion of the closing phase of the call in this case thus involves a non-routine trouble that apparently arises from systematic uncertainty as to whether a form of granting recurrently treated in well-resourced contexts as indicating immediate dispatch of a service can be treated as such in this resource-constrained context. This uncertainty is then resolved – and realignment of the caller and call-taker as help-seeker and help-provider is accomplished – by the call-taker's confirmation that this is indeed so.

### A deviant case

In the cases examined above, and consistently across our data set, the practices used in the granting in addition to the service announcement are systematically treated as arising from the contextual conditions in which the institution is operating. As such, even in cases where there is evidence of misalignment of the caller and call-taker as help-seeker and help-provider, the troubles are treated as arising from the potential uncertainty of the institution's capacity to adequately fulfill service requests that have been granted, rather than from the call-taker's judgments as to the legitimacy of the medical emergency for which service has been requested. In contrast, Excerpt 9a (in which the patient is reportedly experiencing paralysis and severe pain in her legs) includes an extended expansion of the closing phase of the call following a caller's display of dissatisfaction with a granting, which she explicitly links to the contingency component of the granting. Subsequently, the caller explicitly treats the contingent granting as arising from the call-taker's judgment of the (lack of) legitimacy of the emergency, despite the call-taker (as in the cases above) giving no indication of skepticism in this regard.

(9a) Deviant case [10293]
```
01   CT:   .hhhh >Okay ↑ma'am, I'm 'onna send an
02         ambulance out to you< as soon as
03         possible, ↑they?
04   C:    Okay, how soon is 'soon as possible'?
05   CT:   Um:: ↑ma'am I cannot tell you, but as soon
```

```
06                as an ambulance is available, they'll
07                definitely send one through.
08      C:        Is it in an ↑hour, two ↑hours?
09                (1.3)
10      CT:       I cannot tell you but we hope so ma'am:.
11                (.)
12      CT:       [I'll try and do my bes:t for you.
13      C:        [(What-)
14                Okay, 'cause she's l↑aying there >in a lot of
15                pain, she needs< to get to the hospital.
16      CT:       No problem.
17                (0.4)
18      C:        Alright, ↑thank [you.
19      CT:                       [Okay, >thank you so
20                mu[ch for calling.<
21                  [((C hangs up))
```

The granting in this case is much like those in the excerpts shown above, including a service announcement, indication of contingency, and a tag question (lines 01–03). As in the previous excerpts, the caller's response begins with the service receipt O<u>kay</u> (line 04), but the caller initiates an expansion of the granting sequence by requesting a more granular specification of the meaning of *soon* in the contingency component of the granting, thereby explicitly linking her question to this component. In doing so, the caller treats the contingency component as hedging rather than as reassuring, thus treating the granting as being of questionable adequacy and displaying misalignment as a help-seeker in response to the help the call-taker has promised will be provided. Also noteworthy is the low-contingency, high-entitlement form of the caller's question (*how soon is 'soon as possible'?*) which orients to a high degree of entitlement to the information she is requesting – compared, for example, to a form such as *Is it possible to tell me how soon it will be?* (see Curl & Drew, 2008; Drew & Walker, 2010). This further underscores her dissatisfaction with the contingent granting the call-taker has produced, and the attendant misalignment between herself and the call-taker.

In response to the caller's question, the call-taker states that she *cannot tell* the caller how soon it will be (line 05), with the emphasized word *cannot* possibly serving as an appeal to institutional authority or policy over which she personally has no control. She then produces a different form of the contingency component of the granting and indicates that *they'll definitely send* an ambulance (lines 06–07), again grounding her response in institutional constraints while displaying that the responsibility for sending the ambulance rests with an institutional *they* beyond her purview, and hence is a matter of resource (i.e. ambulance) availability rather than her judgment of the legitimacy of the emergency.

The caller then pursues her request in a more specific format that includes candidate estimates of wait times that the caller thereby treats as likely and/or reasonable – *an ↑hour, two ↑hours?* (line 08) – while maintaining her use of a high-entitlement, low-contingency form of the question. The 1.3-second silence (line 09) that follows suggests the call-taker's difficulty in responding to this request and foreshadows a further dispreferred response by the call-taker (Heritage, 1984; Pomerantz, 1984), which she then produces at line 10. In this response, the call-taker maintains her orientation to her (institution-based) inability to answer the question, as she again emphasizes the word *cannot*, before expressing *hope* that the service will be provided within the timeframe proposed by the caller. While the call-taker's use of the collective *we* here does mark a shift (following her prior use of *they*) to include her in the institution on behalf of which she is expressing this hope, it nonetheless continues to show that her personal evaluation of the legitimacy of the emergency is aligned with that of the caller, and thus that any delay in service is solely due to an institutional constraint.

Following a further brief silence (line 11) at a place prepared for the caller to align with the call-taker's assurances, and thus possibly again foreshadowing continued non-alignment by the caller, the call-taker pursues the caller's alignment by shifting from collective to personal pronouns (also see Lerner & Kitzinger, 2007) in producing the further assurance, *I'll try and do my bes:t for you* (line 12). The caller's formulation of this assurance in the first person – and emphasized by the extreme case formulation (Pomerantz, 1986) *my best* – proposes that a potential long wait should be understood as an unavoidable outcome of institutional capacity rather than as resulting from a lack of recognition of the legitimacy of the emergency on the part of the call-taker. Nonetheless, the caller responds by producing (following a second service receipt, *Okay*, in line 14) an account of the seriousness of the patient's condition as in support of a further claim of the urgency of the service request (lines 14–15). She thus appeals to the individual judgment of the call-taker with respect to the legitimacy and seriousness of the emergency as a basis for a less contingent service than the call-taker has thus far promised, thereby treating the contingent granting as a product of skepticism in this regard on the call-taker's part rather than institutional constraints beyond the call-taker's control.

After the call-taker aligns with this appeal by the caller (line 16), the caller produces a third service receipt followed by her first display of appreciation (line 18) – although the brief silence that precedes these tokens (line 17) may display an orientation to her alignment with the call-taker as reluctantly arrived-at. Further evidence of the caller's continued dissatisfaction is observable in her termination of the call prior to the call-taker's completion of a display of appreciation (lines 19–21). While this abrupt termination of the call results in it not being responded to, the call-taker's display of appreciation serves (as in Excerpt 6 above) to reverse default alignment of the caller and call-taker as beneficiary and benefactor. It thereby marks the call-taker's ongoing orientation to the misalignment between herself and the caller throughout this part of the call by thanking the caller for having accepted the diminished service the call-taker could provide.

While the evidence available in the call and dispatch package do not provide for a conclusive account for the basis of the caller's orientation in this case, earlier parts of the call (shown in Excerpt 9b below) do offer some evidence in this regard.

(9b) Deviant case opening [10293]

```
01    CT:    Emergency medical service, Zian ↑speaking?
02    C:     .hhhh W:=what do I do if I need to get an
03           ambulance to come out and fetch somebody,
04           they can't move, their legs are lame, and
05           and their back is also- they can't move at all.
06           (.)
07    CT:    tch ↑Okay, you've ↓got the right number,
08           ma'am. .hhh I'm speaking ↑to?
09           (.)
10    C:     Nicole.
11    CT:    .hh Nicole, tell me, do you have a contact
12           detail for me? <Cell phone number for me,
13           ↑please?
14    C:     .hh Um: (.) okay, the person that i- that it's
15           for, can I give you their details?
16    CT:    Okay, please.
17           ((1:47 omitted, CT gathers further details))
18    CT:    Ma'am tell me, the patient is it a male or
19           ↑female?
20    C:     Female.
21    CT:    How old is she?
22    C:     She::'s about forty nine I think.
```

Following the institutional and personal identifications produced by the call-taker in the call opening (line 01), the caller requests information about how to request an ambulance (lines 02–03) rather than (as is typical in other calls in the data set, and as reported in the literature discussed above) simply issuing an immediate request for an ambulance. In this way, the caller overtly displays a lack of knowledge (cf. Heritage, 2012) relating to the process of requesting an ambulance from a service-provision institution such as this one. The caller then refers to the patient using the 'generic' person reference form (Whitehead & Lerner, 2020) *somebody* (line 03), rather than using a more informative reference form – for example, a kinship term or another categorical reference form – that would provide an account for her calling on the patient's behalf (Kitzinger, 2005). Moreover, the caller subsequently maintains this distancing from the patient (cf. Jackson, 2013) by referring to her as *the person that i- that it's for* (lines 14–15) and by offering the patient's phone number rather than her own (line 15) in response to the call-taker's request for a contact number (lines 11–13). Moreover, the caller displays her limited familiarity with the patient by providing a hedged estimate of her age through the turn-final *I think* (line 22), rather than offering an exact number.

Although the available evidence is tacit and therefore inconclusive, this consistent distancing of herself from the patient by the caller may be evidence that she is oriented to asymmetries in their respective social statuses and/or categories, such that she is seeking to secure an emergency service for a patient who is reliant on an under-resourced (public) institution, in contrast to her own taken-for-granted access to well-resourced (private) services. Similarly, the caller's displayed unfamiliarity with the institution, the high-entitlement, low-contingency form of her requests for information, and the dissatisfaction she displays with the call-taker's contingent granting of the service, may be evidence for her orientation to occupying a position in South Africa's stratified social order associated with eligibility for more immediate emergency services than a public institution in this context could promise to provide. In short, the misalignment between the caller and call-taker in this case may indicate the caller's tacit orientation to a set of class and/or race-based privileges that other callers to this institution typically do not take for granted (cf. Dominguez-Whitehead & Whitehead, 2014; Whitehead, 2020).[7]

## Discussion and Conclusion

Our analysis has demonstrated call-takers' use of components of grantings – namely indications of contingency and tag questions – that are routinely present in our data but rarely reported in previous studies. In contrast to the potential for such additional components to be treated as indicative of the call-taker's assessment of the legitimacy of a request for service as questionable (as in Excerpts 3 and 9), their routine uses and uptake suggest that they are 'artful practices' (Garfinkel, 1967: 32) designed to manage the issues of trust associated with granting requests for service in a highly resource-constrained context. Our findings thus demonstrate the additional interactional burdens that participants (but most especially call-takers) may bear in managing systematic uncertainties with respect to the institution's capacity to immediately provide a service that has been granted – including their management of additional interactional troubles and associated call expansions that may arise from their deployment of these practices. In this way, it demonstrates one way in which matters understood to be 'public issues of social structure' nevertheless come to be experienced as 'personal troubles' (Mills, 1959: 8), through participants' efforts to manage the interactional contingencies these issues give rise to.

In revealing some of the pervasive interactional burdens associated with global and national-level inequalities, our findings serve to distinguish the type of 'critical CA' we have conducted in this research with what has been called 'applied CA' (Antaki, 2011) – or what we could call 'interventionist CA'. The latter type of work offers critical findings on the workings of talk-in-interaction that can serve as bases for interventions designed to alter the interactional conduct of participants as a means of bringing about more favorable outcomes. In contrast, a more favorable set of outcomes in relation to the issues of inequality revealed by our analysis is unlikely to result from changes in the interactional conduct of the participants, since the problems it addresses do not arise in the first instance from the interaction in the call, or from the call-taker's evaluation of the legitimacy or seriousness of the emergency at hand. Instead, call-takers can only seek to address the threats to trust associated with potentially systematically delayed services by inviting callers to anticipate and acknowledge or accept them. In this respect, they are by all appearances doing the best they can to address these difficult circumstances one caller at a time, thereby temporarily papering over problems that, to be adequately resolved, require broader structural changes to improve the resource capacity of the institution – interventions that would require forms of expertise that extend beyond what CA can offer. We have thereby shown how critical CA can identify structural problems that are visible *in* the interaction, but are not *of* the interaction – though they must nevertheless be managed there.

## Acknowledgements

We are indebted to the staff of the Health Communication Research Unit (School of Human and Community Development, University of the Witwatersrand), and especially its Director, Claire Penn, for their facilitation of the collection of the data used for this research, and for their support and encouragement. We would also like to thank Dexter Timm for his assistance in providing the data, and for offering valuable insights into the call center's processes. A report of this study was presented to the 5th International Conference on Conversation Analysis (ICCA-18) in Loughborough, United Kingdom, July 2018. We are grateful to Sandy Thompson for her assistance in developing the analysis, and to Hansun Zhang Waring, Nadja Tadic and three anonymous reviewers for their helpful suggestions on earlier drafts of the chapter.

## Notes

(1) In a case reported by Garcia and Parmer (1999: 301–302), after making a service announcement similar to those shown in Excerpts 1–2 (*we'll send someone there sir*), the call-taker instructs the caller to *stay on thuh phone with me, okay?* Since the tag question *okay* in that case is appended to an additional instruction not associated with provision of the service, but instead contributing to the project of keeping the caller on the line after the service request has been granted, it is designed to manage a different contingency than those on which we focus.

(2) It is important to note that we are not claiming that the use of these components is unique to the national context from which our data are drawn, nor that they are necessarily more common in this context (or others like it) than in those represented in the literature we have reviewed here. Distributional claims of this nature are beyond the scope of our analysis, which instead focuses on how these practices are used by the participants in our data. Future research could consider whether and/or how frequently they occur in particular contexts, and/or whether their deployment in other contexts is designed to manage the contingencies that they evidently manage in our data as opposed to being used in the ways evident in Excerpt 3, or in other ways altogether.

(3) A reviewer suggested that the authors include a 'positionality statement' in the Data and Method section. The analytic viability of a pre-positioned, generalized statement focused on our positioning in relation to this research is not clear to us, since it would not consequentially inform readers about the bases for analyses that we have developed by reference to the specifics of the cases and practices at hand. Such a statement would instead invite readers to substitute common-sense reasoning about these analyses based on the unavoidably selective set of considerations we might include in the statement for evaluations of the analyses on the basis of their empirical merits (cf. Schegloff, 1997, 2005; Whitehead, 2020). If our analyses are found wanting in some way, then readers should attend to those shortcomings, which only then might raise questions about their possible bases, including *whether* they may relate to some feature of our positionality – that is, beyond our membership in the only category of generalized relevance for the work we have done here, namely *conversation analyst*.

(4) The dispatch packages in our data set indicate that in some cases callers/patients make use of alternative, private, forms of transport after waiting for some time for an ambulance to arrive, resulting in the patient no longer being at the location to which the ambulance was dispatched when it arrives. The use of tag questions may thus also be a method for prompting callers to tacitly commit to waiting for the ambulance to arrive rather than seeking alternative transport after terminating the call.

(5) Silences such as this, at places prepared for alignment by the caller, may be evidence for incipient trouble in relation to the alignment of the caller and call-taker as help-seeker and help-provider (cf. e.g. Heritage, 1984; Pomerantz, 1984). However, there is no explicit indication of disalignment by the caller, either in this case or in numerous others in the data in which silences are present at similar places (see Excerpts 5 and 6), and even in calls where the granting does not include a contingency component (see Excerpt 7). Thus, even if such silences do indicate a degree of dissatisfaction on the part of callers, the callers in these cases recurrently opt not to 'go on record' as such.

(6) In this case, the address has been provided by a call-taker from a general emergency service line, 117, that the caller contacted to report the emergency prior to being connected to this call center. In such cases, the 117 call-taker provides the EMS call-taker with the relevant information that they have received from the caller, before providing the EMS call-taker with the opportunity to speak directly to the caller. In this case, the EMS call-taker has taken up this opportunity in order to gather further details of the patient's medical condition from the caller, before issuing the granting shown in the excerpt. The caller's request for confirmation that the EMS call-taker has the address thus displays uncertainty as to whether this information was shared (accurately) by the 117 call-taker.

(7) These features of the call may strike those familiar with South Africa – including ourselves – as characteristic of a middle-class white person calling on behalf of her Black domestic worker. However, the tacit nature of the evidence is such that a claim of this degree of specificity is necessarily speculative.

## References

Antaki, C. (2011) *Applied Conversation Analysis: Intervention and Change in Institutional Talk*. Palgrave Macmillan.

Bell, M.C. (2017) Police reform and the dismantling of legal estrangement. *The Yale Law Journal* 126 (7), 2054–2150.

Clayman, S. and Heritage, J. (2014) Benefactors and beneficiaries: Benefactive status and stance in the management of offers and requests. In P. Drew and E. Couper-Kuhlen (eds) *Requesting in Social Interaction* (pp. 55–86). Benjamins.

Coovadia, H., Jewkes, R., Barron, P., Sanders, D. and McIntyre, D. (2009) The health and health system of South Africa: Historical roots of current public health challenges. *The Lancet* 374 (9692), 817–834.

Curl, T.S. and Drew, P. (2008) Contingency and action: A comparison of two forms of requesting. *Research on Language and Social Interaction* 41 (2), 129–153.

Desmond, M., Papachristos, A.V. and Kirk, D.S. (2016) Police violence and citizen crime reporting in the black community. *American Sociological Review* 81 (5), 857–876.

Dominguez-Whitehead, Y. and Whitehead, K.A. (2014) Food talk: A window into inequality among university students. *Text & Talk* 34 (1), 49–68.

Drew, P. and Walker, T. (2010) Citizens' emergency calls: Requesting assistance in calls to the police. In M. Coulthard and A. Johnson (eds) *The Routledge Handbook of Forensic Linguistics* (pp. 95–110). Routledge.
Garcia, A.C. and Parmer, P.A. (1999) Misplaced mistrust: The collaborative construction of doubt in 911 emergency calls. *Symbolic Interaction* 22 (4), 297–324.
Garfinkel, H. (1963) A conception of, and experiments with, 'trust' as a condition of stable concerted actions. In O.J. Harvey (ed.) *Motivation and Social Interaction* (pp. 187–238). Ronald Press.
Garfinkel, H. (1967) *Studies in Ethnomethodology*. Prentice-Hall.
Hepburn, A. and Potter, J. (2010) Interrogating tears: Some uses of 'tag questions' in a child protection helpline. In A.F. Freed and S. Ehrlich (eds) *Why Do You Ask? The Function of Questions in Institutional Discourse* (pp. 69–86). Oxford University Press.
Heritage, J. (1984) *Garfinkel and Ethnomethodology*. Polity.
Heritage, J. (2002) The limits of questioning: Negative interrogatives and hostile question content. *Journal of Pragmatics* 34, 1427–1446.
Heritage, J. (2012) Epistemics in action: Action formation and territories of knowledge. *Research on Language & Social Interaction* 45 (1), 1–29.
Heritage, J. and Clayman, S. (2010) *Talk in Action: Interactions, Identities, and Institutions*. Wiley-Blackwell.
Horwitz, S. (2009) *Health and Health Care Under Apartheid*. Adler Museum of Medicine, University of the Witwatersrand.
Jackson, C. (2013) 'Why do these people's opinions matter?' Positioning known referents as unnameable others. *Discourse Studies* 15 (3), 299–317.
Kevoe-Feldman, H. (2019) Inside the emergency service call-center: Reviewing thirty years of language and social interaction research. *Research on Language and Social Interaction* 52 (3), 227–240.
Kitzinger, C. (2005) Heteronormativity in action: Reproducing the heterosexual nuclear family in after-hours medical calls. *Social Problems* 52 (4), 477–498.
Lerner, G.H. and Kitzinger, C. (2007) Extraction and aggregation in the repair of individual and collective self-reference. *Discourse Studies* 9 (4), 526–557.
Mills, C.W. (1959) *The Sociological Imagination*. Oxford University Press.
Moskos, P. (2008) *Cop in the Hood: My Year Policing Baltimore's Eastern District*. Princeton University Press.
Pomerantz, A. (1984) Agreeing and disagreeing with assessments: Some features of preferred/dispreferred turn shapes. In J.M. Atkinson and J. Heritage (eds) *Structures of Social Action: Studies in Conversation Analysis* (pp. 57–101). Cambridge University Press.
Pomerantz, A. (1986) Extreme case formulations: A way of legitimizing claims. *Human Studies* 9, 219–229.
Raymond, G. (2003) Grammar and social organization: Yes/no interrogatives and the structure of responding. *American Sociological Review* 68 (6), 939–967.
Raymond, G. and Zimmerman, D.H. (2007) Rights and responsibilities in calls for help: The case of the mountain glade fire. *Research on Language and Social Interaction* 40 (1), 33–61.
Raymond, G. and Zimmerman, D.H. (2016) Closing matters: Alignment and misalignment in sequence and call closings in institutional interaction. *Discourse Studies* 18 (6), 716–736.
Sacks, H., Schegloff, E.A. and Jefferson, G. (1974) A simplest systematics for the organization of turn taking in conversation. *Language* 50, 696–735.

Schegloff, E.A. (1996) Confirming allusions: Toward an empirical account of action. *American Journal of Sociology* 102 (1), 161–216.
Schegloff, E.A. (1997) Whose text? Whose context? *Discourse & Society* 8 (2), 165–187.
Schegloff, E.A. (2004) On dispensability. *Research on Language and Social Interaction* 37 (2), 95–149.
Schegloff, E.A. (2005) On integrity in inquiry…of the investigated, not the investigator. *Discourse Studies* 7 (4–5), 455–480.
Schegloff, E.A. (2013) Ten operations in self-initiated, same-turn repair. In M. Hayashi, G. Raymond and J. Sidnell (eds) *Conversational Repair and Human Understanding* (pp. 41–70). Cambridge University Press.
Schegloff, E.A., Jefferson, G. and Sacks, H. (1977) The preference for self-correction in the organization of repair in conversation. *Language* 53 (2), 361–382.
Schütz, A. (1953) Common-sense and scientific interpretation of human action. *Philosophy and Phenomenological Research* 14, 1–38.
Watson, R. (2009) Constitutive practices and Garfinkel's notion of trust: Revisited. *Journal of Classical Sociology* 9 (4), 475–499.
Whalen, J., Zimmerman, D.H. and Whalen, M.R. (1988) When words fail: A single case analysis. *Social Problems* 35 (4), 335–362.
Whalen, M.R. and Zimmerman, D.H. (1990) Describing trouble: Practical epistemology in citizen calls to the police. *Language in Society* 19 (4), 465–492.
Whitehead, K.A. (2020) The problem of context in the analysis of talk-in-interaction: The case of implicit whiteness in post-apartheid South Africa. *Social Psychology Quarterly* 83 (3), 294–313.
Whitehead, K.A. and Lerner, G.H. (2020) Referring to *somebody*: Generic person reference as an interactional resource. *Journal of Pragmatics* 161, 46–56.
Zimmerman, D.H. (1984) Talk and its occasion: The case of calling the police. In D. Schiffrin (ed.) *Meaning, form and Use in Context: Linguistic Applications* (pp. 210–228). Georgetown University Roundtable on Language and Linguistics.
Zimmerman, D.H. (1992) The interactional organization of calls for emergency assistance. In P. Drew and J. Heritage (eds) *Talk at Work: Interaction in Institutional Settings* (pp. 418–469). Cambridge University Press.

# 6 Delegitimizing the 'Other' at US Congressional Town Hall Meetings

Di Yu

## Introduction

Participatory democracy has long been viewed by political scientists as 'real democracy' (Bryan, 2003) wherein ordinary people exercise their rights of citizenship by directly participating in, deliberating and voting on policy matters. Citizens' participation and voting decisions, however, can become heavily influenced by partisan rhetoric and varying sources of information (Schudson, 1998), particularly during times of volatile political change. In the current sociohistorical context of the US, we observe extreme partisan and ideological divides among political parties and ordinary citizens alike, threatening the health and stability of the democratic structure itself (Levitsky & Ziblatt, 2018). The issues of negative partisanship and who belongs in the political decision-making process are among the four major threats that keep the American democracy under siege today (Mettler & Lieberman, 2020).

A prevailing manifestation of today's toxic polarization (Coleman, 2021) among ordinary citizens is the 'us versus them' dynamic where those who are perceived as different in various ways are treated as dangerous and illegitimate. There are a number of strategies by which the 'us versus them' realities are created, including constructing the 'us' as victims by different measures and various groups of 'them' as lawless, dangerous or deviant (Stanley, 2020). Crucially, these strategies are considered essential mechanisms for fascist politics to divide the population and gain power (Stanley, 2020). The aim of this chapter is to document how ordinary citizens construe those with different backgrounds or views as illegitimate during their participation at town hall meetings.

In the critical discourse analysis approach, one central theme concerns how various 'us versus them' realities are produced discursively to achieve inclusion/exclusion (Wodak, 2008). It has been well documented that governmental representatives or media personnel would use the 'good us versus bad them' discourse as ways to justify questionable legislative or military actions (Mehan, 1997; Oktar, 2001; van Dijk, 2006), exerting dominance and persuasive power over ordinary citizens. Mehan (1997) describes the production of immigrants as enemies in public debates around a piece of new legislation in California. Oktar (2001) outlines how two Turkish newspapers with opposing ideologies use the 'positive self and negative other' to construct the divide between secularists and antisecularists. Van Dijk (2006: 380) illustrates several key components of discursive manipulation such as asserting one's own 'moral superiority and credibility' while 'discrediting' that of one's dissidents and 'vilifying' the opposition.

Apart from the practices of institutional representatives, scholars have also examined ordinary people's encounters of specific forms of 'us versus them' talk-in-action, such as heteronormativity and racism, from the perspectives of critically informed conversation analysis (CCA), membership categorization analysis (MCA) and ethnomethodology (Kitzinger, 2005; Rawls & Duck, 2020; Whitehead, 2013). Heteronormativity can be (re)produced in talk by casual use of reference terms typical to the heterosexual nuclear family structure, thus implicitly excluding those in LGBTQA+ communities (Kitzinger, 2005). In racialized complaint sequences, the racial category memberships of participants are made relevant and serve to (re)produce racialized ideologies in ordinary interaction (Whitehead, 2013). Particularly, as Rawls and Duck (2020) argue, interactions based on different and conflicting interactional orders (e.g. 'white people are nosey' and 'black people are rude') between racialized social groups are constitutive of unequal social realities and continue to sustain and reproduce such realities.

This study focuses on congressional town hall meetings as an institutional setting and ordinary citizens as a party to this interactional setting, given that both have received considerably less attention in past research. Around issues on political affiliation, immigration, and gender equality, it is observed that citizens delegitimize the 'other', namely those from different backgrounds or with opposing views, by treating them as threats to their own rights, freedoms or interests.

## Data and Method

The data corpus comprises publicly available video recordings of 50 congressional town hall events from 24 states in the US occurring in

2019 and 2020. Participants include members of the US Congress (both the House of Representatives and the Senate) and their constituents in attendance. Typically, each meeting includes an opening segment in which the Member of Congress (MOC) gives a report of their recent work, and then individual citizens (CIT) address questions to the MOC one by one. On average, the question-and-answer segment is around 45 minutes featuring 10–15 individual citizen contributions. An individual citizen contribution on average is around 1–2 minutes, comprising a preface segment and an 'ask' segment – usually a question, complaint, request, etc. The data excerpts for this chapter are gathered from two sub-collections for two of the author's dissertation chapters, one on partisanship (39 cases) and the other on exclusion (23 cases). The chapter draws on critical CA which enables the analysis of how 'we "do" power and powerlessness, oppression, and resistance' (Kitzinger, 2000: 174), as well as MCA for analyzing how membership categories and attributes are used in producing local social orders (Houseley & Fitzgerald, 2009). Finally, it is helpful to clarify that the data analysis process does rely on inferences made based on the author's lay knowledge of current US politics, and the selection of excerpts is influenced by the author's political leaning. While this is the case, the analysis remains solely rooted in what the participants produce in the interaction, and there is absolutely no political, moral or epistemic judgment made on the participants in the analysis.

## Analysis

In the following analysis, I showcase five excerpts of citizens, often joined by the MOC or other attendees, delegitimizing 'others' who come from different backgrounds or hold opposing views by portraying them as threatening, dangerous, uninformed and biased, or potentially harmful: be it migrants, Democratic Socialists, or those supporting or benefiting from gender equality. In some cases, citizens use such portrayals as the basis for advocating for legislative actions against the 'other'.

The first instance features CIT12, a Texas resident, who expresses concerns over migrants who cross over the southern border as the basis for her initial questioning of the MOC's limited work on immigration – an apparent misunderstanding that is immediately corrected by the MOC (line 20). In the excerpt here, we focus on how the citizen formulates the 'other' – migrants coming over the border – as threats to the safety and property ownership of local residents.

(1) Squatter
```
01    STF:       holding mic-°I will hold-°
02    CIT12:     okay. I'm (syl syl syl) from Holland, Texas,
03    MOC:       hah.
04    CIT12:     yes. I live in the country. a:nd .HH
05               there's a lot of people that live in the
06               country in Texas, as you well know.
07    MOC:       yes ma'am.=
08    CIT12:  →  =and we are afraid of the people coming over
09               here in the- from the border. ↓now I have a
10               property that's right next door to ours.
11               and it's been vacant for 15 to 20 years. and
12            →  we're- I'm afraid that some (.) migrant is
13               going to come in there and squat. and you
14            →  can't get squatters out. and cause all kinds
15               of ruckus in our (.) little part of the (.) world.
16               and I want to know, you said at the
17               beginning, that you would not try to do
18               anything on immigration because of Pelosi
19               was being all- [(        )]
20    MOC:                      [no ma'am.] I said Nancy Pelosi
21               won't take anything on immigration on the
22               floor of the House, because she wants it to be
23               a political issue in the presidential race. Not
24               wa- I won't; I work on immigration everyday.
25               ((4 lines omitted as CIT checks on mic volume))
26    CIT12:     okay, um- my question is, I was thought-
27               I thought that you- you should be a lit-
28               you should have been working on immigration
29               so the voters will know that you are really
30               doing something and you're- you're- you're
31               blocked every which way.
32    MOC:       yes [ma'am.
```

The citizen's work of delegitimizing the 'other' by portraying them as unlawful and dangerous is notable in several aspects. First, she uses place references (*from Holland Texas, in the country* in lines 02 and 04) and person references (*we*, line 08, and *a lot of people that live in the country*, lines 05–07) to create a specific in-group of 'us' – importantly, the MOC acknowledges both sets of references right away (lines 03 and 07), treating both as recognitionals and displaying his familiarity with the group of residents in the area. In contrast to 'us', the migrants as the 'other' are first formulated as *the people coming over here from the border* (lines 08–09), problematizing the category of migrants as those entering the country from the southern border with Mexico. In addition, the fear of migrants is formulated first as a commonly shared fear by the in-group – *we are afraid of the people coming over here from the border* (lines 08–09) and then as a fear specific to her as a property owner: *I'm afraid that some migrant is going to come in here and squat* (lines 09–14). The migrant category is now identified as *some migrant* with the singular 'some' conveying negative affect (Esposito & Potts, 2020). The group is also said to *come in there and squat* and *cause all kinds of ruckus* (lines 13–14), further portrayed as unlawful intruders and occupants causing disturbance to property owners in the area. The citizen then shifts back to her in-group person formulation by specifying that migrants cause disturbance in an idyllic land that belongs to the locals only – *in our little part of the world* (line 15).

Furthermore, the citizen's prefacing formulation of migrants as dangerous and unlawful is situated within her larger course of action to request that the MOC *work on immigration*, as demonstrated first in lines 16–19 and then 26–31. Despite the citizen's initial understanding that the MOC *would not try to do anything on immigration* (lines 17–18), which the MOC interrupts and corrects, the citizen's request is made in the clear in her second attempt (lines 28–31): the MOC should work on immigration in order to inform the voters and get reelected. While the wording of 'work on' remains neutral, with the backdrop of portraying migrants as unlawful intruders, the citizen effectively makes a request for political actions against the migrants, treating them as the immigration problem to be solved.

In short, the citizen in this case delegitimizes the migrant category through moral grounds – portraying them as dangerous and unlawful intruders disturbing what rightfully belongs to only the local residents. With such a portrayal, the citizen also makes the case for policy actions targeting the migrant population as part of the immigration problem that she identified. From this extract, it is also necessary to observe that delegitimizing a group of individuals from different backgrounds (i.e. construing them as dangerous or unlawful) is by no means small business – it serves as the steppingstone for suggesting political action and attempting political harm, particularly at a platform of civic participation.

The excerpt below also centers on the immigration issue. Thus far in this event, a number of citizens already voiced their concerns over immigration issues on the country's southern border and their view that House Democrats are the ones to blame for increased illegal immigration close to their homes. CIT17 follows up to support these claims (also see Green, 2016, for town hall participants' 'tag-team' questions in which citizens follow up on previous questions).

(2) One world order

```
01      MOC:            points-yes, ma'am. Let's- this lady right here.
02      CIT17:          [holding up hand ]
03      STAFF:          [walking to CIT17]
04      CIT17:          holding mic-I'm not gonna stand.=I'm Linda
05                      (syl) from (syl syl), .h one of the problems
06          →           is, there's a lot of people want- one world
07                      order. and they- have- and Trump upset that,
08          →           and that's why Pelosi ain't gonna do anything
09                      and a:ll other her cronies up there,
10                      alternating gaze between CITS & MOC-
11          →           they want one world o:rder, they
12                      want at least one thi:rd of the population
13                      o' the world go:ne. if not half. they don't
14          →           want no borders. if (.) Clinton had gotten in,
15                      we would not have a border (.) points down-
16                      this day,=we would not points down-
17                      recogni:ze our nation. [and it's not-  ]
18      MOC:    →                              [an' I'm against] the
19                      one world order, [I promise you.]
20      CIT17:                           [that's right.  ] you better
21                      believe it, if by- that's what it all boils down
22                      to be. turns to mic-they want one world order.
23                      20(.)30. Look it up. they'll tell- it- that's their
24                      target date there. It was 20(.h)21. that's why
25                      they are mad at (.) Trump and everybody else,
26                      because they points up-upset that becau-
27                      because they were hoping to have it all done.
28      MOC:    →       well they won't get it done, thank you ma'am,
29                      [we'll fi]ght them. [okay.
30      CIT17:          [no.    ]           [no.
31      MOC:            (we'll       ) to make sure that-=
32                      =one more question-
```

In this excerpt, the citizen formulates the 'other', namely the Democrats, as a threat, not just to a local community, but to the country and the world. The Democrats' alleged political inaction is said to be due to retaliating against President Trump (lines 07–08) and endorsing the *one world order* (lines 11–14) (a documented right-wing conspiracy theory on a socialist movement of suppressing dissent, reducing the population and enslaving the world; see Anti-Defamation League, 2017). In addition to accusing the opposing party of having genocidal tendencies and being against the country's national security, the citizen also describes the dire consequences that would have occurred if Hilary Clinton had won the presidential race as a Democratic candidate (lines 14–17), once again creating a causal relationship between the country's democratic leadership and the loss of national security (*we would not have a border this day,* lines 15–16) and even the loss of national identity (*we would not recognize our nation,* lines 16–17). Thus far, the citizen delegitimizes the opposing party by formulating it as detrimental to the country and its people with factually unfounded claims.

Also worthy of note is the MOC's responses affirming the citizen's report on the One World Order and officially supporting her opposition towards the Democrats. In lines 18–19, the MOC not only swiftly, explicitly affirms his stance against the One World Order (*I'm against the one world order, I promise you*), but more importantly, he confirms his knowledgeable status and even the validity of the One World Order by using the definite article *the*. As the citizen continues to elaborate, the MOC also endorses her opposition by committing that *we'll fight them* (line 29), further supporting the citizen's effort in formulating the opposing party as dangerous and threatening. Instead of acknowledging that differing political views might lead to divergent actions, the MOC explicitly joins the citizen in associating the opposing party with an unfounded conspiracy theory and commits to fight against them because of it.

Thus, we observe here a joint portrayal of those who hold politically different views as threats, again degrading them to a morally inferior position. The lack of tolerance for political opponents to the extent of delegitimizing them, as Levitsky and Ziblatt (2018) warned us, indicates politicians' authoritarian tendencies. It is equally, if not more, concerning when these tendencies are observed among ordinary citizens.

The 'threat' featured in the third extract takes on a more organized flavor, where a citizen from Virginia (CIT5) inquires about the MOC's view of the ongoing *socialist movement* on university campuses and then of the *new blood* in the US Congress.

(3) Socialist movement

```
01    MOC:          uh yes sir.-points
02    CIT5:         (syl syl syl)? um clears throat
03         →        there's a lot of chatter going on about- u:m
04                  on campuses throughout the country about a
05                  socialist ↓movement, a:nd was wondering is
06                  that m- ey: real threat to America or is that
07                  more of a red herring just to disturb (.) thee
08                  conflicts of uh people's opinions.
09    MOC:    →     I- I wish that the threat of socialism was u:h
10                  (0.2) in theory rather than a reality? but when
```

122  Part 1: Reproducing Inequality and Injustice

```
11              ((75 lines omitted; MOC elaborates on
12              socialist threat on university campuses))
13              and uh so (.) we need tuh (.) do our best to
14              try and break through that u:h bubble that
15              exists on the campuses.
16    CIT5:  →  (follow up on it-) what about the new blood
17              that's coming in now.=like (.) AOC n' (0.2)
18              people like her who are of that ilk, uh along-
19              as well as y'know some of thee uh the
20              Muslim interests that are- (.) being there in
21              congress as well.
22    MOC:   →  well? u:m (1.0) I- I think that u:h (.) my
23              colleagues (.) have been elected by their
24              constituents and have every right to:
25           →  share their opinions (.) on (.) policy,
26           →  no matter $how misguided they are.$
27           →  and (.) a lot of those views that I'm
28              hearing are pretty misguided. u:m a:nd
29              some of them are just from a- a lack
30              of information. ((continues))
```

In his line of inquiry, the citizen formulates the 'other' – those affiliated with democratic socialist views and/or with Islam – as *a real threat to America* (line 06). First, the citizen formulates the political view of the group in question as *a socialist movement* (line 05), indicating that this political ideology, according to the citizen, has gained such popularity as to become a movement *on campuses throughout the country* (lines 04–05), highlighting its extremely wide impact and the potential danger of exposing a generation of young people across the nation to an opposing political ideology. Importantly, while the *real threat to America* depiction is first presented as a candidate formulation by the citizen (line 06) with an alternative *more of a red herring* (line 07), the MOC not only decidedly confirms *the threat* formulation but also legitimizes it by upgrading it as *the threat of socialism* (line 09), further validating the citizen's concern.

Second, in his follow-up question regarding *the new blood that is coming in now* (lines 16–17), certain newcomers to the political stage are specified as *AOC and people like her who are of that ilk* (lines 17–18) and *the Muslim interests ... in congress as well* (line 20). Notably, the Congressperson Alexandria Ocasio-Cortez's initials 'AOC' are used as a shorthand here to encode the category of the then-newly elected public officials who share democratic socialist views, while *the Muslim interests* categorizes the then-freshmen congresspersons solely based on their religious affiliation, suggesting that they only represent either the political agenda of those following democratic socialism or the interests of those affiliated with Islam.

Note that, instead of diffusing the citizen's concerns, the MOC's initial responses to both queries serve to confirm if not upgrade the concerns. In his response regarding the socialist movement, the MOC confirms the citizen's worry of the threat of socialism as true (lines 09–10). In his response to the citizen's concerns about the new congresspersons, despite reasserting their rights as publicly elected officials (lines 23–25), the MOC reaffirms the citizen's concerns by characterizing the new congresspersons' views as misguided or uninformed (lines 28–30). In this excerpt, we observe that the citizen and MOC jointly create the sense of threat of the 'other' by depicting a widely popular political movement impacting young people across the country as a real threat and then formulating new congresspersons representing different interests in the US Congress as misguided and uninformed. While in prior excerpts the participants delegitimize the 'other' through minimizing their moral standing, participants delegitimize the 'political other' here by downgrading them as epistemically 'lesser than' – less informed and misguided.

The excerpt below revolves around a different type of threat – the threat to one's religious freedom. Prior to the excerpt, the MOC evades responding to a potential tension brought up by a citizen of Utah (CIT20) between the Equal Rights Amendment (ERA), which guarantees people gender equality, and the First Amendment, which protects people's freedom of religion (data not shown). The citizen then expresses his concern about the *gender movement* and the potential passing of ERA.

(4) Determining my religion is a hate group
```
01      MOC:         ((continues)) okay, we're equal, but we're
02                   different. and- and to- and figuring out how
03                   we define that is- is what (.) is ahead of us.
04      CIT20:   →   so here's my- my concern. it's apparent that
05                   the gender movement and I'm dis- I'm
06                   distinguishing (.) people from a movement.
07               →   'kay? um the movement is- is latching on to
08               →   the ERA and pushing it hard. article after
09                   article I've read (.) indicates that there('s
10                   a) real push in this. so at some point,
11               →   if it passes, I can see a ninth circuit
12                   judge uh determining that my religion is a
13                   hate group. a:nd not allowing me to practice
14                   my religion. that's deeply concerning to me.
```

124   Part 1: Reproducing Inequality and Injustice

```
15            →    .h and so: I uh (0.5) hence my concern about
16                 your votes, u:h I see where you're coming
17                 from, but I'm conce:rned that (.) we're
18                 buying into really old language that was first
19                 proposed in the 20s, and then reintroduced
20                 in the 70s. a:nd it's a trap. and we just got to
21                 be awake. [°that's my concern-°
22     MOC:                  [so I join you in your concern, I
23                 do. I've spoken about religious uh liberty
24                 and religious freedom, .h as it relates to uh
25                 rights of the LGBT community, ((continues))
```

In this instance, we observe that the citizen delegitimizes the 'other' through several steps. First, the citizen identifies *gender movement* (line 07) as a distinct categorial label, presumably referencing those holding progressive views on gender issues. He builds his case against the *gender movement* by claiming to *distinguish people from a movement* (line 06), referencing it as *latching on* and releasing *article after article* (line lines 07–09), and concluding that there is *a real push in this* (line 10). This string of specific word choices serves to portray the 'other' as organized, persistent and single-minded political actors with a clear agenda, and paves the way for the next steps of constructing 'threat'. The citizen then immediately moves to formulate ERA's potential passing as a threat to his religious freedom (lines 10–14). The impact of this threat is formulated as extreme – he foresees his religion being legally, formally determined as *a hate group* and disallowed by a federal judge (lines 11–13) due to the passing of the ERA. Finally, repeating several times his concern (*deeply concerning, hence my concern* and *I'm concerned* in lines 14–17), he denounces the progress of the ERA from the 1920's and the 1970's as *really old language* that *we are buying into* (lines 17–19), suggesting that ordinary citizens like himself are being deceived into believing a backward political agenda. He then warns others of the *trap* of the ERA and urges the audience to stay alert (lines 20), driving home the portrayal of the ERA's impending danger for people like him. It is worth noting that the citizen summarizes the issues expressed so far to account for his concerns over the MOC's political action (*hence my concern about your votes*, lines 15–16).

In short, in this case the citizen first constructs those who may support or benefit from the ERA and gender equality as the 'other' – menacing political agents with clear agendas and established methods; he then constructs the threat of the 'other' as directly putting his own constitutional right in grave danger. Both serve to delegitimate those who may support or benefit from gender equality and legitimate his concerns as morally grounded. Again, we see here that downgrading others' moral grounds or upgrading one's own plays a key role in the organization of delegitimizing as a social practice.

The last excerpt is taken from a longer exchange between a citizen who is a self-proclaimed educator from California (CIT7) and their MOC. CIT7's main concern centers on a state-level legislation entitled California Healthy Youth Act and its component on providing comprehensive education on gender, sexuality, sexual health, etc. to young students. Prior to the excerpt, the citizen has already produced a lengthy multi-unit contribution on the harm of teaching gender fluidity to children. We join the discussion as another citizen reminds CIT7 to ask a question.

(5) It takes away freedom of deeply held beliefs

```
01    CIT7:      ((continues)) there's a whole thing called the
02               genderbread [person. ]
03    CIT?:                  [you have] a question [(or)-
04    CIT7:                                        [I-
05               yes. I'm getting [back to    ] my question.=
06    CIT?:                       [thank you.]
07    CIT7:      =thank you. so, it was- I'm just saying it was
08         →     voted on. I looked at the voting record. 100%
09               by the democrats in California. zero
10               Republicans. okay, so. there are obviously I
11               think- I do believe there is a s- an agenda
12               being pushed here. now I called your uh
13               offices and asked that you please vote no on
14               H.R.5. that's the national (.) basically push
15         →     for this entire thing. .hh um a:nd I just said,
16               it does not provide quality for all and the
17               greater citizens, uh it takes away freedom
18               of deeply held beliefs and religious beliefs
19               and traditional family. so I got an- an email
20               from ↓you, tsk- stating that uh >religious
21               liberty is a sacred right in this country, and
22               every American should be able to practice
23               their ↓faith< .h without interference.
24               (0.5)
25    CIT7:      where is that in section six. when men are
26               able to compete in women's sports.= where
27               is that in section nine when men have access
28               to >bathrooms, locker rooms, dressing
```

126  Part 1: Reproducing Inequality and Injustice

```
29                      rooms.< .h where is that in section five,
30                      when we're to teach a̱ll K through 12, and
31                      universities gender fluidity. so my question
32                      is, when you wrote to me, you said m̱ore
33              →       unites us than divides us. this is v̱ery,
34                      v̱ery ḏifficult situation >and very divisive.<
35                      =but we're talking about the cẖildren of our
36                      communities, the parents who very trustingly
37                      drop their children and grandchildren off
38                      at school. and ṉow this is a̱ll in question.
39      MOC:            thank you.
40      CITS:           applause, cheering
```

In this excerpt, the citizen mainly delegitimizes the notion of gender fluidity through several distinct ways. First, the ideological divide based on one's belief in gender fluidity is transformed into a politically motivated partisan issue (lines 08–11). Similar to the 'real push' argument in the prior extract, the citizen here also treats the allegedly drastic difference in voting records between Democrats and Republicans as politically motivated – *I do believe there is an agenda being pushed here* (lines 10–11). Instead of interpreting the voting records as part of the normal political process, the citizen now firmly believes that the legislation comes with a Democrat-backed exterior political motive rather than actually serving ordinary people in the state, thus treating those of different political leanings as illegitimate and potentially harmful to oneself. This is also one of the moments in the data that highlights the intersectional nature of political communication where partisanship and other types of beliefs are often intertwined.

In addition, as the citizen resumes the report on the harm of gender fluidity, she continues to construct it as a threat to one's beliefs and freedoms (lines 17–19). The 'threat' of gender fluidity, according to the citizen, has now escalated to the national level as evidenced in her objection to the *national…push for this entire thing* (lines 14–15). Not only does it not provide inclusive *quality* education as evidenced in *for all and the greater citizens* (lines 16–17), but it also strips ordinary people of their religious freedom and beliefs in *traditional family* (lines 18–19). To formulate the threat of gender fluidity, the citizen here creates an extreme contrast between the freedom of gender expression and identity and the freedom of religious beliefs and traditional family structure, suggesting that her faith-based values are inherently against freedom of gender expression and identity. With a series of rhetorical questions, she elaborates on the evidence of the legislation not allowing for *religious liberty* (lines 25–31), further strengthening the case of victimhood and formulating the danger of gender fluidity as specifically transgender persons entering heteronormative spaces – i.e. participating in sports and using public facilities. The construal of the 'other' as a threat is also evidenced in the citizen's persistent mis-gendering of transgender women as men who would now have undeserving access to women's sports and spaces (lines 25–29), excluding their presence as inappropriate or unacceptable rather than treating them as ordinary members of one's communities.

Finally, the citizen further produces the sense of threat through the perspectives of vulnerable children and trusting family members (lines 30–34). Endorsing gender fluidity is not only said to break the unity among citizens – *this is very difficult situation and very divisive* (lines 33–34) – but putting those most important and vulnerable members in the society (children of our communities) at risk (lines 35–36). While the MOC does not move to endorse the citizen's view (data not shown), we do observe that many attendees cheer and applaud her contribution (line 40), suggesting their agreement and endorsement. In sum, the citizen delegitimizes (those benefiting from or supporting) gender fluidity via one's moral grounding – constructing it as politically suspect and dangerous to one's religious freedom and family values as well as to ordinary community members.

## Discussion and Conclusion

In this chapter, we observed instances of citizens delegitimizing the 'other' who come from different backgrounds or hold opposing views by portraying them as threats. As I have demonstrated, citizens are often joined by the MOC or other attendees to collaboratively delegitimize the 'other'. Citizens use categorial shorthands (e.g. gender movement, AOC, Muslim interest, Pelosi) to encode the 'other' as threatening, dangerous, uninformed, biased or potentially harmful, and such portrayals of the 'other' can also be used as bases for requesting political action against them.

Scholars who study participatory democracy and public deliberation identify both the essential role of public participation in policy discussions as well as challenges such as level of inclusivity and the premise of consensus seeking (Blacksher *et al.*, 2012; Levine *et al.*, 2005), which are exemplified in the instances we observed above. On the one hand, inclusivity of diverse perspectives in deliberation and policy making can facilitate the achievement of more equitable outcomes; therefore, the inclusion of diverse opinions seems to be a required component of public deliberation forums such as congressional town halls. On the other hand, as we have witnessed above, practices exemplifying deeply rooted differences among citizens abound, and those who have access to the town hall floor have the potential opportunity to assert power over the 'other' and even enact political actions against them. This brings into question the feasibility of Rawls' reasonable pluralism ideal with 'a diversity of opposing irreconcilable religious, philosophical, and moral doctrines' (Rawls, 2005: 2), particularly during such volatile, divided and challenging times.

To move citizens out of the extreme divisiveness, those hosting such events can consider instituting deliberative structures to facilitate citizens' participation toward productive, inclusive outcomes and creating opportunities for further civic education for citizens (Knobloch & Gastil, 2015). For citizens, more important are the tasks of healing from the wounds of toxic polarization and rising above extreme political and ideological divides. While the existence of political and ideological differences would likely continue, they do not necessarily need to become absolute obstacles for achieving the goals of democratic deliberation and civic renewal (Levine, 2015). To end on a positive note, elucidating practices of divisiveness creates the hope for remediating the divide and creating unity. In this spirit, perhaps this analytic exercise can also be considered 'a (small) step toward interrupting this social reproductive potentiality' (Talmy, 2009: 205).

## References

Blacksher, E., Diebel, A., Forest, P.G., Goold, S.D. and Abelson, J. (2012) What is public deliberation. *Hastings Center Report* 42 (2), 14–17.
Bryan, F.M. (2003) *Real Democracy: The New England Town Meeting and How it Works*. University of Chicago Press.
Coleman, P.T. (2021) *The Way Out: How to Overcome Toxic Polarization*. Columbia University Press.
Esposito, L. and Potts, C. (2020) A probabilistic pragmatics for English singular *some*. *Proceedings of Semantics and Linguistic Theory (SALT)* 30, 22–42.
Green, R.J. (2016) The politics of town hall meetings: Analyzing constituent relations-in-interaction. Unpublished doctoral dissertation, Purdue University.
Kitzinger, C. (2000) Doing feminist conversation analysis. *Feminism & Psychology* 10 (2), 163–193.
Kitzinger, C. (2005) Heteronormativity in action: Reproducing the heterosexual nuclear family in after-hours medical calls. *Social problems* 52 (4), 477–498.
Knobloch, K.R. and Gastil, J. (2015) Civic (re)socialization: The educative effects of deliberative participation. *Politics* 35 (2), 183–200.
Levine, P. (2015) *We are The Ones We Have Been Waiting for: The Promise of Civic Renewal in America*. Oxford University Press.

Levine, P., Fung, A. and Gastil, J.W. (2005) Future directions for public deliberation. *Journal of Public Deliberation* 1 (1), 1–11.
Levitsky, S. and Ziblatt, D. (2018) *How Democracies Die*. Penguin Random House LLC.
Mettler, S. and Lieberman, R.C. (2020) *Four Threats: The Recurring Crises of American Democracy*. St. Martin's Press.
Oktar, L. (2001) The ideological organization of representational processes in the presentation of us and them. *Discourse & Society* 12 (3), 313–346.
Rawls, J. (2005) *Political Liberalism*. Columbia University Press.
Rawls, A.W. and Duck, W. (2020) *Tacit Racism*. University of Chicago Press.
Schudson, M. (1998) *The Good Citizen: A History of American Civic Life*. Free Press.
Stanley, J. (2020) *How Fascism Works: The Politics of Us and Them*. Random House Trade Paperbacks.
Talmy, S. (2009) Resisting ESL: Categories and sequence in a critically 'motivated' analysis of classroom interaction. In H.T. Nguyen and G. Kasper (eds) *Talk-in-Interaction: Multilingual Perspectives* (pp. 181–213). National Foreign Language Resource Center.
van Dijk, T.A. (2006) Discourse and manipulation. *Discourse & Society* 17 (3), 359–383.
Whitehead, K.A. (2013) Managing self/other relations in complaint sequences: The use of self-deprecating and affiliative racial categorizations. *Research on Language & Social Interaction* 46 (2), 186–203.
Wodak, R. (2008) 'Us' and 'them': Inclusion and exclusion–Discrimination via discourse. In G. Delanty, R. Wodak and P. Jones (eds) *Identity, Belonging and Migration* (pp. 54–77). Cambridge University Press.

# Part 2
# Resisting Inequality and Injustice

# 7 Negotiating Power Inequalities in Joint Decision-Making in a Faculty Meeting

Innhwa Park and Santoi Wagner

## Introduction

Meetings are essential to various types of organizations including informal gatherings and formal institutions (Brown et al., 2017). In particular, faculty meetings, the context of this study, constitute a large amount of work time for many teachers and are a significant channel of organizational communication. Effective faculty meetings play a central role in improving professional competence, fostering communication and building community (Jennings, 2007). During meetings, participants regularly make decisions about a future course of action, and there is a shared ideal that they should reach decisions through a consensus-oriented, collaborative process (Wasson, 2016). A key aspect of this collaborative process is the inclusion of all participants, giving them the potential to influence decisions. At the same time, decisions in the workplace involve a negotiation of social relationships anchored to institutional roles and professional hierarchies (Clifton, 2009). In the context of faculty meetings, a hierarchical leadership structure present in education underlies the decision-making process (Stosich, 2021). In the US public school leadership structure, the school board and the superintendent occupy the higher rank, and classroom teachers occupy the lower rank, with various administrators such as directors, principals and department heads in the middle. Accordingly, different institutional roles are ascribed with varying levels of institutional power to influence decisions at a programmatic or a district level. Of particular relevance to the current study are the institutional roles of assistant superintendent, department head and classroom teacher.

The assistant superintendent possesses a broad range of rights and responsibilities to oversee curricular and instructional needs in the entire school district. A department head's rights and responsibilities also concern the entire school district, but they are limited to a particular educational program. On the other hand, a classroom teacher is given a narrow set of rights and responsibilities concerning a specific group of students within a single school building. While ascribed with minimal institutional power, as a person who directly interacts with students and their families, a teacher has intimate knowledge of their specific needs. Thus, decision-making at faculty meetings can involve an ongoing power struggle (Stevanovic & Peräkylä, 2012; Stevanovic & Svennevig, 2015; Weiste et al., 2020) among participants with varying levels of institutional authority and domain-specific knowledge. In this chapter, we examine how unequal power relations are enacted and negotiated on a turn-by-turn basis in the decision-making process through the lens of deontic authority (Stevanovic, 2018; Stevanovic & Peräkylä, 2012). We focus on the ways in which the proposer of a future action with less institutional power negotiates this power inequality by balancing compliance and resistance of the deontic authority displayed by higher ranking participants with more institutional power as a means to move her proposal forward to reach a decision.

The chapter draws upon conversation analytic work on decision-making in workplace meetings (Asmuß & Oshima, 2012; Boden, 1994, 1995; Clifton, 2009; Ford, 2008; Huisman, 2001; Mehan, 1983; among others). From a conversation analysis (CA) perspective, decision-making is an emergent process (Huisman, 2001) that consists of incremental activities in which different participants may pursue different agendas (Boden, 1994). It involves local and collaborative work among the participants and is achieved through the turn-by-turn unfolding of interaction (Boden, 1994; Clifton, 2009; Deppermann et al., 2010; Huisman 2001; Pomerantz & Denvir, 2007). The process routinely begins with a proposal for a future action and ends when a consensus is reached (Maynard, 1984; Stevanovic, 2012; Wasson, 2000). As noted above, power to influence the decision is embedded within the institutional hierarchy. That is, institutional roles, often externally defined, grant category-bound rights to certain participants relative to others (Holmes & Stubbe, 2015). For example, managers and chairs may influence the decision in overt ways such as by announcing the decision (e.g. 'no screendumps'), stating the desired decision (e.g. 'we'll put that against Ms. Banks'), and ratifying the decision (e.g. 'okay, that sounds good') (2015: 75–78). However, access to category-bound rights themselves is not sufficient in determining future actions.

Other participants can and do exert power in distinct ways such as by displaying expertise (Holmes & Stubbe, 2015: 5–7), contesting ideas (Ford, 2008) and seeking the chair's alignment and using laughter (Clifton, 2009). In other words, power inequalities based on the institutional hierarchy manifest in the different ways in which participants influence decisions for future actions. The participants' orientation to their respective rights to influence future actions can be examined with the notion of deontic authority (Stevanovic & Peräkylä, 2012).

Within the conversation analytic literature, authority is recognized as having two connected domains: epistemic and deontic. Epistemic authority, relating to relative access and rights to knowledge, is now an established area of research (e.g. Heritage, 2012; Heritage & Raymond, 2005). More recently, deontic authority, that is 'a person's legitimate power to determine action' (Stevanovic, 2018: 371), has been subjected to the CA lens (e.g. Kent, 2012; Nissi, 2016; Stevanovic, 2012, 2013, 2015, 2018, 2021; Stevanovic & Peräkylä, 2012; Stevanovic & Svennevig, 2015). Rather than focusing on power derived purely from a formal position (e.g. from an institutionally ascribed role such as chair or manager), analysts are concerned with how this legitimacy is constructed in interaction, and thus open to local negotiation. Stevanovic (2018: 375) distinguishes between deontic status as 'the relative power that a participant is considered to have or not to have' (e.g. arising from an institutional role) and deontic stance as 'participants' publicly displayed implicit claims of how authoritative they are' (2018: 375). She gives the example of trying to get a spouse to stop humming: Possibilities range from a strong claim of deontic authority ('Shut up!') to a mitigated claim ('Would you please be quiet?') to a weak deontic stance ('I'm sorry, I can't hear the radio weather report') (2018: 377). Given any type of deontic stance display, a recipient's response may not only range from full compliance (e.g. the cessation of humming) to active resistance (e.g. the continuation of humming), but also simultaneously doing both compliance and resistance (e.g. the cessation of humming along with a verbal reformulation, 'I was about to stop') (see also Kent, 2012; Stevanovic & Monzoni, 2016). In such cases, the spouse challenges the implicit deontic claim of the speaker to place a constraint on their behavior and asserts their own deontic authority. A further distinction can be made in regard to the scope of deontic claims: they can be distal, relating to 'people's rights to control and decide about their own and others' future doings' or proximal, relating to 'people's rights to initiate, maintain, or close up local sequences of conversational action' (Stevanovic, 2015: 85–86). Clearly then, joint decision-making when faced with proposals for future action is a locus for claiming, displaying and negotiating deontic authority (Stevanovic, 2018). By deploying the concept of deontic authority to examine the interactional unfolding of decision-making, the current study examines how power is exercised and negotiated on a turn-by-turn basis in a consensus-oriented and collaborative context where participants have differing levels of ascribed institutional power. We examine specific ways in which power inequalities grounded in a hierarchical leadership structure are reproduced and resisted in the context of a faculty meeting.

## Data and Method

Taken from a larger data set of 12 hours and 30 minutes of video-recorded faculty meetings in a US K-12 public school district, a decision-making episode lasting approximately 16 minutes is used as data for this study. The participants include one assistant superintendent of curriculum and instruction and eight English as a Second Language (ESL) teachers who work at different school buildings in the district. One of the teachers is the head of the ESL department and chairs the meeting. The focal participants in the target sequence are Sarah, the assistant superintendent of the school district, Julia, the ESL department head, and Anna, one of the four elementary school ESL teachers. Sarah is one of the highest-ranking members of the administration and oversees curricular and instructional needs encompassing student growth and achievement, technology and communication, and organizational leadership in the entire school district. Julia oversees curricular, instructional and sociocultural needs of English Language Learners (ELLs) throughout the school district and supervises other ESL teachers. Anna, as an ESL teacher, identifies, instructs and monitors ELLs in her school building. All the data were collected with the informed consent of the participants; the participants' names and other identifiers have been anonymized. As teacher trainers, both authors work closely with ESL teachers at large and, as regular participants of faculty meetings, both authors possess members' knowledge of institutional norms in such settings. Nonetheless, we acknowledge that we have limited access to the participants' knowledge of the specific institution and its members' ongoing interactions outside of the recorded meetings, which may have enhanced our understanding of the analyzed data.

The context of the study is as follows. Fifteen minutes into the meeting, the participants began their discussion on a new agenda item – on the possibility of having bilingual high school students act as volunteer interpreters for the district's open house evening. Julia, the department head, introduced the topic by nominating Anna, one of the teachers, to further explain. Anna first produced a problem presentation regarding the lack of interpreters to meet the needs of Spanish-speaking ELL families at her school and proposed the creation of a volunteer program, possibly utilizing bilingual high school students. In response, Mary, a high school ESL teacher, suggested that they invite all the Spanish-speaking families to come early and listen to a Spanish translated presentation before they attend the open house. Anna accepted Mary's suggestion with a positive assessment, thereby adopting and proposing it as a solution to the problem she had presented. Our analysis begins at this point and focuses on the interactional practices by which unequal power relations (based on the participants' distinct statuses in the institutional hierarchy) are reproduced and resisted in the extended decision-making process.

The analysis is conducted within a critical CA framework. We use CA to examine how unequal power relations in the workplace are enacted in interaction. We adopt a single case analysis approach as we investigate how a single proposal is responded to by the participants as they progress towards a decision for future action. Single case analysis 'involves tracking in detail the production of some aspect of talk [...] to observe the ways in which particular conversational devices are used in its production' (Hutchby & Wooffitt, 2008: 114). It can promote a deeper understanding of an existing phenomenon and uncover unnoticed but significant aspects of interaction for professionals in institutional contexts (Waring, 2009). After viewing and transcribing the data, we observed that the participants recurrently pursue a joint decision over an extended sequence involving multiple tellings from various participants. We chose the current decision-making episode as it showcases how the participants' specific institutional roles and power relations intersect with their participation in the interaction. In the analysis that follows, we present extracts from the decision-making episode that illustrate how claims of deontic authority are produced and responded to on a moment-by-moment basis.

## Analysis

The extracts presented share a number of features: firstly, there is an initial display of deontic authority by either Sarah, the assistant superintendent, or Julia, the department head, that seeks to direct focus and subsequent talk to various issues concerning Anna's (an elementary school teacher) proposal; secondly, Anna balances compliance and resistance to the claim of deontic authority; and thirdly, Anna pivots the talk back to her proposal from the issues to move it forward.

Extract 1 shows how Sarah (Sar) directs the talk to a broader problematization, and how this is met with Anna (Ann) moving between complying with the directive and rejecting the problematization, culminating in a refocusing on her proposal. The extract begins immediately after Anna has positively assessed Mary's (Mar; a high school teacher) suggestion to provide a Spanish translation for Spanish-speaking ELL families before they attend the open house. In doing so, Anna proposes providing the Spanish translation as a possible solution to overcome the communication barrier with them. Sarah, the assistant superintendent, begins her turn, *I was thinking that-*, in line 01, but this is overlapped by Rachel (Rac) (an elementary school teacher).

(1) exclusion (3.46)

```
01    Sar:         >I was think[ing that-<
02    Rac:                     [Do you think that's
03                 doable, with (.) either (.)
04    Sar:         Well so the issue i:s [it- it- it-=
05    Rac:                               [high schoolers=
06    Sar:         [=me- it'll be grea:t meeting=
07    Rac:         [=or or grown-ups in the district?
08    Sar:         =the needs of the Spanish speaking
09                 population<which is a (.) larger
10                 population [but in some buildings=
11    Hel:                    [Mm-hmm,
12    Sar:         =it may not [be.
13    Rac:                     [Right,
14    Mar:                     [Mm-hmm,
15    Sar:         [So then, [you're excluding- you're=
16    Car:                   [You have other languages.
17    Sar:         =excluding the parents from India,
18                 [you're excluding the parents=
19    Hel:         [Mm-hmm,
20    Sar:         [=fro::m
21    Ann:   →     [But most of our Indian families
22           →     [seems to:: to kno:w English,
23    Hel:         [Our Arabic speaking
24    Rac:         Yeah ( )
25    Ann:   →     >It's hard,< I mean just- we have a
26           →     la:rge group that we can meet, so
27           →     why not,
28    Sar:         Right,
29    Ann:   →     I do understand, we can- and we can
30           →     always put out, [if we have someone=
31    Jul:                         [I think there are=
```

```
32    Ann:   →    =fo:r
33    Jul:        =Indian American fam- <and we're
34                getting more Arabic speaking
35                [families [too, to where (.) we=
36    Mar:        [Mm-hmm,
37    Hel:                   [Yes, we are.
38    Jul:        =even have a couple parents right
39                now, if they had- (.) agai:n, it's
40                about the ti:ming, but if they had
41                known, .h I think we have a couple
42                of mo:thers, [(who would) like=
43    Mar:                     [°For sure.°
44    Jul:        =((throws arms above head)) they
45                would've been there
46                tra:n[slating, right,
47    Car:             [Y(hh)up. [Abdulla's mom hh
48    Ann:   →                   [So what maybe-
49           →    maybe we can- even if we start it
50           →    (0.8) because Spanish is easy to
51           →    fi:nd, [I mean ((turns to Rac)) Do=
52    Jul:               [It's easy, but it's not.
53    Ann:   →    =↑you speak Spanish?
54    Rac:        No (I don't) huh huh huh huh
55    Ann:   →    Well the two- ((open hand towards
56           →    Nat/Kat) the two of you could do
57           →    it, for you:r buildings, right so
58           →    then it's just- we just need two
59           →    mo:re, if we get two: East Foster,
```

Rachel's question starting in line 02 develops the proposal further. However, Sarah restarts her turn in line 04 at a non-possible completion point of Rachel's talk, with slightly increased volume. She upgrades her claim of deontic authority from a thought (Stevanovic, 2013) to the shell-noun construction (Schmid, 2000), *the issue is*. This not only indexes a shift in the trajectory of the talk (Delahunty, 2012), but it displays a unilaterally-oriented decision of the importance of her nominated topic. Its sequential position as the first topic raised after the proposal is made, the definite article *the*, and the lexical choice of *issue*, which conveys a negative valence, contribute to its strength as a claim of deontic authority. Sarah provides a positive assessment of the proposal, *it'll be grea:t*, but she follows with a problematization in lines 10, 12, 15 and 17–18. The problematization focuses on (a) a Spanish-speaking family majority not existing in all buildings in the district, and (b) Indian families (and other families as implicated by the repetition of *you're excluding* and the continuing prosody that projects more items to come) not being helped by a Spanish translation. Thus, Sarah highlights aspects of the proposal that are more related to district-wide knowledge and concerns rather than those of a single school building. She draws attention to all families, not just Spanish-speaking families, and to the possibility of exclusion, thereby widening the scope of the discussion to the proposal's broader consequences. Her problematization is both reflective and constitutive of her institutional knowledge, rights and responsibilities as the assistant superintendent.

In responding to Sarah's identification of the two issues, Anna addresses the sequentially contiguous one (Sacks, 1987) – that Indian families will be excluded. She makes an epistemic claim and rejects the presupposition of the problematization in lines 21–22, that Indian families don't speak English. She starts her turn in overlap with the contrastive marker *but*, and then mitigates a wholesale rejection with *most* and *seems to know* in *most of our Indian families seems to:: to kno:w English*, and thus conveys that they will not be excluded by the proposal. Noticeably, her overlap in line 21 precedes the hearable mention of other possible languages projected by Sarah's ongoing turn. In line 25, she produces a quick concessive >*it's hard*<, acknowledging the complexity of meeting all families' needs, and then, she pivots back to refocus on her proposal to meet the needs of the Spanish-speaking families, with the rhetorical question *why not*, possibly challenging (Koshik, 2005) Sarah's prior turn. Subsequently, Sarah produces an acknowledgement, *right*, in line 28. Anna's use of do-emphasis in her expression of affiliation, *I do understand*, and her suggestion, *we can always put out, if we have someone fo:r* (another language presumably – as evidenced by Julia's subsequent suggestion of Arabic-speaking mothers) display understanding and affiliation with Sarah's *issue* of exclusion. After the other teachers take up the suggestion of potential interpreters for Arabic (lines 33–47), Anna self-selects, in overlap with Carrie (Car), to again return the focus of the talk to her proposal related to Spanish-speaking families (lines 48–59).

Thus, in this extract, Sarah's strong claim to proximal deontic authority in directing the talk to her problematization is met with a series of turns by Anna that show both compliance and resistance. Anna displays compliance in topicalizing and claiming understanding of the issue of families who speak languages other than Spanish. This aspect of her response endorses Sarah's deontic claim as legitimate (Stevanovic, 2015). At the same time, Anna resists the basis and the relevance of the problematization to her specific proposal, treating it as external to her proposal. She narrows her rejection to Sarah's presumption regarding Indian families, and she pivots the talk to detailing possible arrangements for her proposal, and thus bolsters her own claim to deontic authority (Clinton, 2009). Her balancing of compliance and resistance with her multiple self-repairs and restarts highlight the delicacy of this negotiation.

Similar to Extract 1, the next extract also sees Sarah problematizing an issue external to the proposal. In this case, another elementary school teacher, Natalie (Nat), responds first. Anna follows Natalie's telling with a pivot back to her proposal. The extract begins just after Anna has given a detailed rationale for the proposal.

(2) principal's message (6.33)

```
01    Ann:    cuz we know the needs in our
02            schools (.) pretty much.
03    Sar:    So let me ask you a question <I kno:w,
04            for instance, i:n most- what I- my
05            impression was that (.) in most of
06            the elementary schools, .h the
07            principal speaks for about twenty
08            minutes?
09    Ann:    Yeah, [((nods))
10    Sar:         [Befo:re? (1.5) cause in that
11            case, they're also coming to a
12            presentation by the principal,
13    Rac:    Correct [((nods))
14    Sar:            [that they don't know what
15            th- is being said,
16    Ann:    Yeah,
17    Sar:    and the principal, .h is the one who
18            goes o:ver .h really the important
19            da:tes and ru:les, in terms of the
20            general school, so it's not just
21            what's happen[ing in the,=
22    Ann:                 [Right,
23    Sar:    =presentation fo::r u::m (1.0)
24            [you know for a class[room,=
25    Ann:    [Classroom,
26    Mar:                         [Mm-hmm,
27    Sar:    =so: [(.) let's think about that.
28    Nat:         [U:m ((raises hand))
29            Well I- I actually ha:d the idea of
30            doing tha:t, and I talked to: Carl,
31            about doing something like prior to:
32            (0.5) like a half an hour
33            ear[lier,
```

142   Part 2: Resisting Inequality and Injustice

```
34    Mar:        [°The [Spanish presentation?°
35    Sar:              [Right,
36    Nat:        and I ha:d and I was like >don't hold
37                me to it< but like this is what I
38                would like to do, you know and then
39                like have all the Spanish speaking
40                families that I could communicate
41                important information to, but
42                honestly like- like you were saying
43                like, beginning of the ye- because
44                I didn't think of it (.)
45                [right from the get ↑g[o:::
46    Sar:        [Soon enough.     [Right.
47    Mar:        Yeah,
48    Nat:        And only- like maybe two weeks
49                befo::re, I just- I couldn't (.) get
50                together, everything that I needed
51                from a:ll the teachers, [and I=
52    Mar:                                [Mm-hmm,
53    Nat:        =was like .h if I'm gonna do it, I
54                wanna do it well,
55    Ann:        Right,
56    Nat:        A::nd I didn't wanna just t- bring
57                them in to just be like
58                [(((waves)) So [u::h
59    Sar:        [Hi.
60    Rac:                       [(Don't have anything
61                to share)
62    Nat:        Yeah, so I mean but I- so I agree:.
63                like if we- if I (0.2) had planned
64                it, early enough. like I think
65                [(an-)
66    Ann:   →    [And the first year would be the
67           →    ha:rdest, because once we had that,
68           →    then we go back every year, and say
69           →    is there any- to the classroom
70           →    teachers, what else do you want us to
71           →    a:dd per grade level, that is
72           →    important,
73    Jul:        [That's true.
74    Hel:        [Yeah,
```

In a multi-unit turn in lines 03–08, 10–12, 14–15, 17–21 and 23–24, Sarah brings up the issue of the principal's presentation, a separate event from the classroom presentation being discussed. Her sequence-initial *so* suggests a new topic that has emerged from incipiency (Bolden, 2006) – in other words, its origin does not lie in prior talk. The turn continues with *let me ask you a question* which projects a forthcoming action (Schegloff, 1980) and displays self-authorization of the projected action (Hoey, 2022). Sarah prefaces her description of the issue initially with a strong claim of knowledgeability (Heritage & Raymond, 2005), *I know*, but after a series of cut-offs, she self-repairs, downgrading the strength of her assertion of knowledge (Kärkkäinen, 2003) to *my impression* (lines 04–05). The teachers (in lines 09 and 13) confirm her description. In lines 14–15, Sarah draws the parallel between her issue (the principal's address) and Anna's proposal: in both cases, the Spanish-speaking families *don't know what th- is being said*. Anna responds with acknowledgement tokens (lines 16, 22) and collaboratively completes Sarah's turn, *classroom*, in line 25. Although the core proposal is still being discussed, Sarah has claimed that her parallel issue is relevant to the interactional agenda, and in line 27, she produces a so-prefaced directive, *so: (.) let's think about that*. This marks the completion of her complex multi-unit turn (Raymond, 2004), and the directive embodies a strong proximal deontic claim that directs the teachers to engage with this topic in the here and now (Stevanovic, 2015).

Natalie self-selects to speak, beginning in line 28, and produces an extended multi-unit turn that, instead of addressing the issue of the principal's presentation, describes her difficulties with a course of action similar to Anna's proposal that she has already tried. In line 66, Anna begins at a point during Natalie's turn not projectably at a possible completion point. With the possible interruptiveness of Anna's turn mitigated by the conjunction *And*, the turn pivots from Natalie's telling to Anna's current proposal. Anna's assessment *the first year would be the ha:rdest* (line 66–67) does double duty: it acknowledges Natalie's difficulties while simultaneously referring to her own proposal. Anna continues to make claims to epistemic authority and produces an implied claim that subsequent years would not be as difficult. By self-selecting early, Anna blocks further talk on Natalie's telling and focuses on the relative ease of implementing her proposal after the first year. Subsequently, Julia and Helen express agreement (lines 73–74).

In this extract, Sarah produces a strong proximal deontic claim (Stevanovic, 2015) in problematizing a parallel issue and directing others to specifically address the newly raised issue in the here and now. Although Natalie responds first with a telling of her own experience in trying out her own idea, Anna moves, as she does in Extract 1, to pivot the ongoing talk to her own proposal and underlines her own distal deontic authority in explicating its future implementation.

The third extract shows how Sarah, again, broadens the scope of the discussion. Here, she also directs the expansion and the closure of the sequence. While Anna acknowledges the issue raised by Sarah, she aligns with Sarah's move towards sequence closing and thus contributes to pivoting the talk away from the broad issue. Just prior to the interaction shown below, Helen (Hel; an elementary school teacher), in explaining how she communicates information with her ELL families, has noted that some parents do not attend the open house.

(3) communicating with all parents (10.30)
```
01   Sar:    So that- the issue is (0.5)
02           the purpose is that you wanna
03           communicate (.) with all parents.
04   Hel:    Mm-hmm,
05   Sar:    information that they should all
06           know, [and how do we best make sure=
07   Hel:          [Mm-hmm,
08   Jul:          [Yes.
09   Sar:    =(.) that all our parents are
10           getting that communica[tion,=
11   Hel:                          [Mm-hmm,
12   Sar:    [=so if- if it's offering=
13   Nat:    [((raises hand))
14   Sar:    =some bilingual information at open
15           house, it- it goes beyond that
16           even. So what can we do to make
17           sure that we're bringing all the
18           parents- it's like- it's bigger.
19   Hel:    [It is bigger.
20   Jul:    [Right, °yeah, it is.°
21   Sar:    Yes. ((hand gestures towards Nat))
22   Nat:    U:m one of the huge issues at
23           Forestbrook, too, was I think that
24           a lot of parents couldn't be in
25           attendance (0.5) because they
26           didn't have childcare, [and because=
27   Hel:                           [((nods))
28   Nat:    =they're not supposed to bring their
29           child[ren,
30   Sar:         [Right,
```
(26 lines omitted: The participants discuss issues concerning the open house/lack of childcare at their school buildings.)

| | | |
|---|---|---|
| 57 | Ann: | There were lots of kids running |
| 58 | | around this time, and then (0.5) |
| 59 | | they were bringing it up to our |
| 60 | | principal, some people were saying, |
| 61 | | you know you have to be careful, |
| 62 | | because then, other people get |
| 63 | | upset, they took the time to fi:nd |
| 64 | | [( ) |
| 65 | Jul: | [Yea::h, [oh my go::sh. it's so= |
| 66 | Sar: |          [I think- |
| 67 | Jul: | [=complicated. |
| 68 | Sar: | [so that's something [that I have to= |
| 69 | Nat: |                            [So::: hhhhh |
| 70 | Sar: | =bring up with the [principals, |
| 71 | Hel: |                     [It's a who:le |
| 72 | | different issue, hehehe |
| 73 | Sar: | U:m and let's- yeah, let's move on, |
| 74 | | [because we're like- [we're really- |
| 75 | Nat: | [But- |
| 76 | Jul: |                     [That we are |
| 77 | | not gonna solve. |
| 78 | Nat: | [Okay. |
| 79 | Sar: | [No. ↑But- but- we- but ↑that is |
| 80 | | a- that is a discussion. |
| 81 | | [abou:t the issue: I- it's been a= |
| 82 | Jul: | [Mm-hmm, |
| 83 | Sar: | =discussion for yea:rs now in the |
| 84 | | district, [in terms o:f parents,= |
| 85 | Hel: |       [Mm-hmm, |
| 86 | Sar: | =there are parents, in- in all |
| 87 | | honesty, that don't under- that |
| 88 | | nee:d help with chi:ldcare, and |
| 89 | | that don't understand, but there's |
| 90 | | also parents that choo:se |
| 91 | | [not to (1.5) follow [(the rules.) |
| 92 | Jul: | [Again it's just- |
| 93 | Ann: → |                     [Right, you're |
| 94 | → | never gonna change [all that. |
| 95 | Jul: |                    [So I- the |
| 96 | | consensus I hear is that it's |
| 97 | | complicated, and that I real- at |
| 98 | | lea:st from my perspective, I think |
| 99 | | we need to work within our |
| 100 | | particular build[ing, |
| 101 | Hel: |                [Mm-hmm, |
| 102 | Jul: | [because the context is gonna be= |

103  Nat:      [Yeah, yeah,
104  Jul:      =different,

In lines 01–03, Sarah conveys her deontic authority again using the shell-noun construction (Schmid, 2000), 'the issue (repaired to *purpose*) is', projecting her upcoming talk as the focal point (Aijmer, 2007). With the shell-noun construction and the repeated emphasis on the lexical item <u>all</u>, Sarah broadens the scope of the discussion from communicating information with Spanish-speaking ELL parents, the focal issue raised by Anna, to all parents. She invites the participants to discuss ways to communicate information with all parents (lines 05–18). In doing so, she explicitly and repeatedly refers to the shifted focus that goes beyond offering bilingual information at the open house, *So what can we do to make sure that we're bringing <u>all</u> the parents- it's like- it's bigger.*

In line 21, Sarah nominates Natalie, who brings up an issue that deters parents from attending the open house at her school (lines 22–29). In the omitted lines, Natalie problematizes different aspects of the issue including a lack of childcare and a communication barrier. Other participants share relevant experiences at their own schools. As part of this discussion, Anna shares what happened at her school (lines 57–64), thus displaying affiliation with the preceding comments and compliance with Sarah's refocus to discuss communication with all parents and not just Spanish-speaking ELL parents. In lines 66, 68 and 70, Sarah produces an upshot conveying her authority and responsibility as the assistant superintendent, *I think- so that's something that I have to bring up with the principals.* In alignment with the participants' collaborative moves towards sequence closing, Sarah then explicitly directs topic transition, *U:m and let's- yeah, let's move on, because we're like- we're really-* (lines 73–74). The use of directive conveys her strong claim to proximal deontic authority in shifting the local interactional agenda (Stevanovic, 2015), this time, closing down a topical sequence. In response to Julia's (the ESL department head) summary statement that conveys her resistance to further engage with the discussion of this broader concern, *Th<u>at</u> we are not gonna solve* (lines 76–77), Sarah first agrees with the content of Julia's turn, *No*, then continues with her turn, conveying her historical knowledge of issues with parents in the district (lines 79–91). In an overlap, while Julia starts but halts her turn with a cut-off (line 92), Anna acknowledges Sarah's turn, *Right*, and produces an aphoristic summary implicative of topic closure (Schegloff, 2007: 181–194), *you're never gonna change <u>all</u> that* (lines 93–94). In doing so, she intensifies her assessment with an extreme case formulation (Pomerantz, 1986) and conveys that the current discussion prompted by Sarah is beyond their control and efforts, thereby affiliating and aligning with Sarah's move to close the sequence. In overlap, Julia returns the focus to their joint decision regarding Anna's proposal, presenting it as a consensus (Wasson, 2016).

In this extract, Sarah exercises proximal deontic authority in managing the local interactional agenda (Stevanovic, 2015); she shifts the focus of the talk by broadening the scope of the discussion, eliciting contributions from other participants. Further, Sarah directs the closure and the expansion of the topical sequence. Anna's response includes elements of compliance with Sarah's deontic authority with her affiliative participation in the broader discussion initiated by Sarah. Although she does not directly display resistance, her extreme case formulation summary aligns with the progression of Sarah's sequence-closing moves and thus pivots the talk away from this broader proposal.

In the final extract, it is Julia, the ESL department head, who displays her deontic authority in controlling the local interactional agenda towards the end of the decision-making episode. Anna again shows compliance and resistance, producing her own distal deontic claim for the future piloting of her proposal. Just prior to the interaction below, the participants have been discussing the district-wide resources for translation help (e.g. the availability of a bilingual intern).

(4) building level plan (13.51)

```
01    Jul:    ((gazes at laptop)) so I guess what
02            I put is >explore how we can meet
03            the diverse needs of parents at
04            open house, [using the existing
05    Rac:                [((nods))
06    Jul:    resources we have, [early
07    Nat:                       [((nods))
08    Jul:    preparation consent from principals
09            ((gazes up from laptop)) needed.<=
10            [=.hhh but if- if I knew in August,
11    Ann:    [((nods))
12    Jul:    [I could (.) you know offer it as
13    Ann:    [((nods)) Yes.
14    Jul:    extra credit [to some of the
15    Ann:                 [((nods))
16    Jul:    East Foster [university students=
17    Sar:                [Absolutely absolutely.
18    Hel:                [((nods)) Mm-hmm,
```

| | | |
|---|---|---|
| 19 | Jul: | =even if they're not bilingual. |
| 20 | | It's about ha:ving cage:r .h |
| 21 | | education majo:rs, you know, I mean |
| 22 | | I know we would like them |
| 23 | | [to be bilingual, |
| 24 | Sar: | [They really need to be bilingual. |
| 25 | | [I think. |
| 26 | Jul: | [hhh I don't- I don't kno:w. |
| 27 | Sar: | [Well I mean if- how are they= |
| 28 | Jul: | [I would rather have some help,= |
| 29 | Sar: | [=gonna explai:n [(0.5) the= |
| 30 | Jul: | [=than no help. |
| 31 | Ann: | [Yeah, |
| 32 | Sar: | =information [we have. |
| 33 | Ann: | [For this (.) purpose, |
| 34 | | we need [them to be bilingual. |
| 35 | Jul: | [Yea:h, for this purpose, |
| 36 | | I- I don't know. |
| 37 | Sar: | I mean I'd like it that way, if |
| 38 | | it's possible, because .h (0.5) I |
| 39 | | think if I was a [parent- |
| 40 | Jul: | [but even parents |
| 41 | | getting to their rooms, |
| 42 | | [sometimes is difficult, like you= |
| 43 | Mar: | [°I was gonna say just guid[es.° |
| 44 | Sar: | [Yes. |
| 45 | Jul: | =can't even get them to the right |
| 46 | | ↑roo::m. [And just having- |
| 47 | Kat: | [I couldn't get here. |
| 48 | | [I'll be honest. |
| 49 | Hel: | [hehe[hehehe |
| 50 | Sar: | [hahahaha[hahahaha |
| 51 | Kat: | [$I was like$ ((hand |
| 52 | | gestures circling motion)) (°walked |
| 53 | | around°) |
| 54 | Hel: | [$I was having palpitations coming= |
| 55 | Jul: | [No I know the preference is for= |
| 56 | Hel: | [=in this mor:ning,$ |
| 57 | Jul: | [=bilingual. and- and I'm sure |
| 58 | | the language department would (.) |
| 59 | | you know send out an email, |
| 60 | | and offer probably extra credit, |
| 61 | | but we rea:lly would need to get on |
| 62 | | this like in .h ea:rly august, to |

```
63                      make it [happen.
64      Hel:            [If-
65      Ann:    →       [So maybe: we talk to-
66              →       I wouldn't mind try:ing it, thee:
67              →       ((points to Mar)) your suggestion
68              →       (.) about having them come early,
69              →       so I ca- we can pilot it ourselves,
70              →       [in ou:r [in our own buildings,=
71      Mar:            [((nods))
72      Jul:                     [Okay,
73      Ann:    →       =what's gonna work for us.
74              →       [We'll try it.
75      Jul:            [Sounds good. Sounds good.
76                      ((gazes at laptop)) Alright, and
77                      so:: okay, ((starts typing))
78                      each (.) so building level plan
79                      ((types)) <°building level plan.°>
```

At the beginning of line 01, Julia directs her gaze towards her laptop screen on which the meeting notes are displayed. She produces a so-prefaced upshot of the discussion (Raymond, 2004) by reading aloud what she typed earlier (cf. Lindholm *et al.*, 2020). In doing so, Julia marks the completion of the topical sequence and initiates a sequence-closing sequence (Schegloff, 2007: 181–194; Schegloff & Sacks, 1973). In alignment with Julia's move towards closing, multiple participants acknowledge Julia's turn, without expanding on the sequence, via head nods. In line 10, it is Julia who expands the sequence by re-introducing the issue of early preparation, which the participants previously discussed (Extract 2). She latches onto the preceding unit of talk with an audible inbreath and projects more talk (Schegloff, 1996). Once again, multiple participants, including Anna, acknowledge Julia's turn without expanding on the sequence, this time via head nods along with verbal acknowledgements (lines 13, 15, 17, 18). Notably, Sarah produces multiple sayings (Stivers, 2004) of the acknowledgement token, *Absolutely absolutely* (line 17), indicating her stance that Julia's turn, and possibly the topical sequence itself, may have persisted beyond what is necessary. Nonetheless, Julia further extends her turn in line 19, raising a new issue concerning sources of help. Similar to her earlier practice (line 10), Julia latches onto the preceding unit of talk as a way to hold the floor. Further, she adds an increment (Schegloff, 1996; Walker, 2004), producing a grammatically contiguous turn, *even if they're not bilingual*. In overlap with Julia's turn, Sarah produces a direct counter, *they really need to be bilingual* (line 24). While she initially mitigates the counter with a post-positioned epistemic downgrade, *I think*, in continued overlap, Sarah supports her counter with an account (lines 27, 29, 32). Subsequently, Anna affiliates with Sarah in opposition to Julia's proposal and emphasizes the specific focus, *For th<u>is</u> (.) purpose, we need them to be bilingual* (lines 33–34). In overlap, Julia produces a partial repeat of Anna's turn followed by an epistemic hedge, *I- I don't know*, conveying a disaffiliative stance (Keevallik, 2011). As Sarah further mitigates her earlier counter (lines 37–39), Julia accounts for her stance by broadening the issue from the need for translators to general guides (lines 40–42, 45–46). Multiple participants affiliate with Julia with acknowledgement, laughter and a supportive telling (lines 43, 44, 47–54, 56). In line 55, Julia deploys a no-preface, indexing a shift from non-serious to serious (Schegloff, 2001), and brings the post-expansion sequence to a close with a reiteration of the summary statement highlighting the need for early preparation (lines 55, 57–63).

Anna, in lines 65–74, bypasses the issue of early preparation; instead, she refocuses the discussion on the specific proposal, providing a Spanish interpretation to ELL families. After the restart, she initially constructs her turn as an individual decision, *I wouldn't mind try:ing it* (line 66). But at the end of her turn, she presents a claim of joint future action, *We'll try it* (line 74), invoking shared decisional accountability (Thompson & McCabe, 2018). She also aligns herself with Julia's stance towards varied contexts across different school buildings, recycling elements of Julia's earlier turn (Extract 3, lines 99–100), *in ou:r in our <u>own</u> buildings* (line 70) (Clifton, 2009). In overlap, Julia makes the closing of the sequence relevant in multiple ways. She first produces positive assessments (Schegloff, 2007: 123–127), *sounds good*, followed by a series of transition-relevant markers (e.g. *alright*) (Beach, 1993; Ford, 2008: 53–57) and conjunctions (e.g. *so*) (Clayman, 2012) (lines 75–79). At the same time, she embodies her disengagement from the discussion by directing her gaze towards her laptop screen and starting to type.

In this extract, Julia conveys her proximal deontic authority (Stevanovic, 2015) by opening, expanding and closing the sequence-closing sequence (Schegloff, 2007: 181–194; Schegloff & Sacks, 1973). In particular, she expands the sequence by repeatedly claiming the floor via multi-unit turns to raise issues that go beyond the scope of the specific proposal. Anna's response includes elements of compliance with and resistance to Julia's deontic authority. In response to Julia's re-introduction of the importance of early preparation, Anna produces acknowledgement without a substantive response to engage in the discussion. When Julia raises a new issue concerning non-bilingual help, Anna rejects the idea through agreement with Sarah's direct counter. Julia's series of turns that initiate sequence closing draw on her institutional role as chair and the accompanying power to influence the decision through announcing it (Clifton, 2009; Holmes & Stubbe, 2005). Her sequence-closing moves make future planning relevant, and Anna takes this opportunity to pivot back to specifying the decision and its implementation as a joint future action, an explicit display of her own distal deontic authority.

## Discussion and Conclusion

In this study, we have examined how power inequalities manifest in a decision-making process during a faculty meeting in which the participants occupy varying statuses in an organizational hierarchy, and thus have different levels of ascribed institutional power. By deploying the concept of deontic authority, we have shown that institutional power inequalities are reproduced and resisted through distinct interactional practices by which the participants influence a decision for future action. Following the teacher's specific proposal (in this case, providing an interpretation for Spanish-speaking ELL families), the assistant superintendent and the department head exhibit their institutional power by shifting the local interactional agenda. They recurrently orient to the proposal's broader implications and consequences (e.g. exclusion of other families) and problematize different aspects of the proposal. While such broader district-wide concerns are relevant to their own institutional responsibilities, the impact of these problematizations is to inhibit or possibly derail the progression of the proposal's discussion (e.g. Extract 3).

How then does the teacher, who has less institutional power, overcome the power inequalities grounded in the organizational hierarchy and manage to pursue her interactional agenda to have her proposal accepted? The teacher responds to deontic authority displayed by other participants with more institutional power by balancing compliance and resistance. She shows compliance by acknowledging the broader issues raised by the assistant superintendent and/or the department head and affiliating with their stance towards these issues. At the same time, she conveys resistance by challenging the relevance of the broader issues to her specific proposal and moving to close the sequences concerning them. Notably, the teacher orients to her display of resistance as delicate: she delivers disagreements in a dispreferred manner with mitigations and self-repairs (Pomerantz, 1984) and/or rejects problematizations by aligning with the more powerful institutional voice (Ford, 2008: 53–91). This balancing act enables her to pivot the talk back to her proposal and achieve a favorable decision. That is, rather than relying on those with more institutional power to push forward the proposal, the teacher continually brings the focus back to the narrow scope of the agenda item in pursuit of specifying future arrangements for the proposed action. Overall, our findings show how power inequalities based on the participants' distinct institutional roles manifest in the different ways in which participants influence decisions for future actions, and support that the claims of deontic authority are continuously negotiated in the 'laminations of actions and reactions' in real time (Boden, 1994: 22).

## References

Aijmer, K. (2007) The interface between discourse and grammar: *The fact is that*. In A. Celle and R. Huart (eds) *Connectives as Discourse Markers* (pp. 31–46). John Benjamins.

Asmuß, B. and Oshima, S. (2012) Negotiation of entitlement in proposal sequences. *Discourse Studies* 14 (1), 107–126.

Beach, W.A. (1993) Transitional regularities for 'casual' 'okay' usages. *Journal of Pragmatics* 19 (4), 325–352.

Boden, D. (1994) *The Business of Talk: Organizations in Action*. Polity Press.

Boden, D. (1995) Agendas and arrangements: Everyday negotiations in meetings. In A. Firth (ed.) *The Discourse of Negotiation: Studies of Language in the Workplace* (pp. 83–99). Pergamon.

Bolden, G.B. (2006) Little words that matter: Discourse markers 'so' and 'oh' and the doing of other-attentiveness in social interaction. *Journal of Communication* 56 (4), 661–688.

Brown, H., Reed, A. and Yarrow, T. (2017) Introduction: Towards an ethnography of meeting. *Journal of the Royal Anthropological Institute* 21 (S1), 10–26.

Clayman, S.E. (2012) Address terms in the organization of turns at talk: The case of pivotal turn extensions. *Journal of Pragmatics* 44 (13), 1853–1867.

Clifton, J. (2009) Beyond taxonomies of influence: 'Doing' influence and making decisions in management team meetings. *Journal of Business Communication* 46 (1), 57–79.

Delahunty, G.P. (2012) An analysis of the thing is that S sentences. *Pragmatics* 22 (1), 41–78.

Deppermann, A., Schmitt, R. and Mondada, L. (2010) Agenda and emergence: Contingent and planned activities in a meeting. *Journal of Pragmatics* 42 (6), 1700–1718.

Ford, C.E. (2008) *Women Speaking Up: Getting and Using Turns in Workplace Meetings*. Palgrave Macmillan.

Heritage, J. (2012) Epistemics in action: Action formation and territories of knowledge. *Research on Language and Social Interaction* 45 (1), 1–29.

Heritage, J. and Raymond, G. (2005) The terms of agreement: Indexing epistemic authority and subordination in talk-in-interaction. *Social Psychology Quarterly* 68 (1), 15–38.

Hoey, E.M. (2022) Self-authorizing action: On let me X in English social interaction. *Language in Society* 51 (1), 95–118.

Holmes, J. and Stubbe, M. (2015) *Power and Politeness in the Workplace: A Sociolinguistic Analysis of Talk at Work* (2nd edn). Routledge.
Huisman, M. (2001) Decision-making in meetings as talk-in-interaction. *International Studies of Management & Organization* 31 (3), 69–90.
Hutchby, I. and Wooffitt, R. (2008) *Conversation Analysis* (2nd edn). Polity Press.
Jennings, M. (2007) *Leading Effective Meetings, Teams, and Work Groups in Districts and Schools.* Association for Supervision and Curriculum Development.
Kärkkäinen, E. (2003) *Epistemic Stance in English Conversation: A Description of it Interactional Functions, with a Focus on I Think.* John Benjamins.
Keevallik, L. (2011) The terms of not knowing. In L. Mondada, J. Steensig and T. Stivers (eds) *The Morality of Knowledge in Conversation* (pp. 184–206). Cambridge University Press.
Kent, A. (2012) Compliance, resistance, and incipient compliance when responding to directives. *Discourse Studies* 14 (6) 711–730.
Koshik, I. (2005) *Beyond Rhetorical Questions: Assertive Questions in Everyday Interaction.* John Benjamins.
Lindholm, C., Stevanovic, M., Valkeapää, T. and Weiste, E. (2020) Writing: A versatile resource in the treatment of the clients' proposals. In C. Lindholm, M. Stevanovic and E. Weiste (eds) *Joint Decision Making in Mental Health* (pp. 187–210). Palgrave Macmillan.
Maynard, D.W. (1984) *Inside Plea Bargaining: The Language of Negotiation.* Plenum.
Mehan, H. (1983) The role of language and the language of role in institutional decision making. *Language in Society* 12 (2), 187–211.
Nissi, R. (2016) Spelling out consequences: Conditional constructions as a means to resist proposals in organisational planning process. *Discourse Studies* 18 (3), 311–329.
Pomerantz, A. (1984) Agreeing and disagreeing with assessments: Some features of preferred/dispreferred turn shapes. In J.M. Atkinson and J. Heritage (eds) *Structures of Social Action* (pp. 57–101). Cambridge University Press.
Pomerantz, A. (1986) Extreme case formulations: A way of legitimizing claims. *Human Studies* 9 (2–3), 219–230.
Pomerantz, A. and Denvir, P. (2007) Enacting the institutional role of chairperson in upper management meetings: The interactional realization of provisional authority. In F. Cooren (ed.) *Interacting and Organizing: Analyses of a Management Meeting* (pp. 31–51). Lawrence Erlbaum.
Raymond, G. (2004) Prompting action: The stand-alone 'so' in ordinary conversation. *Research on Language and Social Interaction* 37 (2), 185–218.
Sacks, H. (1987) On the preferences for agreement and contiguity in sequences in conversation. In G. Button and J.R.E. Lee (eds) *Talk and Social Organisation* (pp. 54–69). Multilingual Matters.
Schegloff, E.A. (1980) Preliminaries to preliminaries: 'Can I ask you a question?'. *Sociological Inquiry* 50 (3–4), 104–152.
Schegloff, E.A. (1996) Turn organization: One intersection of grammar and interaction. In E. Ochs, E.A. Schegloff and S.A. Thompson (eds) *Interaction and Grammar* (pp. 52–133). Cambridge University Press.
Schegloff, E.A. (2001) Getting serious: Joke → serious 'no'. *Journal of Pragmatics* 33 (12), 1947–1955.
Schegloff, E.A. (2007) *Sequence Organization in Interaction.* Cambridge University Press.
Schegloff, E.A. and Sacks, H. (1973) Opening up closings. *Semiotica* 8 (4), 289–327.

Schmid, H.-J. (2000) *English Abstract Nouns as Conceptual Shells: From Corpus to Cognition.* Mouton de Gruyter.
Stevanovic, M. (2012) Establishing joint decisions in a dyad. *Discourse Studies* 14 (6), 779–803.
Stevanovic, M. (2013) Constructing a proposal as a thought: A way to manage problems in the initiation of joint decision-making in Finnish workplace interaction. *Pragmatics* 23 (3), 519–544.
Stevanovic, M. (2015) Displays of uncertainty and proximal deontic claims: The case of proposal sequences. *Journal of Pragmatics* 78, 84–97.
Stevanovic, M. (2018) Social deontics: A nano-level approach to human power play. *Journal for the Theory of Social Behaviour* 48 (3), 369–389.
Stevanovic, M. (2021) Deontic authority and the maintenance of lay and expert identities during joint decision making: Balancing resistance and compliance. *Discourse Studies* 23 (5), 670–689.
Stevanovic, M. and Peräkylä, A. (2012) Deontic authority in interaction: The right to announce, propose and decide. *Research on Language and Social Interaction* 45 (3), 297–321.
Stevanovic, M. and Svennevig, J. (2015) Introduction: Epistemics and deontics in conversational directives. *Journal of Pragmatics* 78, 1–6.
Stevanovic, M. and Monzoni, C. (2016) On the hierarchy of interactional resources: Embodied and verbal behavior in the management of joint activities with material objects. *Journal of Pragmatics* 103, 15–32.
Stivers, T. (2004) 'No no no' and other types of multiple sayings in social interaction. *Human Communication Research* 30 (2), 260–293.
Stosich, E.L. (2021) 'Are we an advisory board or a decision making entity?': Teachers' involvement in decision making in instructional leadership teams. *Leadership and Policy in Schools* 22 (3), 638–656.
Thompson, L. and McCabe, R. (2018) How psychiatrists recommend treatment and its relationship with patient uptake. *Health Communication* 33 (11), 1345–1354.
Walker, G. (2004) On some interactional and phonetic properties of increments to turns in talk-in-interaction. In E. Couper-Kuhlen and C.E. Ford (eds) *Sound Patterns in Interaction: Cross-Linguistic Studies from Conversation* (pp. 147 – 170). John Benjamins.
Waring, H.Z. (2009) Moving out of IRF: A single case analysis. *Language Learning* 59 (4), 796–824.
Wasson, C. (2000) Caution and consensus in American business meetings. *Pragmatics* 10, 457–481.
Wasson, C. (2016) Integrating conversation analysis and issue framing to illuminate collaborative decision-making activities. *Discourse & Communication* 10 (4), 378–411.
Weiste, E., Stevanovic, M. and Lindholm, C. (2020) Introduction: Social inclusion as an interactional phenomenon. In C. Lindholm, M. Stevanovic and E. Weiste (eds) *Joint Decision Making in Mental Health* (pp. 1–41). Palgrave Macmillan.

# 8 I'm Just Saying: Being Explicit in a Mixed-Race Conversation about Racism

Sarah Chepkirui Creider

> *To expose racism in the system we must analyze ambiguous meanings, expose hidden currents, and generally question what seems normal or acceptable.*
> —Essed, 1991: 10

> *We are capable of bearing a great burden, once we discover that the burden is reality and arrive where reality is.*
> —Baldwin, 1992: 91

## Introduction

In this chapter, I look at a conversation where a mixed-Race[1] group of speakers discuss topics related to racism. In order to better understand the work these participants engage in, I use early ethnomethodological work on the unspoken assumptions that underlie most everyday conversations. Below, I start with a brief exploration of Garfinkel's (1967: 30) work on a 'shared agreement' which allows conversations to unfold relatively seamlessly. I then discuss how this agreement, related to an assumption of shared backgrounds and experiences, cannot hold in a conversation about Race and racism among participants from differing racial backgrounds. Next, I turn to the interaction at the center of this chapter, investigating how two speakers resist a racist ideology of sameness by being explicit about both semantic meaning and conversational actions. I attempt to show that seemingly unnecessary explanations serve to signal that understanding cannot be taken for granted, and to highlight the individual experiences of Race and racism brought by each participant to the conversation.

In his research on interaction, Harold Garfinkel (1967) argues that the actual words we use in a conversation are not sufficient to do the work of creating meaning. Instead, participants rely on an unspoken shared context in order to understand: (1) what is being talked about and (2) what is being accomplished via that talk (1967: 29). For instance, most interactions are based on the belief that all participants share a basic vocabulary. Thus, we rarely pause in the midst of a conversation in order to define the words and phrases we are using. Instead, we assume that our recipients understand which objects, ideas and actions we are referring to. We can see this certainty in the lack of explanations and the lack of questions about meaning in a typical interaction. On a more fundamental level, we are also confident in a mutual ability to understand why we say what we say, or the actions that our talk accomplishes. For instance, if I pass a colleague in the hall and say, 'How are you?', I don't usually start by announcing that 'I'm greeting you now'. Nor does my colleague need to say, 'I understand that what you just said was a greeting'. Instead, she simply responds in kind, showing by her continued engagement that we both understand what's happening – or what we are doing – in that brief moment (Garfinkel & Sacks, 1970). Moments when speakers do stop to explicitly name what they are engaged in, or to 'say in so many words what (they) are doing' (1970: 179), are called *formulations* by Garfinkel and Sacks. In the case of interaction, one description of 'what (we) are doing' is 'having a conversation', or – even 'saying something'. Thus, when participants explicitly name what they are doing as 'saying', 'talking' or 'having a conversation', they are formulating their actions. The fact that people don't constantly stop to explain themselves via formulations suggests that they trust such explanations are unnecessary.

What happens though, when there is no shared background from which to understand each other's actions – when the only possible common context is one that is based on a denial of participants' actual experiences? For the participants whose conversation I explore below, one such situation may be a conversation about racism. As generations of scholars have reminded us, the history of Race and racism in the United States is also a history of denial (Baldwin, 1992; Essed, 1991; Rawls & Duck, 2020). For many researchers (and for many US residents), the fact of racism (Essed, 1991; Rawls & Duck, 2020; Whitehead, 2015) is, as Baldwin (1992: 88) writes, a 'reality'. However, this is not a belief shared by all who live in the United States. Thus, we see multiple layers of denial. First, there is the belief that racism no longer exists and that 'everything is working just fine now' (Rawls & Duck, 2020: 18). A second – perhaps less obvious but equally dangerous – fantasy is that we all share the same racial context, i.e. that people are people, regardless of their backgrounds (Robles & Shrikant, 2022: 274; Sue, 2015). In fact, daily life is not the same for people of different Races in the United States. Put simply, a speaker who has spent her whole life being seen and spoken to as a White person will bring a radically different background to conversation from one who has spent her life being seen and spoken to as a Black person. In other words, we may not share a context from which to understand each other when we are talking about Race and racism. The very idea of a single, objective reality denies the lived experience of racism (Essed, 1991).

This understanding may seem obvious for those who think of themselves as being anti-racist. However, because we tend to take the act of conversation for granted, the agreements described by Garfinkel (1967) can lead to an unspoken denial of the differences we bring to our interactions, even among those who seem to hold similar beliefs. By allowing a mixed-Race conversation about racism to unfold like any other everyday conversation, we essentially deny the profoundly different understandings participants may bring to such an interaction. The references and understandings that we take for granted in most everyday conversations are not necessarily shared when people of differing racialized backgrounds talk about Race and racism.

Thus, refusing to allow a conversation to continue as if everyone understood each other can be seen as a form of resistance, a way to highlight the individual differences that each speaker brings to the interaction. It is this kind of resistance that I explore in this chapter. I suggest that being explicit, via definitions and formulations, combats a false assumption of understanding by insisting on the possibility of misunderstanding – or, at least, of differing understandings. In a sense, then, our colloquial understanding of 'conversation' is not sufficient to describe the complex and subtle actions necessary to engage in the act of talking about Race in mixed-Race settings. Indeed, it is important to note that the very fact of segregation and discrimination is, as Turowetz and Rawls (2021: 21) point out, a violation of Garfinkel's trust argument – without which 'parties cannot assume they are operating by the same constitutive rules'.

Below, I describe two related ways that speakers in the conversation explored here resist a racist ideology of a shared context: (1) with *definitions*, or explicit explanations for presumably familiar terms; and (2) with *formulations*, or explicit references to the act of having a conversation. I start by analyzing three extracts where speakers use definitions to clarify terminology related to racism – despite the fact that the word or phrase in question is one which recipients could be expected to understand. Next, I look at three examples where speakers use formulations to explicitly name what they are doing, either by announcing what action a specific turn is designed to accomplish (e.g. *saying*), or by framing the activity at hand as a *conversation*. My focus is on how this extra work emphasizes individual points-of-view, and resists the idea that there is a single, non-racialized context that all speakers can draw on as they interact with each other. Finally, in the conclusion, I suggest that by being explicit about what they mean and what they are doing, these activists build resources which can be used both in their own interaction and in conversations with their wider community.

## Data and Method

This conversation is part of a larger corpus of materials gathered from meetings, written communications, and interactions among a loose group of community members from a rural county in the Midwestern United States. The group has been working together in various formations since 2016 in order to respond to what they see as unjust, racist and sexist policies and actions enacted in their community. This particular interaction was a Zoom call to discuss a shooting (seen by group members as racially-motivated) that had taken place about six months before the call, in the members' home county. There were eight people on the call, but this chapter includes talk from only four speakers: A and G, who identify as African American men; L, who identifies as a White man; and, P, who identifies as a White, Jewish woman. The other four participants (not mentioned in this chapter) all identify as White.

With participants' permission, the Zoom call was recorded, and later transcribed, using an adaptation of Jefferson's (1983) transcription notation (see Appendix). Initial transcriptions were then examined, line-by-line, following the conversation-analytic tradition of 'unmotivated looking' (Psathas, 1995). Thus, although this conversation was chosen for analysis because of participants' focus on topics related to racism, no attempt was made to concentrate on talk that seemed related to Race, racism or racialized identities in the initial analysis. Instead, I looked at how participants responded to each other, and at the actions that they seemed to be accomplishing via their talk. Initial analysis led to an interest in moments when participants seemed to be doing extra work to explain themselves. In line with critical CA, I began to look more closely at these moments, focusing on the work participants themselves were doing as they resisted racist ideologies within the context of a conversation explicitly focused on racism. That said, although I attempted to stay with the emic perspective of conversation analysis, it is worth noting that I am from the same county as these participants, some of whom are members of my own family. I am also a White woman who grew up as a member of a Black family in this region. Thus, just as these participants bring their specific contexts to their conversation, I bring my own context and background to this analysis. Because of my personal relationship with these data, I have checked my initial understandings with two of the participants in this conversation: G (a Black man) and P (a White woman).

## Analysis

In this section, I look at two ways in which participants orient to a lack of shared context and emphasize the reality that each speaker has their own individual perspective. Throughout the analysis, I highlight how this orientation resists the ideology of a single, non-racialized reality from which a mixed-Race conversation can be undertaken. I start by looking at three examples of *definitions*, where speakers explicitly unpack terminology associated with racism. Next, I offer three examples of *formulations*, or moments when speakers explicitly reference the fact that they are engaged in a conversation.

## Definitions: Explicitly unpacking terms

This section starts with three examples of how these participants explain – or unpack – words and phrases that would seem, at first glance, to be easily comprehensible by their recipients. I conclude with an extract where one of the terms that is carefully defined is used by another speaker, later in the conversation. The first example relates to a word that is associated with the participants' local context. Next, I look at two phrases associated with a national conversation regarding Race and racism.

Extract 1 begins just a few minutes into this one-hour conversation. Speaker A has been discussing unconscious bias – specifically on the part of police officers in African American neighborhoods.

(1) incident
01    A:      that is present, (0.4) in our subconscious, an-
02                    and we're not acknowledging it until we have
03                    an incident like this.
04    G:      [right]

```
05   A:   →   [and ] what's an incident like this, Daunte
06               Wright, (0.2) um the uh- [name]'s brother
07               getting shot in the face (.) u:m George Floyd
08               (.) ya [know  ]
09   G:          [so bas-]
10               so- if I could excus- interrupt so basically
11               you can take any (.) not any there's a bunch
12               of different the:mes that could be put on top
13               of these .h incidents
```

As I note above, this Zoom conversation was called in order for participants to discuss a shooting that had taken place in their county. The events surrounding the shooting were referred to by group members as 'the [placename] incident', or 'the incident'. At this point in the conversation, the phrase had been used multiple times, and it had also been part of group members' interactions for several months (personal conversation). In line 03, A refers to *an incident like this*. It is interesting to note that he does not say something like 'this incident'. Instead, his use of the indefinite pronoun plus the phrase *like this* seems to set up the idea that this is one of a group of possible incidents, all of which might be *like* something. Then, despite no sign of misunderstanding on the part of his recipients – the only response is G's affirmative 'right' in line 04 – A goes on to explain the *incident* more explicitly.

In line 05, A again prefaces *incident* with the indefinite article, this time in the context of asking a rhetorical question. The verb 'to be' in *what's* also sets up recipients to expect a noun phrase – thus, *an incident like this* seems to be treated as an article plus noun. That is, rather than asking something like 'what kind of incident', A treats the phrase as a term in need of an explanation. Next, he lists three African American men: two were murdered by police officers in Minnesota, and one was shot at in A's own community (lines 05–07). By naming the victim of a local shooting in between the names of two victims of shootings that were reported on the national stage, A makes it clear that he sees the local event as part of a national pattern. Thus, his additional explanation seems designed to provide context for both the word *incident* and for the topic of this call. At the same time, by offering additional explanation, he makes it clear that he sees such work as necessary. That is, his work to define this term alerts his recipients that they should not take the word for granted, and that A's understanding may be different from theirs. In response, G comes in seamlessly (line 09), building on A's work to define and provide context for 'these incidents' (line 13). In fact, as we will see in Extract 5, G seems to treat A's explanation as reasonable and necessary, as he moves on to suggest a variety of different ways to understand the three incidents referenced by A. Thus, A's work in these turns allows the conversation to unfold based on a presumably shared foundation.

In the next extract, we see similar work on the part of A, but this time in relation to a phrase associated with the national context. This excerpt occurs at the very beginning of the recording. Apparently, shortly before the recording had started, A had used the phrase 'two justice systems'. In line 01, G starts to explain how A is using the term, which then sparks an extended explication on the part of A.

(2) two justice systems
```
01    G:           so when A says there's two justice
02                 systems, (0.8) and now, thank god, finally,
03                 after 53 years, people on TV are saying this,
04                 s- a few, not many and they're all
05                 black, but it w- it-
06                 (0.2)
07    G:           [ you're mute- ]
08    P:           [ya- you're mut]ed A.
09    A:           a lot of people are saying it. Uh all the
10                 sensitivity going on in Minnesota, is about
11         →       that whole topic. There's two justice
12                 systems,
13    G:           right. >right right.<=
14    A:   →       =there's two, (.) kinds of treatment on a- on
15                 a- on a vehicle stop. (0.4) There's-
16    P:           coughs
17    A:   →       there's even the notion that vehicle stops
18                 occur, because you're driving while Black.
19    G:           right A but that they and we have tuh- tease
20                 out like- when people say that
```

In lines 09 through 11, A refers to the Minnesota protests against police brutality which were, at the time of this conversation, receiving extensive coverage in national news media. He explains that the protests were related to *that whole topic* (line 11), referring back to G's use of *two justice systems* (lines 01–02). This could be a reasonable stopping point. Speaker a has made the point that many people are talking about *two justice systems,* and has also connected the idea of unequal justice to protests in Minnesota. However, he goes on. First, he repeats the phrase in question, as if to emphasize its importance – despite the fact that there is no sign of trouble or confusion on the part of his recipients. If anything, G's multiple uses of *right* in line 13 may suggest some impatience (Stivers,

2004). A goes on to give *vehicle stops* as an example of unequal justice (lines 14 and 15) and then to clarify that Black people are more likely to be stopped while driving in the first place (lines 17 and 18). His use of *there's even the notion* (line 17) seems to add still more emphasis, or to upgrade the importance of what he is saying. Throughout these lines, A provides multiple layers of explanation for a phrase that, in fact, has been part of both local and national conversations for months. A, however, does not let these three words slide by, unexplored. The fact that he offers such a detailed explanation of what *he* means by 'two justice systems' suggests that he does not trust that the others in the conversation share his understanding of this important concept. G then goes on to provide a similar clarification, this time of the phrase *driving while Black*. We see this in Extract 3, below.

This next extract, taken from a longer turn on the part of G, starts where Extract 2 ends, with G responding to A's discussion of *driving while Black*. G begins by offering the kind of theoretical explanation we saw from A above, but then moves to a more personal reflection.

(3) the driving while black

```
01      G:            right A but that they and we have tuh- tease
02                    out like- when people say that like with the
03           →        driving while Black some African
04                    Americans are saying that like hey- this-
05                    they're just waking up tuh that, (0.2) but
06           →        some people are saying like (.) it's inevitable
07                    like it's predictable, like the number of stops
08           →        that I've gotten which is >quite a few,< um,
09                    (.) because of this or that, it doesn't end.
10                    eye roll Um, they'll say it's because
11                    you're Black. (.) so, when people s- >some
12                    people say< it's two justice systems that's
13                    what they mean (.) by it's two justice systems.
14      A:            [a- XX]
15      G:            [so     ] of course when a police officer
```

In lines 01 and 02, G starts by explicitly stating how important it is to *tease out* the use of phrases such as *driving while Black*. In line 02, he prefaces the phrase with the definite pronoun *the*, as if the words, when used together, become an object. This seems to add to the sense that the phrase is in need of special treatment, and that it cannot be simply tossed into a conversation without careful work. And, indeed, G shows his lack of trust in a shared understanding of the meaning of *driving while Black* by offering several accounts for how the term is used (lines 03–07). With his use of *some African Americans* (lines 03–04) and then *some people* (line 06), G clearly and unequivocally states that the phrase might be used differently by different groups of people. Even more importantly, he goes on to describe his own experiences as a Black man of being pulled over while driving (lines 07 and 08). This move is particularly powerful given that only one of the other participants on the call is Black. For the White community members with whom G is speaking, *driving while Black* is, at most, a theoretical idea. While they may or may not have experienced traffic stops, the *inevitable* and *predictable* (lines 06 and 07) nature of G's experience is not part of their lived reality. Thus, by taking the time to dig into a phrase that seems, on the surface, not to need further explanation, G makes it clear that there is no way that the phrase *driving while Black* could be understood from a single shared context for the participants in this conversation. He both brings his own context for the phrase into the conversation and resists the idea that all speakers on the call could understand *driving while Black* in the same way. Because G continues his turn at this point, going on to discuss how police officers might react to the phrase 'two justice systems', we do not see how others in the conversation react to his explanation. What is clear is that G makes the choice to offer a detailed exploration of what *driving while Black* means to him, a choice which suggests that he, at least, believes that an explanation is necessary.

By carefully explicating words and phrases that are commonly used in conversations about racism, A and G offer the terms back into the interaction as potential resources for further discussion (Goodwin, 2013). Extract 4, which takes place about 30 minutes into this conversation, shows an example of this process.

Line 01, below, comes at the end of an extended turn, where L has been describing what he sees as two possible paths for the group.

(4) travesty of justice
```
01    L:         that's ano- you know we're- we're sorta
02               on uh- a caught in this dilemma, I think.
03               (0.2) on the one hand we wanna reach out
04               and communicate, and build bridges and (.)
05               at- the- on the other hand ya'know we see
06               this (.) ya'know (0.2) travesty of justice
07        →      that's the laughing-$two justice
08               systems.$
```

In lines 03 and 04, L describes the possibility of *build*(ing) *bridges* with members of the community who may not share similar political views. He then contrasts that with fighting what he calls a *travesty of justice* (line 06). Then, in lines 07 and 08, he clarifies that the *travesty* is an example of *two justice systems*. His use of the definite article and his laughter suggest that he is aware of using a term that has been referred to earlier in the conversation. Importantly, not only do we see the phrase *two justice systems* reappearing in the conversation, but it is used in order to connect a local event with a national pattern. This connection is exactly what A seemed to be emphasizing in his careful explication of this and other phrases earlier in the conversation (see Extracts 1 and 3).

## Formulations: Explicitly referencing conversation

In this section, I look at another form of being explicit used by these participants. Here, speakers directly reference the fact that they are engaged in a conversation. As Garfinkel and Sacks (1970) write, and as I describe above, such moments can be described as formulations, in that speakers are offering a formulation of whatever activity they are engaged in.

Extract 5 seems to show a subtle misalignment between G and A, the source of which was an exchange we saw above, in Extract 2. G had suggested that the phrase *two justice systems* was not in common usage, especially among White people (Extract 2, line 04), and A then disagreed, saying that *a lot of people* were using the phrase (Extract 2, line 09). G, however, simply went on to discuss what people mean by the phrase. In this extract, as line 01 begins, G is suggesting that a police officer who hears *that* (referring to the phrase *two justice systems*) will probably be offended.

```
(5) what I'm saying
    01    G:              of course, when a police officer or a DA
    02                    hears that, (.) they're gonna be naturally
    03                    offended, [a:s, ] a person, [and] then
    04    A:              [yes.].            [yes ]
    05    G:              they'll also be offended as (.) officers of
    06                    the court, [bec]ause no one thinks that
    07    A:              [b- ]
    08    G:              they're doing the wrong thing. We
    09                    really have tuh absorb that into our bones
    10                    like nobody >if we think that we are
    11                    convincing someone hey finger
    12                    point-you're wrong, you're head
    13                    shake-(0.2), head shake-you're-
    14    A:     →        no [I- and what I'm saying is] (0.2)
    15    G:              [not ( )                     ]
```

```
16      A:              they're ta:lking about it.
17      G:              yeah >I agree with you A, I- we I've moved
18          →           on.< I'm just saying that
19      A:              [yeah.]
20      G:              [like w]hen [we when-]
21      A:                          [yeah-   ]
22      G:              an- an- I'm glad we're talking about it. and
23                      when A says to us, there's two justice
24                      systems, like, the police officers are
25                      immediately going tuh be defensive.
```

After a relatively quick disagreement regarding whether or not the phrase *two justice systems* is in general use (Extract 2), we see here a broader misalignment about the direction of the conversation. A attempts to continue discussing how many people are using the phrase *two justice systems*, and G focuses on how people will respond to hearing the phrase (lines 01–03, 05–06 and 08–13). While these speakers' almost anthropological concern with talk in their broader communities is fascinating, it is outside the scope of this chapter. Instead, my focus is on the work involved in this particular conversation. Rather than making their statements as if they were neutral, objective facts, A and G emphasize that they are only providing their points of view. This is accomplished in two ways. First, both speakers use the first-person pronoun in their formulations. A and G do not talk about what 'we' are saying, or what the conversation is about in general (as in 'we were talking about…'). Instead, they refer only to what they, as individuals, are saying. Here, it is interesting to note G's self-repair in line 17, where he uses the plural pronoun *we* and then quickly changes to *I*, as he discusses his own trajectory within the conversation. We can also note that when G does use *we* in line 22, announcing that he's glad *we're talking about it*, he is referring to the broader discussion of *two justice systems*, rather than to this particular interaction. In these brief turns, then, A and G emphasize the fact that they are speaking from a subjective, personal reality – rather than from a false and unexplored shared context.

Secondly, by essentially using reported speech to account for their own actions, A and G metaphorically take a step outside of the conversation. More importantly, they ask their recipients to do the same. They explicitly name what they are accomplishing as *saying that* X. This work makes space for disagreement, not just about meaning, but also about the direction of the conversation as a whole, and thus serves to resist the idea that all participants have similar, invisible beliefs about how a conversation about racism should unfold.

We see similar work in the next extract, which begins right after Extract 1, described above. As line 01 begins, A is explaining what he means by the word *incident*, making clear that it is part of a pattern of young African American men being shot.

(6) jump in
```
01    A:          Duante Wright, (0.2) um the uh- [name]'s
02                brother getting shot in the face (.) u:m
03                George Floyd, (.) ya [know. ]
04    G:                               [so bas-]
05          →     so- if I could excus- interrupt so basically
06                you can take any (.) not any there's a bunch
07                of different the:mes that could be put on top
08                of these .h incidents incidents .h that make
09                them fit into the system >when they say<
10                systematic racism (0.2) that's it- you could
11                look at it sociologically. You could look at
12                it. (.) like when he says microaggression
13                >that's <psychologically.> eh-
14                psychoeducational °frame°. Like um
15                (.) socialpsycho- euhm you could look at it
16                anthropologically. .h you could look at it
17                through feminism. so whenever something
18                is a system it means it's (0.2) <part of>
19                your ecology of your l↑ife right? And that
20                means its >everywhere.< And you can,
21                [>things  ]
22    A:    →     [>so let me] jump in.<
23                (0.2)
24    G:          things that are [everywhere]
25    A:                          [so what   ]
26    G:          can be looked at in different ways is
27          →     what I'm trying to say.
28    A:    →     and [when I jump in] on that, it says that,
29    P:              [(          )  ]
30    A:          when you're in one of those incidents,
31                your adrenaline is flying, what's in
32                control?
```

In line 04, G overlaps with the end of A's turn. The use of *so* in line 04 may provide a way to connect with what A has been saying. However, in a self-repair, G interrupts himself and inserts a formulation for the action he is taking (line 05). That is, whether or not he actually was interrupting A (and whether or not A takes G's turn as an interruption), G formulates his own turn as 'interrupting'. He also uses the conditional, saying *if I could* (line 05), which seems to further emphasize the delicate nature of his turn. Then, in line 22, in overlap with G, A provides his own formulation with the phrase *jump in,* colloquially used to describe taking a turn in a conversation.

These turns suggest an attentiveness to the possibility of differing interpretations in several ways. First, conversational actions which could be seen as dispreferred are clearly defined. It's as if the possible trouble caused by overlap might be diminished if the speaker at least makes clear that he is aware of what he is doing. Secondly, both of these turns (lines 05 and 22) highlight the speaker's own interpretation of their conversational actions, which may or may not be shared by their recipients. We can also note that A's use of 'let me' may suggest an orientation to the fact that he is prioritizing his own proposed trajectory for the conversation over that of G's (Hoey, 2020). In this way, his turn subtly emphasizes that he has his own point of view about where the conversation should go.

The next few turns provide additional examples of formulations. Despite A's attempt to gain the floor in line 22, G continues speaking, finishing with an announcement that this *is what I've been trying to say* (line 27). G's use of a formulation here, along with the addition of *trying,* may be in response to A's multiple attempts to speak, including his overlap in line 25. In any case, the addition of *what I'm trying to say* emphasizes that G is speaking from his own point of view, and the word *trying* seems to make the possibility of misunderstanding – or different understandings – even more explicit. In line 25, A tries to speak again. It is possible that his *so what* is the first part of something like *so what I'm trying to say,* but of course there is no way of knowing this. When A does gain the floor, he uses a similar structure as in his earlier attempt in line 22: *and when I jump in … it says that* (line 28). It is unclear whether the phrase *it says* is an unmarked and unrepaired misspeaking of *I say,* or whether A is describing more generally what *it means* when he takes a turn. In either case, we see here yet another example of a speaker prefacing a turn by saying that they are saying something.

Throughout this excerpt, both A and G are careful to attend to possible misinterpretations of their conversational actions. While their formulations may be designed to help them get the floor, they also signal the importance of not taking for granted that all participants on this call orient to the same expectations and rules regarding conversation (Turowetz & Rawls, 2021). In addition, these formulations draw attention to the fact of turn taking. By announcing that they are speaking (*interrupting, jumping in*), A and G remind recipients that a conversation is not an undifferentiated pile of words and actions, but rather consists of specific, authored turns, spoken by specific individuals.

In the final extract in this section, we see another kind of formulation. Here, along with formulating what a specific turn is accomplishing, a speaker explicitly names the larger action that is occurring as *having a conversation*. Line 01, below, is the continuation of an extended turn on the part of A. He has been discussing unconscious bias and has just suggested that the only way to 'deal with it' is via discussion.

(7) have a conversation with me

```
01    A:              until that gets to the conscious level to be
02                    discussed, you'll never, (0.2) you'll never,
03                    you'll never deal with it. (0.8) an- and right
04                    now it's not being dealt with. And the only
05                    conversation we're getting is on cable
06                    television, where they spend hours on it,
07                    whe:re, my wife gets tired of hearing
08                    about it.
09    G:              I do [too.]
10    A:       →      [but ] I'm sayin, there's a singular
11                    conversation, that- other people are turning
12                    the station, whereas we should be having
13             →      focus groups just like this one, and havin'
14             →      a conversation, between Races, jus' like
15                    this one, an- an not that everybody on this
16                    call agrees with what's being said, anuh
17             →      an- please speak up, (0.4) because I am.
18             →      An' I'm trying to say it flat out, that-
19                    anytime you have one of these incidents
20                    the only thing that's operating is your
21                    training, and that's automatic, and guess
22                    what? They're trained tuh have that bias.
23                    (0.8)
24    A:              tell me I'm wrong. have a conversation
25                    with me. Get on-
26    P:              I think that-
27    A:              Get on that level.
28    P:              I think you're very clear A, and I agree the
29                    way tuh um- kind've like get rid of the pus,
30                    is tuh open the thing up and acknowledge
31                    that there is all the pus there,
```

In line 10, we see A use a formulation similar to those in Extracts 5 and 6, when he explicitly describes his current action as *saying*. A goes on to offer a formulation of the overall activity he and others are engaged in, first describing it as a *focus group* and then as a *conversation between Races* (lines 13–15). Notably, he pauses there, and acknowledges that others may disagree with him – although it's not clear if the disagreement he imagines relates to his previous remarks about bias, or to the fact that what is occurring is a *focus group/conversation between Races*. Next, we see two more formulations of A's own actions. The first, in line 17, comes at the end of a TCU and the second, immediately following the first (line 18), seems to start off a new turn. Interestingly, A's construction in line 18 is similar to a formulation used by G earlier in the conversation (Extract 6, line 27) – in both cases, the speaker announces that he is *trying* to say something. Here, A adds the phrase *flat out*, as if to emphasize that he is being direct and explicit.

Throughout this excerpt, then, A makes room for multiple points of view via his formulations and requests. Additionally, while he orients to potential disagreement, his focus here is not just on what people may say. Rather, he does not seem to be sure that they will say anything at all. As I will discuss below, it is as if his trust in the act of conversation is eroded. At the same time, the numerous references to *saying*, *speaking* and *conversation* are a way of resisting the idea that all speakers have a common interpretation of what is occurring in this moment. By explicitly naming his actions, A makes it clear that his beliefs about what a *conversation* about racism should look like may differ from those of his fellow participants.

## Discussion and Conclusion

In this chapter, I have explored a conversation where speakers coming from differing racial backgrounds discussed topics related to racism. I have tried to show how participants oriented to a lack of the shared expectations that underlie most conversations (Garfinkel, 1967). More importantly, I have suggested that resisting these expectations is a way of resisting the racist fantasy of an objective, non-racialized reality to which all humans can refer, regardless of their backgrounds. For these speakers, this resistance took the form of being explicit in ways that, at first glance, might seem unnecessary. In some cases, which I am calling definitions, terms which might be assumed to have a shared referent for fellow participants were treated as in need of an account. In other situations, participants used formulations to be explicit about the fact that they were individual speakers with their own point of view. Below, I start with an exploration of the first set of cases, and then move on to discuss the second. I then describe some of the possible implications of this project, both for these participants and for conversations about racism more generally.

As Garfinkel and Sacks (1970) make clear, the words we use in most conversations are not treated as problematic. Thus, the extra explanations given to phrases associated with racism in this interaction seem noteworthy. Here, it is important to note that this conversation took place almost one year after the murder of George Floyd and the protests that followed that murder. Phrases such as *two justice systems* and *driving while Black* were part of a nationwide exploration of the pattern of African American men being murdered by police officers. In addition, at the time of this specific interaction, the participants had been working together for approximately half a year: Race, racism and the justice system had been topics for their shared conversations throughout that time. Thus, A and G had every reason to believe that their fellow participants were familiar with the words and phrases *the incident, two justice systems* and *driving while Black*. Even so, they were explicit and precise regarding their meaning. This precision points to a lack of trust in a shared context. Neither A nor G seems to take for granted that others in the conversation will construct meaning from a common set of experiences and understandings. At the same time, by carefully defining these words and phrases, G and A signal to their recipients that being explicit is necessary – that they should not take shared understanding as a given. Thus, their work can be seen as a way to resist and transform the insidious fantasy that there is a common, objective racial reality to which we can all refer (Baldwin, 1962; Rawls & Duck, 2020; Sue, 2015).

Along with being explicit regarding meaning, A and G use formulations to explicitly refer to the fact that they are engaged in a conversation. These formulations work to resist the assumption of a shared background by alerting recipients that a conversation about racism may not be a simple event, and that talking about racism may mean different things for different speakers. Thus, in their use of the first-person pronoun and in their emphasis on the action of *saying*, A and G highlight the idea of a personal point of view. These turns highlight the speaker behind the words, emphasizing the fact that there is an 'I' who has something to say – something that reflects a set of personal experiences and beliefs. Such formulations are simultaneously a reminder that these speakers do not rely on a shared set of understandings and rules for conversation *and* a powerful way for them to resist the essentially racist idea that such a shared understanding exists.

Finally, it is important to note that although there were eight speakers on this call, this analysis highlights the work of A and G – the only two African Americans in the interaction. Given that both A and G are Black men, their concern with how others are using and responding to talk about racism may be related to the kind of outsider perspective (or 'double consciousness') described by Du Bois (2003 [1903]), and also discussed by Turowetz and Rawls (2021) in their work on Garfinkel's trust argument. In fact, particularly in their explanations of terms, A and G seem to emphasize the differences between how White and Black people may understand language related to racism. In Extract 1, we see A describing the relationship between a local incident and a national issue. In Extract 2, A gets more and more specific about the ways that a relatively abstract term *(two justice systems)* plays itself out in the daily life of African Americans. And, in Extract 3, G describes not just the theoretical meaning of *driving while Black* but also his embodied experiences of driving as a Black man. In all three of these cases, then, the speakers highlight the ways that terms related to racism reflect patterns – patterns which are part of their own lived experiences. Regardless of their theoretical or political beliefs regarding racism, there is no way that the White participants in this call could share these experiences – and thus, these understandings of the words and phrases in question. Of course, there is no way to know if A and G would have engaged in this kind of extra work to explain themselves among an all-Black group of participants. And it is also unclear whether or not A and G were addressing each other along with the other speakers on their call. Indeed, as we see in Extracts 5 and 6, A and G do use formulations when speaking to each other. It is, of course, possible that this work is designed as a performance for the other recipients on the call. However, we can also remember that while G and A both identify as Black men, they bring differing specific and personal contexts into this conversation. Their work during this conversation can be seen as a way to transform two sets of assumptions regarding sameness. One is that there is an objective, non-racialized backdrop for conversations about racism, and the other is that all members of the same background would understand such a conversation in the same ways. Not taking a shared context for granted may mean hearing and acknowledging many kinds of differences we bring to our interactions, related to Race and to other aspects of our personal histories.

For analysts, this study builds on previous work related to mixed-Race conversations and to conversations about racism. It also provides another example of the way that, as Rawls and Duck (2020: 7) write, 'racism disrupts interaction'. In practical and personal terms, and as a member of the same community as these speakers, studying this interaction has been an exercise in experiencing hopelessness and hope at the same time. My sense is that by explicitly talking about their talk, these rural activists implicitly recognize a lack of trust in their ability to talk about racism. It is as if the world where conversation is built on shared understanding fades further away with each reference to 'two justice systems', 'driving while Black' or 'implicit bias'. At the same time, the very conversational choices that bring attention to a lack of common ground may serve to move forward the conversations that A so strongly calls for. Below, I briefly discuss this implication for the work of A and G, in terms of possible conversations with the wider community.

On a broader level, by designing their turns to highlight their understanding of what *conversation* consists of, these speakers offer a path towards conversations about racism with other members of their community. In fact, one reason I was initially interested in looking closely at a mixed-Race conversation about racism was because these participants are so clear that one of their goals is conversation across different backgrounds and viewpoints. Thus, the idea of conversation as political action comes up multiple times in this interaction (see, for instance, Extracts 4 and 7). Since the time of this conversation, these speakers, along with others in their group, have continued to work towards community conversations about Race and racism.

Throughout this chapter, I have tried to show how such conversations may ask us to rethink taken-for-granted aspects of interaction. That is, one first step in talking about racism may be to acknowledge that speakers from differing racial backgrounds do not and cannot share an understanding of either 'racism' *or* 'talking'. The definitions and formulations used by A and G might seem like tiny, unimportant ripples in an otherwise smooth stream of conversation – but they can also serve as reminders of the chasm between worlds created by our racist history. Thus, rather than pretending that they understand each other, these participants ask for a conversation that is precise, complex and often painful in the inequality, segregation and separation it uncovers. In this way, they offer us an example of what it might look like to start a conversation from 'where reality is' (Baldwin, 1992: 91).

### Note

(1) I follow the work of Rawls and Duck (2020) in capitalizing the words 'Race', 'White' and 'Black'. I do so in order to emphasize the fact that these words are based on social constructs, or as Rawls and Duck write, 'social facts'.

## Appendix: Transcription symbols for embodied actions

*words*         (italicised) embodied action
words-*words*   (dash) co-occurrence of embodied and verbal conduct

## References

Baldwin, J. (1962) As much truth as one can bear. *New York Times*, 14 January, p. 11. https://www.nytimes.com/1962/01/14/archives/as-much-truth-as-one-can-bear-to-speak-out-about-the-world-as-it-is.html
Baldwin, J. (1992) *The Fire Next Time*. Random House.
Du Bois, W.E.B. (2003 [1903]) *The Souls of Black Folk*. Signet Classic.
Essed, P. (1991) Understanding everyday racism: An interdisciplinary theory. Sage.
Garfinkel, H. (1967) *Studies in Ethnomethodology*. Prentice-Hall.
Garfinkel, H. and Sacks, H. (1970) On formal structures of practical actions. In J.D. McKinney and E.A. Tiryakian (eds) *Theoretical Sociology* (pp. 337–366). Appleton-Century Crofts.
Goodwin, C. (2013) The co-operative, transformative organization of human action and knowledge. *Journal of Pragmatics* 46 (1), 8–23.
Hoey, E.M. (2020) Self-authorizing action: On *let me X* in English social interaction. *Language in Society* 51, (95–118).
Jefferson, G. (1983) Notes on some orderliness of overlap onset. *Tilburg Papers in Language and Literature*, No. 28.
Psathas, G. (1995) *Conversation Analysis: The Study of Talk-in-Interaction*. Sage. https://doi.org/10.4135/9781412983792
Robles, J.S. and Shrikant, N. (2022) Interactional approaches to discrimination and racism in everyday life. In C. Tileaga, M. Augoustinos and K. Durrheim (eds) *The Routledge International Handbook of Discrimination, Prejudice and Stereotyping* (pp. 273–286). Routledge.
Rawls, A.W. and Duck, W. (2020) *Tacit Racism*. The University of Chicago Press.
Stivers, T. (2004) "No no no" and other types of multiple sayings in social nteraction. *Human Communication Research* 30, 260–293.
Sue, D.W. (2015) *Race Talk and the Conspiracy of Silence: Understanding and Facilitating Difficult Dialogues on Race*. Wiley.
Turowetz, J. and Rawls, A.W. (2021) The development of Garfinkel's 'Trust' argument from 1947 to 1967: Demonstrating how inequality disrupts sense and self-making. *Journal of Classical Sociology* 21 (1) 3 – 47.
Whitehead, K.A. (2015) Everyday antiracism in action: Preference organization in responses to racism. *Journal of Language and Social Psychology* 34, 374–389.

# 9 Using Racial Incompetence as a Comedic Device and Tacit Method of Anti-Racist Education

Lillian Cheeks and Kevin A. Whitehead

**Introduction**

A key contribution of Garfinkel's (1956:) early development of ethnomethodology is his demonstration of the systematic moral enforcement of common-sense knowledge – which Garfinkel describes as the 'socially sanctioned grounds of inference and action that people use in everyday life, and which they assume that other members of the group use in the same way' (1956: 185). As Garfinkel's famous 'breaching experiments' and other related research demonstrated, those who fail to use common-sense knowledge in designing their actions and interpreting the actions of others risk being seen as incompetent or even malicious (see e.g. Garfinkel, 1963, 1964, 1967; Heritage, 1984a).

Similar insights are evident in Sacks's (e.g. 1972a, 1972b, 1992) pioneering work on membership categorization devices. In demonstrating how membership categories serve as 'the store house and the filing system for the common-sense knowledge that ordinary people – that means ALL people in their capacity as ordinary people – have about what people are like, how they behave, etc.' (Schegloff, 2007: 469), Sacks's work describes the range of morally-enforced expectations, entitlements and obligations associated with categories. Consistent with Garfinkel's findings, these features of common-sense knowledge about categories provide a set of systematic resources that members of particular categories can use in designing their social actions, and observers can use in making inferences – including moral – about the nature and bases of their actions (also see e.g. Hester & Eglin, 1997; Kitzinger, 2005; Raymond, 2019; Raymond & Heritage, 2006; Whitehead, 2020).

These foundational insights are also consistent with Rawls and Duck's (2020) recent account of tacit racism, which takes inspiration from Garfinkel's work, combined with Du Bois's (2003 [1903]) theory of 'double consciousness', to describe how asymmetries of knowledge with respect to morally-enforced expectations associated with Black versus white participants are a systematic basis for the tacit (re)production of structural racism in everyday interactions. As Du Bois (2003 [1903]) notes, Black people, by virtue of their subjugated position in a racialized social order, are required as a matter of survival to know how white people see them and expect them to act. White people, on the other hand, are not similarly required to see themselves through Black people's eyes, or to contend with the severe consequences of not knowing about the world of the racial Other that Black people pervasively face. In examining how these racialized asymmetries of knowledge feature in everyday interactions, Rawls and Duck (2020) specify how racism may be tacitly produced in ways that are stark and painful for the Black people subjected to it, but to which the white people involved are able to remain completely oblivious (also see Mueller, 2017, 2020).

These common-sense race-based expectations and entitlements can also structure and/or serve as a set of resources for the production and reception of humor. For example, Scarpetta and Spagnoli's (2009) study of stand-up comedy demonstrates the importance of the respective categorial (including racial) identities of the comedian and audience members in shaping the treatment of jokes as humorous as opposed to offensive (including racist). More generally, there is long-standing recognition of incongruity between an expected action and an actually-produced one being a systematic device for the production of humor (see e.g. Glenn, 2003; Okazawa, 2021, 2022; Stokoe, 2008).

In using interactions portrayed in television situational comedies ('sitcoms'), Stokoe (2008) and Okazawa (2021, 2022) demonstrate how conversation analytic methods and findings can offer insights into how writers and actors of these scripted interactions display and exploit common-sense knowledge as a device for producing humorous incongruities. Specifically, Stokoe (2008) shows how sitcoms use portrayals of characters breaching the rules of turn-taking (Sacks *et al.*, 1974) and the expectations associated with preference organization (Pomerantz, 1984); Okazawa (2021) examines portrayals of characters' resisting categorization before acting in recognizably category-bound (Sacks, 1972a, 1972b, 1992) ways; and Okazawa (2022) examines how characters' utterances that are ambiguous with respect to whether they serve to categorize others are used to portray humorous misunderstandings that implicate category-related moral orders.

In this chapter, we build on these lines of research, and thereby contribute to critical conversation analytic research on race and racism, by considering how television sitcom and comedy sketch show writers and actors exploit features of the asymmetrical distribution of common-sense knowledge about race as a device for producing humor. Specifically, we consider cases in which white characters are portrayed as laughably incompetent with respect to common-sense knowledge about categories of people of color, thereby constructing humorous incongruities between expectations for how such knowledge *should* be used in designing and interpreting actions, and the ignorance portrayed through the characters' *actual* actions. In addition, we examine how this device serves as a tacit critique of the types of 'clueless' actions by white people – and the associated privilege and power they serve to (re)produce – that may be well-intentioned while nonetheless being experienced by recipients of color as hostile or racist (cf. Essed, 1991; Rawls & Duck, 2020).[1] We thus consider how these scripted exchanges tacitly provide anti-racist education, with the portrayed actions of the characters serving as cautionary tales of racial and/or racist incompetence.

## Data and Method

Our data set consists of recordings from interactional exchanges depicted in sitcoms and comedy sketch shows in which racial categories are treated as relevant, either through explicit mentions or via implicit allusions to race (see Whitehead, 2009) produced by the characters portrayed in the shows. The recordings were collected both from shows in which race is consistently topicalized ('racial comedies') and those in which it is made relevant more fleetingly while not being a consistent topical theme. Through repeated viewing of the recordings, we identified a range of ways in which common-sense knowledge about race was deployed and/or subverted in the portrayed interactions. The analysis we report below focuses on a collection (see Schegloff, 1996) of 87 cases in which characters are portrayed as exhibiting various forms of the racial incompetence described in the foregoing discussion. These cases were transcribed using Jefferson's (2004) conventions and subjected to detailed critical analysis grounded in ethnomethodological and conversation analytic principles.

As is unavoidably the case in undertaking any sociological analysis, we necessarily used our own members' knowledge in order to recognize the members' knowledge being used, often tacitly, by the writers and actors who produced our data (cf. Garfinkel, 1967). We have worked throughout our analysis, on a case-by-case basis, to describe such members' knowledge as explicitly as possible, especially when analyzing details that may be opaque for readers who are unfamiliar with the features of common-sense knowledge about race that are evidently being mobilized in portraying characters' racial incompetence.

The use of interactions portrayed in sitcoms as a data source departs from the focus on unscripted, naturally-occurring interactional data on which conversation analytic research was historically developed (see e.g. Heritage, 1984a; Sacks, 1984; Sacks *et al.*, 1974). However, in following a similar approach to that used by Stokoe (2008) and Okazawa (2021, 2022), as noted above, we treat these shows as scripted but nonetheless naturally-occurring products of writers' and actors' professional activities – as opposed to being generated by researchers, or for research purposes (cf. Potter, 2002; Speer, 2002). That is, we examine them for the ethnomethods and social resources evidently used to produce them, without proposing them to be equivalent to or a substitute for the types of 'real-world' interactions they portray.

## Analysis

The extracts we examine in this section were selected so as to include both cases that most clearly illustrate the core features of the phenomenon of portrayed racial incompetence around which our collection was built, and that demonstrate the range of variation in terms of specific types of racial incompetence evident across the collection (cf. Schegloff, 1996). We begin with relatively simple cases, characterized by the portrayal of characters' deficiency in one specific domain of common-sense racial knowledge, before progressing to cases that include more complex intersections of multiple domains of such incompetence.

Extract 1 shows an instance of the racial incompetence of *The Office's* main character, Michael Scott,[2] in relation to his lack of knowledge of race-based entitlement to produce particular actions – in this case, jokes. This is portrayed in Michael's reflections on the positive reception of a comedic routine performed by Black comedian Chris Rock in contrast to its negative reception when performed by Michael himself. Michael's reflections are contextualized by the portrayal of an all-staff diversity training, in which the trainer, Mr Brown, asks the participants about their familiarity with *the Chris Rock routine* (line 05), which he identifies as the *exact incident* he *was brought in here to respond to* (lines 03–04). Michael's role in the incident is then tacitly revealed by the camera panning to his concerned face (lines 08–09) after showing the other participants' unanimous displays of familiarity with the incident (line 06), before cutting to a documentary-style interview in which Michael provides his reflections (lines 13–20).

(1) *The Office*; S1, E2
```
01    Bro:    Um, so looking through the cards I've noticed that
02            many of you wrote down the same incident, which is
03            ironic because it's the exact incident I was brought
04            in here to respond to. Now how many of you are
05            familiar with the Chris Rock routine?
06            (3.0) ((camera pans to participants raising hands))
07    Bro:    Hm:.
08            (0.5) ((camera zooms in on Michael's concerned
09            facial expression))
10    Bro:    Very good.
11            (.)
12    Bro:    Okay.
13    Mic:    .hhh How come Chris Rock can ↑do a rou↓tine, (.)
14            and everybody finds it hilarious and groundbreaki:ng,
15            (0.5) ((swallows)) then I: go and do the exact ↑same
16            rout↓ine >↑same comedic timing,< .hh and people file
17            a complaint to corporate.
18            (1.2)
19            °Is it because I'm white, and Chris is Black?°
20            (2.0) ((looks upward, then tilts head))
```

Michael's reflections are formulated as a puzzle, as he questions why there was a difference between receptions of Rock's performance of the routine and his own. He uses the extreme case formulations (see Edwards, 2000; Pomerantz, 1986) *everybody, hilarious* and *groundbreaking* in characterizing the positive reception of Rock's performance of the routine (line 14), as well as in emphasizing that he had performed *the exact same routine* (lines 15–16) only to have it met with a *complaint to corporate* (line 17). Viewers with even passing familiarity with Rock's racial identity and his highly racialized and profane style of comedy could readily infer that race is the solution to the puzzle Michael has posed (cf. Whitehead, 2009). That is, as a white person, Michael lacks the race-based entitlement to make the kind of racialized jokes that Rock's routines typically include (also see Scarpetta & Spagnoli, 2009), and thus Michael's violation of this entitlement is what occasioned the complaint. Michael is thus portrayed as lacking basic awareness of these race-based entitlements, and as having failed to gain such awareness over an extended period of time following his performance of the routine, spanning the filing of the complaint and the completion of the diversity training.

Michael's portrayed racial incompetence is also underscored by two further features of his formulation of the puzzle, and his ongoing efforts to solve it. First, in noting that his performance of the routine was done with the *same comedic timing* (line 16) as Rock's, Michael conveys that he has entertained and ruled out the possibility that his performance was deficient in terms of its technical features. He is thereby portrayed as being able to reflect on a highly technical basis for comedic failure while being unable to recognize a racial basis that is more fitted to both the negative reception he received and the formal complaint and diversity training that followed. Second, as Michael pivots to speculating about whether he and Rock's respective racial categories constitute the basis for these negative responses (line 19), he is portrayed as having belatedly considered the potential importance of race in this regard. However, his whispering of this speculation portrays him as treating any possible use of a racial account as a delicate action (cf. Lerner, 2013) to which he has diminished entitlement, and thus as possibly implying that it is the people who used race to interpret his performance of the routine who acted inappropriately, rather than his own actions being inappropriate. Moreover, his displays of thoughtful consideration of this possibility that follow (shown in his upward glance and head tilt at line 20) treat this explanation as still a matter of uncertainty. He is thereby portrayed as confirming his inability to recognize race as the obvious solution to the puzzle even after explicitly entertaining it.

Extract 2, from the sketch comedy show *Saturday Night Live*, portrays a (white) British intern, Rob, making an ostensibly innocuous lunchtime suggestion that portrays him – and ultimately all of the other non-Black participants in the scene – as racially incompetent.[3] Like Extract 1, this case shows a character who exhibits incompetence with respect to knowledge of race-based entitlement to produce a particular action, with the proposed action in this case also intersecting with portrayed deficiencies in common-sense knowledge of racialized foods, names and places.

(2) *Saturday Night Live*; S45, E6
```
01    Hei:    Oka:y everybody, the contracts are officially signed.
02    Ego:    (H[AH!)[ALL RI::GHT!
03    Ken:         [WOO[::! ((claps))
04    Mel:              [AWESOME[:!
05    Hei:                      [Yeh, so lunch is on the company
```

| | | |
|---|---|---|
| 06 | | today:, and our:: n<u>e</u>w intern Ro:b from the UK is going |
| 07 | | to p<u>i</u>ck it <u>up</u>, thank you Ro:b! |
| 08 | Rob: | No problem! |
| 09 | | (1.0) ((audience laughter)) |
| 10 | Hei: | <u>So</u>, where we goin'? Any sug<u>ge</u>stions? |
| 11 | Mel: | Oh, there's a new <u>Thai</u> place that's supp<u>o</u>sed to be good. |
| 12 | | (0.2) |
| 13 | Ego: | Or how about p<u>i</u>zza? Th<u>a</u>t's always fun to share. |
| 14 | | (0.2) |
| 15 | Rob: | Sorry, (0.2) can <u>I</u> make a sug<u>ge</u>stion? |
| 16 | | (0.2) |
| 17 | Hei: | Oh, sure! |
| 18 | | (0.5) |
| 19 | Rob: | Cool. Well, uh: <u>I</u> thought we could- <u>I</u> could get us all |
| 20 | | those new ch<u>i</u>cken <u>sa</u>ndwiches from P<u>o</u>peye:'s. |
| 21 | | (4.5) ((audience laughter; dramatic music; camera |
| 22 | | zooms to Kenan's shocked facial expression)) |
| 23 | Ken: | From <u>where</u> now? |
| 24 | | (0.8) ((audience laughter)) |
| 25 | Rob: | From <u>Po</u>peye's. |
| 26 | | (0.2) |
| 27 | Rob: | They don't h<u>a</u>ve one back in England, but it's uh: |
| 28 | | just like KFC, right? |
| 29 | | (0.8) |
| 30 | Ken: | <u>No</u>. |
| 31 | | (1.2) ((audience laughter)) |
| 32 | Ken: | No, it's <u>not</u>. |
| 33 | | (1.0) ((audience laughter)) |
| 34 | Rob: | Well either way I thought I could go there <u>by</u> mys<u>e</u>lf |
| 35 | | and get li:ke (.) fifteen chicken <u>sa</u>ndwiches? |
| 36 | | (2.2) ((audience laughter; dramatic music; camera |
| 37 | | zooms to Ego's shocked facial expression)) |
| 38 | Ego: | <u>By</u> yours<u>elf</u>? |
| 39 | | (0.3) ((audience laughter)) |
| 40 | Ego: | So <u>you</u> wanna go to a <u>Po</u>peye's <u>alone</u>, in the <u>middle</u> of |
| 41 | | lunch <u>ru</u>sh, (.) then <u>bu</u>y up all the ch<u>i</u>cken ↑<u>sa</u>ndwiches? |
| 42 | | (0.8) ((audience murmur)) |
| 43 | Rob: | Yeah. That's the pl<u>a</u>n. |
| 44 | | (0.6) ((audience laughter)) |
| 45 | Ken: | Is there even a <u>Po</u>peye's a<u>round</u> here? |
| 46 | | (0.5) |
| 47 | Rob: | Sure. (0.2) I:: found one just down the street here on |
| 48 | | uh:: Frederick Douglass B<u>ou</u>levard. |
| 49 | | (2.5) ((audience laughter; dramatic music; camera zooms |

| 50 |      | to Ego and Kenan's shocked facial expressions)) |
|----|------|---|
| 51 | Ken: | Did you say (.) Frederick Douglass Boulevard? |
| 52 |      | (0.8) ((audience laughter)) |
| 53 | Rob: | Yeah, th<u>a</u>t's it, it's right betwee:n (.) the l<u>i</u>quor store |
| 54 |      | and thee F<u>oo</u>t Locker. |
| 55 |      | (6.0) ((dramatic music; camera pans to Ego and Kenan's |
| 56 |      | shocked facial expressions; Ego stands up, shaking head)) |
| 57 | Mel: | Sounds great, I l<u>o</u>ve chicken s<u>a</u>ndwiches. |
| 58 |      | (0.8) ((audience laughter)) |
| 59 | Hei: | Sure, I'm down, ((continues)) |

In line 06, Heidi introduces Rob by not only stating that he is the new intern, but also that he is from the UK, thereby using two categories despite, as Sacks's (1972a, 1972b) economy rule notes, only one category being required in order to do adequate reference. The mention of Rob's citizenship category appears to be designed to convey Rob's status as an 'outsider', foreshadowing that this category will account for some future conduct he is going to produce. Following discussion of where they might get lunch from (lines 10–13), Rob suggests getting the *new chicken sandwiches* from the fast-food restaurant, Popeye's (lines 15–20). This suggestion invokes the nationwide phenomenon at this time of extremely high demand for these sandwiches following their introduction in Popeye's franchises, which was accompanied by media reports of numerous Popeye's locations running out of the sandwiches, and of violent conflicts between customers who were waiting to buy them. Rob's suggestion to go there and buy these sandwiches for multiple people (lines 19–20 and 34–35) is thus recognizable as a provocative and potentially recognizably racialized attempt to claim for white consumption an item to which Black people might claim a special entitlement.[4]

The nonchalant way Rob produces this suggestion portrays him as seeing it as a completely unproblematic one – and thus underscores his displays of the privilege and power of one who takes for granted his right to pursue sought-after items without regard to the potential consequences of doing so. In contrast, immediately following Rob's initial delivery of the suggestion, there is a substantial silence (line 21), during which the camera zooms, accompanied by dramatic music, to show the shocked expression on the face of Kenan (a Black character), thereby conveying the problematic nature of the suggestion. While the basis for these contrasting orientations by the characters is not explicitly revealed, their visibly contrasting racial categories, along with Rob having previously been identified as being from the UK, provides for the inference that Rob's suggestion should be immediately recognizable by any 'insider' as ill-advised and/or dangerous. The audience laughter that accompanies this move displays their appreciation of the humor produced by the juxtaposition of Rob's nonchalance and Kenan's shock, and indicates their appreciation of the category-based common-sense this contrast trades on. Moreover, this juxtaposition is further underscored by Kenan's subsequent incredulous question (line 23), which uses other-initiated repair as a vehicle for challenging what Rob has proposed (see Schegloff, 1997) – and is registered as such by the audience's responsive laughter (line 24). As Schegloff (1997) observes, the use of this practice relies on the recipient recognizing that the initiation of repair is also implementing a challenge, which they can display by responding in a way that takes up both the repair and the challenge. Rob's casual repetition of his suggestion (line 25) portrays him as taking up the repair while remaining oblivious to the challenge, and thus as being incompetent both at registering Kenan's shock and at recognizing the deficiency in his own common-sense knowledge that underpins the disjuncture between them.

The nationality-based account for Rob's ignorance is then further elaborated, as he reports the absence of Popeye's in England, before proposing that *it's just like KFC* (lines 27–28). Kenan's immediate and blunt response (line 30) – produced in a preferred turn shape (Pomerantz, 1984) despite its disalignment with what Rob has proposed – conveys the stark contrast between Rob and Kenan's understandings of the implications of Rob's suggestion. Rob's response again portrays him as failing to register Kenan's shock, and the associated asymmetry in their respective category-bound common-sense knowledge, as he produces a modified repeat of his plan, now explicitly proposing to carry it out *by myself* (line 34).

Following this 'doubling down' by Rob, the device of using dramatic music while zooming in on a character's shocked facial expression is used once again, this time showing another Black character, Ego, with such an expression (lines 36–37). Ego's character also uses a similar repair-as-challenge practice to that previously deployed by Kenan's character, displaying similar shock in response to Rob's proposal. Specifically, she uses extreme case formulations to convey the extreme nature of his proposal, problematizing his stated intention to carry out his plan alone, at a particularly busy time, and to *buy up all* the sandwiches (lines 38 and 40–41) – and thus underscoring his extreme incompetence. Once again, Rob nonchalantly re-confirms his plan (line 43), thereby continuing his portrayal as failing to register the basis of Ego's challenge, or even that she has challenged it at all, with the audience's laughter (line 44) showing their recognition and appreciation of Rob's multi-layered incompetence.

As the sketch continues, the specifically racial dimension of Rob's incompetence is made more explicit, as he displays a lack of understanding of the racialized location of the specific Popeye's restaurant that he reports planning on visiting (lines 47–48 and 53–54),⁵ occasioning further displays of shock by both Kenan and Ego, accompanied by the now-familiar camera zoom and dramatic music (lines 49–50 and 55–56), separated by a further round of incredulous questioning by Kenan (line 51). The culmination of the portrayal of Rob's incompetence as primarily race-based, rather than arising first and foremost from his nationality, is produced through a twist in the form of portrayals of similar incompetence by two other characters, Melissa and Heidi, who readily endorse Rob's suggestion (lines 57 and 59). The categorial identities of these characters contrast with Rob's in that both are evidently portrayed as Americans, thus eliminating nationality – both Rob's and theirs – as an adequate account for their ignorance. This leaves race as the 'obvious' account (cf. Whitehead, 2009), highlighted by the recognition of the two Black characters (Kenan and Ego) of the shocking nature of Rob's suggestion, in contrast to the portrayed oblivion of all of the non-Black characters (Rob, Melissa and Heidi).⁶

Extract 3 shows an exchange from *Black-ish* featuring one of the show's main (Black) characters, Andre 'Dre' Johnson, interacting with a (white) colleague, Josh, at the advertising company at which he works, with additional commentary provided by a narrator voiced by Andre's character. Josh is initially (like the characters in Extracts 1 and 2) portrayed as incompetent with respect to knowledge of race-based entitlements in relation to his own actions, before subsequently also exhibiting deficient knowledge of how members of another racial category – specifically, Black people – might typically formulate a mundane action.

(3) *Black-ish*; Pilot
```
01    Jos:    Yo! Doctor DRE:!
02    Nar:    This is Josh.
03            (.)
04    Dre:    Um,
05    Nar:    Not an honorary brother.
06    Dre:    Just Andre.
07    Jos:    Right, sorry Andre? Hey bro, w- oh I mean Andre.
08            Listen, we're workin' on this Folger's copy and
09            we wanted to know how you think °a Black guy°
10            would say (.) 'good morning'.
11    Dre:    Hmm? ((scoffing)) Probably just like that.
12    Jos:    Cool, >cool cool cool.<
```

In greeting Andre (line 01), Josh addresses him using the name of Black rapper Dr. Dre, doing so with increased volume and stretching on the *e* sound evidently designed to portray his adoption of African American English (AAE). Immediately after this greeting, the narrator introduces Josh (line 02) before informing viewers that he is *Not an honorary brother* (line 05). This conveys that Josh lacks the entitlement to use AAE in the way he has just done, with the emphasis on the word *Not* further underscoring the unequivocal nature of this lack of entitlement, and thus the incompetence in the design of Josh's greeting. Also noteworthy is Andre's initial hesitation following the greeting (line 04), which marks the dispreference (Pomerantz, 1984) of the otherwise blunt correction he issues at line 06. In addition to the marked departure from the preference for self-correction (Schegloff *et al.*, 1977) constituted by this utterance, Andre's failure to return Josh's greeting underscores his unequivocal disaffiliation from Josh (cf. Heritage, 1984a), thus further exposing the incompetence Josh has exhibited. Then, after registering Andre's correction, issuing an apology, and repeating Andre's full name with emphasis on the syllable he had omitted in his greeting, Josh immediately exhibits similar incompetence by addressing Andre with the informal term *bro* – which appears to be a further instance of his adoption of AAE – before initiating self-repair (Schegloff *et al.*, 1977) to instead use an emphasized repetition of Andre's name (line 07).

Josh then issues an inquiry (lines 07–10) that portrays the intersection of the type of incompetence in relation to his *own* actions that he has already displayed with further racial incompetence in relation to knowledge of the actions of *others*. With regard to the latter, this inquiry displays that he and the group on behalf of which he reveals he is making the inquiry (through his use of collective pronouns in lines 08 and 09) lack knowledge of Black men's ways of saying *good morning* (lines 9–10) – with this ignorance, as Andre's derisive response (line 11) conveys, involving not knowing that there is no characteristically 'Black' way of doing this. Josh's formulation of the inquiry also further portrays his incompetence in relation to race-based entitlements associated with his own actions, as his whispered reference to a hypothetical *Black guy* (line 09) treats the simple mention of this compound category as a matter of diminished entitlement on his part (cf. Extract 1), while he concurrently fails to register any awareness of how the inquiry itself may implicate his racial incompetence.

In contrast to the incompetence Josh enacts in Extract 3 by incorrectly assuming a category-bound way of producing an action, a character in Extract 4 is portrayed as producing an action in a markedly category-bound way while failing to take into account its ill-fitted 'recipient design' (Sacks et al., 1974: 727) for a recipient who is a member of a different racial category. In this case, from *Fresh off the Boat*, the Huangs, a Taiwanese-American family, are greeted by a group of women from their new neighborhood. During the course of the exchange, one of the women, Deidre, produces a highly personal report in a way portrayed as bound to the racial category (white) of which Deidre is evidently a member (cf. Rawls & Duck, 2020). Deidre also exhibits, throughout the exchange, various intersecting forms of racial incompetence that are similar to – but also extend – those seen in previous extracts. These include deficiencies in common-sense knowledge about the family's racial category in relation to names, physical appearances, geographical origins and linguistic abilities, combined with a complete lack of self-awareness in relation to these deficiencies.

(4) *Fresh off the Boat*; S1, E1

```
01    Dei:    >Hi I'm Deidre, this is Amanda, this is Samantha,
02            this is Lisa, this is Carol Joan.<
03            (.)
04    Dei:    Welcome?
05    Jes:    Thank you. I'm Jessica.
06    Dei:    ↑O:h::, I was expecting something a little more
07            exotic, but I love the name Jessica. I had a
08            sorority sister with that name, she died in a
09            horrible riptide accident. .h ↑We ↓dedicated a
10            section of the highway to her.
11            (.) ((camera pans to Jessica's incredulous stare))
12    Dei:    ↑Anyway ↓where are you guys ↑fro:m?
13            (0.2)
14    Edd:    My parents were born in Taiwa:n, (.) but my brothers
15            and I were born in DC.
16    Dei:    ↑O::h::, <YOUR ENGLISH IS VERY GOOD!> uhuh huh huh!
17    Jes:    Are you all sister?
18    Wom:    UHUH HUH HUH HUH HUH HUH HUH!
19    Dei:    Anywhoo, ((continues, without answering Jessica's
20            question))
```

From the outset of the interaction, the women are evidently portrayed as 'hyper-white:' They are all rollerblading, their outfits are matching or similar in style, they all adopt similar bodily comportment, and they all have blonde hair protruding from their helmets. The fast pace at which Deidre speaks as she introduces them, and the names of the women she lists (lines 01–02), may also be designed to be heard as bound to the compound category 'white woman'. These features thus establish a context in which the women's (and especially Deidre's) subsequent conduct can be understood as possibly similarly bound to this racial category, in contrast to that of the Huangs.

After Jessica speaks for the first time to introduce herself (line 05), Deidre is portrayed as hearing Jessica's name as surprising, as shown by the turn-initial 'change of state' token, *Oh* (Heritage 1984b; also see Wilkinson & Kitzinger, 2006), along with her subsequent report of having expected *something a little more exotic* (lines 06–07). Deidre is thus portrayed as racially incompetent by virtue of failing to recognize that a person of Jessica's evident racial category might have a name like hers. Deidre's subsequent 'touched-off' (Sacks, 1992, Vol. I: 761) report that she *had a sorority sister with that name* (lines 07–08) may be designed as tacitly treating the name Jessica as hearably white, thereby accounting for her portrayed surprise at Jessica's name, with this possibility resting on a common-sense assumption that Deidre's sorority was as white as her current companions.

Deidre then continues, building on the touched-off mention of her sorority sister by reporting her death (lines 08–09). Deidre's rapid transition from greetings and introductions to nonchalantly talking about the death of someone close to her appears designed to portray category-bound 'oversharing', with the camera panning to Jessica's incredulous stare and her lack of any further response (line 11) conveying her treatment of it as such. In addition, her report of the death as arising from swimming in the ocean (an activity apparently portrayed as bound to the category 'white'), and of the group's subsequent naming of a section of highway in her memory (lines 09–10), seem to be designed to reinforce the race-based privilege and power Deidre and her social network are portrayed as enacting.

Deidre then shifts rapidly away from her discussion of the death and its aftermath, thereby further underscoring its nonchalant and poorly recipient-designed character, to launch a query about where the family is from (line 12). After Eddie (Jessica's son) speaks for the first time to answer her (lines 14–15), Deidre's response (line 16) further underscores her racial incompetence, as she again displays surprise with a stretched turn-initial *Oh*, before complimenting Eddie on his good English. She is thereby portrayed as treating his racialized appearance as more salient to her expectations of his English-speaking ability than his just-previous report of his place of birth. This incompetence is also emphasized by the markedly raised volume and slow, careful enunciation of her talk as she speaks to Eddie, which – particularly when contrasted with the previous extremely fast pace of her talk, and despite having just shown her recognition of his competence as an English speaker – portrays her as condescendingly assuming he may have trouble understanding spoken English.

Jessica then remarks on the similar appearance of the group of women by asking if they are *all sister* (line 17), with this question further (although still tacitly) conveying to the audience their uniform appearance and conduct in terms of categories such as race, gender and class. The women's collective laughter in response (line 18), and Deidre's failure to subsequently answer the question (lines 19–20), portrays their treatment of the question as ridiculous, and thus their orientation to Jessica as an incompetent perceiver of the meaning of their similar appearance. This further conveys Deidre's own lack of awareness of her and the other women's own stereotypical white middle-class femininity, despite the inferences they have made about Jessica and Eddie's racialized appearance. They are thus portrayed as exhibiting the type of treatment of whiteness as 'invisible' that scholars building on Du Bois's work (e.g. Frankenberg, 1993; Hill, 2008; Lipsitz, 2006; also see Whitehead & Lerner, 2009) have described.

Our final case, Extract 5, shows further instances of a range of the types of racial incompetence evident in the previous extracts, combined with a portrayal of incompetence in relation to common-sense knowledge associated with accurately racially categorizing others, including intersecting knowledge of racial phenotypes, names and food preferences. This case is from an episode of *Seinfeld* in which one of the show's main characters, Elaine, has been discreetly attempting to investigate the racial identity of her new boyfriend, Darryl. Having gathered inconclusive evidence based on his appearance, home decor and aspects of his conduct, Elaine has concluded that he is indeed Black after he attributed a couple staring at them to their status as a biracial couple. As the extract (showing a subsequent exchange in the diner involving Elaine, Darryl and an evidently Black waitress) unfolds, it is revealed that both Elaine and Darryl had erroneously racially categorized the other.

(5) *Seinfeld*; S9 E15
```
01    Wai:    °Here you go.°
02    Ela:    Long day?
03    Wai:    Yeah, I just worked a triple sh↑ift!
04    Ela:    pt I hear ya sister.
05            (1.0) ((audience laughter))
06    Wai:    Sister?
07            (0.2)
```

| | | |
|---|---|---|
| 08 | Ela: | Yeah.=hh It's ok<u>a</u>y, my <u>boy</u>friend's Bl<u>a</u>ck, here he is, see? |
| 09 | | (0.5) ((audience laughter; waitress has skeptical |
| 10 | | expression)) |
| 11 | Dar: | Hi El<u>ai</u>ne. |
| 12 | | (0.5) |
| 13 | Ela: | °Hey.° |
| 14 | | (0.5) ((Waitress looks quizzically at Daryll; |
| 15 | | audience laughter)) |
| 16 | Wai: | <u>He</u>'s Bl<u>a</u>ck? |
| 17 | Ela: | Y<u>e</u>h. |
| 18 | | (1.5) ((Daryll looks at Waitress, Elaine with surprise)) |
| 19 | Dar: | I'm Bl<u>a</u>ck? |
| 20 | | (1.0) ((audience laughter)) |
| 21 | Ela: | Aren't you? |
| 22 | Wai: | I'll <u>gi</u>ve you a couple minutes to dec<u>i</u>de. |
| 23 | | (2.0) ((audience laughter)) |
| 24 | Dar: | What are you <u>talk</u>ing about. |
| 25 | | (0.2) |
| 26 | Ela: | You're Bl↑a::ck, you <u>said</u> we were an interracial <u>couple</u>. |
| 27 | Dar: | We <u>are</u>. |
| 28 | | (0.2) |
| 29 | Dar: | Because you're His<u>pan</u>ic. |
| 30 | | (3.0) ((audience laughter, Elaine looks surprised)) |
| 32 | Ela: | I <u>am</u>? |
| 33 | Dar: | <u>Are</u>n't you? |
| 34 | Ela: | <u>No</u>::! Why would you th<u>i</u>nk that? |
| 35 | Dar: | Your name's Benes. |
| 36 | | (0.2) |
| 37 | Dar: | Your <u>hair</u>! |
| 38 | | (0.2) |
| 39 | Dar: | And you kept taking me to those <u>Spa</u>nish restaurants. |
| 40 | | (0.6) ((audience laughter)) |
| 41 | Ela: | Huh! That's because I thought you were Bl<u>a</u>::ck. |
| 42 | | (2.0) ((audience laughter, Daryll looks confused)) |
| 43 | Dar: | ↑Why would you take me to a Sp<u>a</u>nish restaurant |
| 44 | | because I'm Bl<u>a</u>ck? |
| 45 | | (0.8) ((audience laughter, Elaine wincing)) |
| 46 | Ela: | °<u>I</u> don't think we should be talking about this.° |
| 47 | | (1.2) ((audience laughter)) |
| 48 | Dar: | So what <u>are</u> you? |
| 49 | Ela: | I'm wh<u>i</u>te. |
| 50 | Dar: | So (0.2) we're just a (0.5) couple of wh<u>i</u>te people? |
| 51 | | (1.2) ((audience laughter)) |
| 52 | Ela: | I <u>g</u>uess. |

```
53                    (1.2) ((audience laughter))
54      Dar:          Huh=hhhhh
55      Ela:          Yeah.=hhh
56                    (1.5) ((audience laughter))
57      Ela:          So do you wanna go to The Gap?
58      Dar:          Sure! ((starts to grab coat and stand up;
59                    audience laughter))
```

In her interaction with the waitress prior to Darryl's arrival at the diner (lines 01–08), Elaine is portrayed as violating a race-based entitlement by using the Black-identified address term *sister* (line 04), with the waitress's delayed and questioning response (lines 05–06) signaling the incompetence Elaine has displayed in doing this. In response, Elaine claims a proxy entitlement to use this term by virtue of Darryl's racial identity just as he arrives (line 08), with the audience's laughter and the waitress's skeptical facial expression marking the dubiousness of both this claim to entitlement and possibly also to Darryl's status as Black, thereby underscoring Elaine's racial incompetence.

The waitress then explicitly conveys the dubiousness of Darryl's claimed membership in the category 'Black' by questioning it directly (line 16), with both her presumed expertise at recognizing co-members of this category and the way in which she is portrayed as immediately recognizing Elaine's error serving as a competent contrast to the painstaking – but ultimately erroneous – efforts Elaine has made to accurately categorize him. Elaine's affirmative and unequivocal response (line 17) serves as the key moment at which Darryl is shown to become aware of how she has mis-categorized him, as conveyed in his surprised look at both the waitress and Elaine (line 18), and his similar questioning of Elaine's assertion (line 19). The waitress's ironic response (which treats their deliberation about Darryl's racial category as akin to deciding what to eat) and accompanying audience laughter (lines 22–23) then further underscore the exposure of Elaine's incompetence portrayed here.

Elaine's protestations (line 26) in the face of Darryl's questioning (line 24) following the waitress's departure then serve as a launching point for exposing Darryl as having similarly incompetently mis-categorized Elaine as Hispanic (lines 27 and 29), with his ensuing account of his reasoning for this categorization listing ambiguous evidence in relation to her name, hair and her repeatedly taking him to Spanish restaurants (lines 34, 36 and 38). Darryl is thereby portrayed as incompetent by virtue of using ambiguous evidence to arrive at an unequivocal – but erroneous – assumption of Elaine's racial category, thereby also solving the puzzle of why he made the comment about them being a biracial couple that she had used as a basis for her own unequivocal assumption about his racial category.

Darryl's mention of Spanish restaurants is then used to further upgrade Elaine's portrayed racial incompetence, as she claims to have taken him to these restaurants because she thought he was Black (line 40). The nonsensical nature of this proposed category-food preference is conveyed in a number of ways in the ensuing moments, including Darryl's confused look and accompanying audience laughter (line 41), his subsequent direct questioning of her reasoning (lines 42–43), Elaine's pained look and further audience laughter (line 44), and her whispered acknowledgment of how being heard talking in this way may be discrediting for them (line 45), followed by another round of audience laughter (line 46).

The path out of the exchange is then begun by Darryl's direct question about Elaine's racial category (line 47), which is produced in a way possibly designed to parody a form of this question stereotypically associated with racially incompetent white people. Following Elaine's unequivocal self-identification as 'white' (line 48), and their reciprocal acknowledgment that they are, as Darryl puts it, *just a couple of white people* (lines 49 and 51), Darryl displays what appears to be designed as a mixture of mild surprise and disappointed resignation at this revelation (line 53), and Elaine aligns with this sentiment (line 54). This may be designed to link back to the proxy entitlement that Elaine claimed in addressing the waitress at the outset of the scene, and the similar social capital claimed by Darryl in his prior remarks on them being an interracial couple, with their displays of disappointment registering their loss of these ostensible benefits, and thereby further exposing the racial incompetence they had embraced in treating their relationship as a source of such benefits.

As a final punchline to the scene, Elaine invites Darryl to *The Gap* (line 56), with the turn-initial *So* in this invitation marking it as an upshot of the preceding exchange (Raymond, 2004), and thus treating the activity of going to this store as bound to the category 'white'. Darryl's enthusiastic acceptance of this invitation (line 57) shows his alignment with this as an activity well-suited to their newly-discovered status as an all-white couple, and the closing of the exchange in this way underscores their unproblematic ability to return to life-as-white-people following the potentially embarrassing racial incompetence they have both exhibited.

## Discussion and Conclusion

As our analysis demonstrates, the writers and actors of exchanges such as these exploit common-sense knowledge about a wide range of features associated with particular racial categories – including category-bound actions and activities, and associated entitlements; foods, names and places; linguistic practices and abilities; interpersonal relationships; and observable (phenotypical) features – in order to portray instances of racial incompetence grounded in deficits with respect to such knowledge. Moreover, this incompetence can be underscored by the derisive or otherwise disaffiliative responses of characters on the receiving end of such displays. The writers thereby exploit ordinary structures and practices of interaction – most centrally in these cases relating to preference organization (Pomerantz, 1984; Heritage, 1984a) – to convey to viewers the unequivocal nature of the breaches that have been portrayed. In doing so, they produce tacit critiques of white racial incompetence and, by extension, of the nonchalant privilege and power that displays of such ignorance render visible (cf. Mueller, 2017, 2020).

For viewers who recognize these types of incompetence from their own real-world observations and experience, their portrayal in exaggerated or parodied ways can serve as a comedic device (cf. Okazawa, 2021, 2022; Stokoe, 2008), converting actions that might be experienced as awkward or harmful in real-world settings into occasions for humor. In order to appreciate the humor in these exchanges, however, viewers must themselves be sufficiently competent to recognize the expectations being breached by characters portrayed as racially incompetent. These portrayals may thus function as cautionary tales for viewers who may have been unaware of their own incompetence, and thus of the ways in which people of color may routinely experience their everyday actions as exhibiting tacit or everyday racism (Essed, 1991; Rawls & Duck, 2020), even when they may be well-intentioned. That is, the exaggerated portrayals of characters' incompetence offer highly exposed and unequivocal indications of the problematic character of exchanges whose real-world realizations may be more equivocal or ambiguous. Also significant in this regard is the possibility for portraying openly disaffiliative responses of the recipients of instances of such incompetence, with fictional characters unencumbered by the constraints to which participants responding to real-world instances of possible racism are evidently systematically oriented (see e.g. Robles, 2015; Stokoe, 2015; Whitehead, 2015). These responses may thus further educate viewers on racial (in)competence, with the fictionalized, comedy-based format facilitating their learning in tacit, less direct and/or confrontational ways than are typically involved in everyday conversational or formal anti-racist educational interventions (cf. Scarpetta & Spagnolli, 2009; Whitehead, 2009; Whitehead & Wittig, 2004). In the process, however, they also serve to keep racial categories and associated common-sense knowledge in 'good repair' (Heritage, 1984a: 210), with their use in this way thus serving as a mechanism for their reproduction as shared bases for competent action and inference, even if in designedly humorous and/or anti-racist ways.

## Acknowledgements

Reports of portions of this chapter were presented at the 7th Annual UC Davis Symposium on Language Research in March 2021; at the 116th Annual Meeting of the American Sociological Association in August 2021; and for the Conversation Analytic Working Group and the Race and Ethnicity Working Group at the University of California, Los Angeles in March 2023. We are grateful to the audiences of these presentations for their constructive feedback, and to Hansun Zhang Waring, Nadja Tadic and the anonymous reviewers for their helpful suggestions on earlier drafts of the chapter.

## Notes

(1) Also cf. Joyce, Humă, Ristimäki, Almeida and Doehring's (2021) analysis of the sexist practices of 'mansplaining'.
(2) Speaker designations in the transcripts throughout our analysis consist of the first three letters of the character's name or (for unnamed characters) situationally relevant category.
(3) Since none of the characters in this sketch other than Rob are named, we have referred to them using the first names of the actors who play them: Heidi (Gardner), Ego (Nwodim), Kenan (Thompson) and Melissa (Villaseñor).
(4) This racialized entitlement is explicitly conveyed in a later part of the sketch (not transcribed), in which Kenan's character explains to Rob's that *there's not many things in this country where our people get first dibs, but the Popeye's chicken sandwich, that's one of 'em.*
(5) The street name and businesses he mentions here appear to be designed to invoke common sense knowledge of these as regular features of predominantly Black neighborhoods.
(6) As the sketch continues, Rob's displays of incompetence are generalized beyond race (while possibly still intersecting with race), including his statement of his intention to cut in line, and his willingness to yell at a hypothetical female cashier in the service of securing the sandwiches.

## References

Du Bois, W.E.B. (2003 [1903]) *The Souls of Black Folk*. Signet Classic.
Edwards, D. (2000) Extreme case formulations: Softeners, investment, and doing nonliteral. *Research on Language and Social Interaction* 33 (4), 347–373.
Essed, P. (1991) *Understanding Everyday Racism: An Interdisciplinary Theory*. Sage.

Frankenberg, R. (1993) *White Women, Race Matters: The Social Construction of Whiteness*. University of Minnesota Press.
Garfinkel, H. (1956) Some sociological concepts and methods for psychiatrists. *Psychiatric Research Reports* 6, 181–195.
Garfinkel, H. (1963) A conception of, and experiments with, 'trust' as a condition of stable concerted actions. In O.J. Harvey (ed.) *Motivation and Social Interaction* (pp. 187–238). Ronald Press.
Garfinkel, H. (1964) Studies of the routine grounds of everyday activities. *Social Problems* 11 (3), 225–250.
Garfinkel, H. (1967) *Studies in Ethnomethodology*. Prentice-Hall.
Glenn, P. (2003) *Laughter in Interaction*. Cambridge University Press.
Heritage, J. (1984a) *Garfinkel and Ethnomethodology*. Polity.
Heritage, J. (1984b) A change of state token and aspects of its sequential placement. In J.M. Atkinson and J. Heritage (eds) *Structures of Social Action* (pp. 299–345). Cambridge University Press.
Hester, S. and Eglin, P. (1997) *Culture in Action: Studies in Membership Categorization Analysis*. University Press of America.
Hill, J.H. (2008) *The Everyday Language of White Racism*. Wiley-Blackwell.
Jefferson, G. (2004) Glossary of transcript symbols with an introduction. In G.H. Lerner (ed.) *Conversation Analysis: Studies from the First Generation* (pp. 13–23). John Benjamins.
Joyce, J.B., Humă, B., Ristimäki, H.-L., Almeida, F.F.d. and Doehring, A. (2021) Speaking out against everyday sexism: Gender and epistemics in accusations of 'mansplaining'. *Feminism & Psychology* 31 (4), 502–529.
Kitzinger, C. (2005) Heteronormativity in action: Reproducing the heterosexual nuclear family in after hours medical calls. *Social Problems* 52 (4), 477–498.
Lerner, G.H. (2013) On the place of hesitating in delicate formulations: A turn-constructional infrastructure for collaborative indiscretion. In J. Sidnell, M. Hayashi and G. Raymond (eds) *Conversational Repair and Human Understanding* (pp. 95–134). Cambridge University Press.
Lipsitz, G. (2006) *The Possessive Investment in Whiteness: How White People Profit from Identity Politics*. Temple University Press.
Mueller, J.C. (2017) Producing colorblindness: Everyday mechanisms of White ignorance. *Social Problems* 64 (2), 219–238.
Mueller, J.C. (2020) Racial ideology or racial ignorance? An alternative theory of racial cognition. *Sociological Theory* 38 (2), 142–169.
Okazawa, R. (2021) Resisting categorization in interaction: Membership categorization analysis of sitcom humor. *Journal of Pragmatics* 186, 33–44.
Okazawa, R. (2022) Membership categorization, humor, and moral order in sitcom interactions. *Discourse, Context & Media* 46, 1–8.
Pomerantz, A. (1984) Agreeing and disagreeing with assessments: Some features of preferred/dispreferred turn shapes. In J.M. Atkinson and J. Heritage (eds) *Structures of Social Action: Studies in Conversation Analysis* (pp. 57–101). Cambridge University Press.
Pomerantz, A. (1986) Extreme case formulations: A way of legitimizing claims. *Human Studies* 9, 219–229.
Potter, J. (2002) Two kinds of natural. *Discourse Studies* 4 (4), 539–542.
Rawls, A.W. and Duck, W. (2020) *Tacit Racism*. University of Chicago Press.

Raymond, C.W. (2019) Category accounts: Identity and normativity in sequences of action. *Language in Society* 49 (4), 585–606.
Raymond, G. (2004) Prompting action: The stand-alone 'so' in ordinary conversation. *Research on Language and Social Interaction* 37 (2), 185–218.
Raymond, G. and Heritage, J. (2006) The epistemics of social relations: Owning grandchildren. *Language in Society* 35 (5), 677–705.
Sacks, H. (1972a) An initial investigation of the usability of conversational data for doing sociology. In D.N. Sudnow (ed.) *Studies in Social Interaction* (pp. 31–74). Free Press.
Sacks, H. (1972b) On the analyzability of stories by children. In J.J. Gumperz and D. Hymes (eds) *Directions in Sociolinguistics: The Ethnography of Communication* (pp. 325–345). Holt, Rinehart and Winston.
Sacks, H. (1984) Notes on methodology. In J.M. Atkinson and J. Heritage (eds) *Structures of Social Action* (pp. 21–27). Cambridge University Press.
Sacks, H. (1992) *Lectures on Conversation*. Blackwell.
Sacks, H., Schegloff, E.A. and Jefferson, G. (1974) A simplest systematics for the organization of turn taking in conversation. *Language* 50, 696–735.
Scarpetta, F. and Spagnolli, A. (2009) The interactional context of humor in stand-up comedy. *Research on Language and Social Interaction* 42 (3), 210–230.
Schegloff, E.A. (1996) Confirming allusions: Toward an empirical account of action. *American Journal of Sociology* 102 (1), 161–216.
Schegloff, E.A. (1997) Practices and actions: Boundary cases of other-initiated repair. *Discourse Processes* 23 (3), 499–545.
Schegloff, E.A. (2007) A tutorial on membership categorization. *Journal of Pragmatics* 39 (3), 462–482.
Schegloff, E.A., Jefferson, G. and Sacks, H. (1977) The preference for self-correction in the organization of repair in conversation. *Language* 53 (2), 361–382.
Speer, S.A. (2002) 'Natural' and 'contrived' data: A sustainable distinction? *Discourse Studies* 4 (4), 511–525.
Stokoe, E. (2008) Dispreferred actions and other interactional breaches as devices for occasioning audience laughter in television 'sitcoms'. *Social Semiotics* 18 (3), 289–307.
Whitehead, K.A. (2009) 'Categorizing the categorizer': The management of racial common sense in interaction. *Social Psychology Quarterly* 72 (4), 325–342.
Whitehead, K.A. (2015) Everyday antiracism in action: Preference organization in responses to racism. *Journal of Language and Social Psychology* 34 (4), 374–389.
Whitehead, K.A. (2020) The problem of context in the analysis of talk-in-interaction: The case of implicit whiteness in post-apartheid South Africa. *Social Psychology Quarterly* 83 (3), 294–313.
Whitehead, K.A. and Wittig, M.A. (2004) Discursive management of resistance to a multicultural education programme. *Qualitative Research in Psychology* 1, 267–284.
Whitehead, K.A. and Lerner, G.H. (2009) When are persons 'white'? On some practical asymmetries of racial reference in talk-in-interaction. *Discourse and Society* 20 (5), 613–641.
Wilkinson, S. and Kitzinger, C. (2006) Surprise as an interactional achievement: Reaction tokens in conversation. *Social Psychology Quarterly* 69 (2), 150–182.

# Part 3
# A Final Argument

# 10 'Just a Method in Search of a Problem?' The Power of Conversation Analysis

Elizabeth Stokoe and Saul Albert

## Introduction

This chapter explores the power of conversation analysis to reveal ethical, moral and other deeply problematic assumptions about communication that have personal, institutional and societal consequences. Such practices would otherwise remain largely unknown, incorrectly imagined, unevidenced, disattended or obscured, since the worlds of communication and conversation and the phenomena of the 'psychological thesaurus' (Edwards & Potter, 2005) – i.e. experience, cognition, attitude, memory, etc. – are usually investigated using artificial or *post-hoc* methods such as simulations, experiments, surveys and interviews (see Stokoe, 2020).

Despite a long tradition of revealing the systematic interactional workings of power, prejudice, resistance and so on, most conversation analysts will recognize the caricatures of their research methods that circulate within critical social science and discourse analysis (Stokoe et al., 2012). These include accusations of 'pointless empiricism'; the 'dangerous adoption of relativism'; focusing on 'nothing but the text'; failing to 'deal with subjectivity'; analyzing features of interaction that 'are of no consequence'; an 'aversion to theory'; and thus of failing to address the 'big and important questions' (e.g. Frosh, 1999; Parker, 2005, 2012; Sarangi, 2018). According to Oliver *et al.* (2005: 1277), 'the conversation analyst wants to learn about talk' while 'the critical discourse analyst wants to learn what this talk says about other aspects of the participant's life'.

We do not recognize conversation analysis in these characterizations. Since its inception, conversation analysis (CA) (along with ethnomethodology, discursive psychology and membership categorization) has explicated the interactional practices – sequential, categorial, multimodal, embodied – that constrain and afford the workings of power, resistance, justice and social change. In contrast to the way it is sometimes caricatured, CA's engagement with and understanding of institutionality, racism and other '-isms', prejudice and power, provides a robust methodological apparatus for their systematic analysis (e.g. Previtali *et al.*, 2023; Rawls *et al.*, 2020; Yu & Sterponi, 2023; see the other chapters in this book).

The aim of this chapter is not to revisit debates about critical inquiry but to argue for and illustrate the power of conversation analysis to explicate, expose and challenge erroneous but widely held views about communication that underpin the interactional procedures, asymmetries and actions that are consequential for people's everyday encounters with social injustice. We will show, through illustrative cases, how, for instance, institutional encounters deviate from the written guidance and standardization that are presumed to underpin and ensure their parity and integrity. We will explore the deeply problematic practice, used by many organizations, of applying normative criteria about what counts as 'good' communication in their training and assessment of employees – from written assessment criteria to algorithmic coding in speech analytics and conversational artificial intelligence (AI). Relatedly, the final section of the chapter will show how communication training can be improved using conversation analytic evidence, including for dealing with '-isms' (Stokoe, 2015).

The fundamental precursor to each case we offer below, and the starting point in our argument for the power of CA, is standard conversation analytic research design: using audio and video recordings of actual encounters illustrated with detailed technical transcripts.

## The Power of Recordings and Transcripts

A commonly articulated reason for doing qualitative research is to enfranchise research participants by eliciting what is important to them in their own voices and words as 'active participants' in research activities (e.g. Hutchinson *et al.*, 2004; Johnston *et al.*, 2021: 544). It is somewhat ironic, therefore, that so much qualitative research collects and analyzes participants' voices by constructing unfamiliar, simulated research settings, or by removing the participants' words and voices from their naturalistic interactional settings. Qualitative approaches often position themselves in contrast to 'alienating' processes of quantification that risk losing vital qualities of the phenomena in question (Jovanović, 2011). However, qualitative analytic accounts *about* people's lives and experiences are often generated through semi-structured interviews that are set up for recording and verbatim transcription without any intrinsic and endogenous connection to participants' everyday communicative practices. Like survey-generated data, interview-generated accounts are necessarily *post-hoc* and consistently oriented to the researcher's agendas, questions or topics (Rapley, 2001) – the 'shadow cast upon the social world by the prior conceptual apparatus deployed by the person who constructed the [questions]' (Harré, 1993). Interview interactions are shot through with epistemic and presentational problems, from the inaccuracy and biases of researchers' memories in producing field notes and analytic accounts, to the particularities of the researchers' stakes in doing the interview in the first place (Potter & Hepburn, 2005).

A related problem with most interview data is their forms of written representation. Quoted data extracts that follow painstaking theoretical and cultural/historical contextualization are typically stripped of their interactional context. Researchers often emphasize the reflexive and co-produced nature of interview data while, at the same time, failing to present and analyze how the interviewers' own questions may guide or constrain the participants' responses. For example, Charmaz and Thornberg (2021) discuss what they cite as an exemplary case of qualitative interview research in which adult victims of school bullying describe their experiences to researchers that have set out to understand the participants 'as social actors and the social interactions they have been involved in' (Thornberg *et al*., 2013: 312). However, only short transcript extracts are presented, without including the questions asked or the features of 'active listening' that 'interviewers were instructed and trained' to do (2013: 312). Thus, there is another kind of stripping away, which is of interviewer and participant voices and embodied conduct that work in aggregate in the sequential organization and production of accounts.

What should these short transcript extracts include? There is much discussion of transcription 'as theory' (Ochs, 1979) and what to represent or not. Oliver *et al*. (2005: 1273–1274) refer to a transcript continuum, from 'naturalism, in which every utterance is transcribed in as much detail as possible', to 'denaturalism, in which idiosyncratic elements of speech (e.g. stutters, pauses, nonverbal involuntary vocalizations) are removed'. On this continuum, Jefferson's (2004) system for conversation analysis is 'natural': it seeks to represent how turns of talk are designed, where they are placed sequentially, timed gaps and pauses, the onset and end of overlapping talk, and aspects such as pitch, emphasis, laughter and crying (Hepburn & Bolden, 2018). Some have criticized CA's use of Jeffersonian transcription for contradictory attachments to incompatible ontologies (e.g. Ashmore & Reed, 2000); as a means of empiricist standardization (Sharrock & Anderson 2017); as structuralist or behaviorist (Atkinson, 1988); or as encoding 'conventional sociological preconceptions' (Hester & Francis, 1990: 398). Others object to 'excessive' and 'surplus' levels of detail (Bogen, 1999). For yet more others, the Jefferson system is not detailed enough, in terms of the phonetic details needed for auditory or acoustic analysis (Walker, 2012).

Relevant to 'giving voice' in qualitative research, Oliver *et al.* (2005) further suggest that 'natural' transcripts may encode bias by, say, attempting to transcribe accents. However, analysts have principled ways of working with accent and generally only encode different ways of pronouncing the same word where that is clearly interactionally relevant, such as when 'participants' pronunciations are the focus of the analysis' or 'when aspects of the speaker's pronunciation become an oriented to feature of interaction' (Hepburn & Bolden, 2018: 53–54). As Schegloff (1997) writes, in conversation analysis, 'it is the orientations, meanings, interpretations, understandings, etc. of the *participants*… which are privileged in the *constitution of social-interactional reality*' and so 'have a prima facie claim to being privileged' (1997: 166–167, emphasis in original). This principle is realized in the Jefferson transcription system.

We want to step back from these debates to make different points about giving voice to participants and the power of conversation analytic transcription. We present two examples. The first comes from a British televised interview in June 2020 between a journalist, Sophy Ridge, and the UK government's Health Secretary, Matt Hancock, in which Hancock named two British Asian politicians (Priti Patel, Home Secretary, and Rishi Sunak, Chancellor), in response to a question about the number of Black people in the cabinet.

(1) Ridge/Hancock 7.6.2020 (See https://youtu.be/lEp0ENBmQLg?t=265)
```
01    Ridge:       .h How many: (0.2) Black people are: (.)
02                 in the current #↓cabinet.#
03                             (2.6)
04    Hancock:     U::m: (0.5) thē:: ↑W'll.
05                             (0.2)
06    Hancock:     ↓#Uh- (in-)# (0.3) W- g- there's a- whole
07                 ↑series of people from a: (0.3)
08                 Black an' maha- minority ethnic
09                 background? .hh u::h the Chancellor of
10                 the Exchequer? (.) the Home Secretary?
11                 .hh u:m as:- (.) £to na(H)me but tw(Hh)o£
12                 [so:: th- it's uh y'know it's uh actually-    ]
13    Ridge:       [I'm just talking about Black- Ss:- >Sorry<]-
```

```
14                  (.) I'm talking about Black people
15                  specifically ...
```

This interview was lauded as a 'gotcha' moment in the British media since, at the time, a factual answer to Ridge's question would have been 'zero Black people'. The aftermath of the murder of George Floyd had prompted a public debate about the disadvantages and disparities experienced by Black people in British society. Media headlines such as 'Matt Hancock Names Two Asians When Asked To Identify Black Cabinet Members' (Singh, 2020), highlighted Hancock's inability to name any Black cabinet members, and academic analysis (e.g. Bankole, 2020) enumerated and discussed the impact of the lack of Black people in powerful governmental roles. However, the verbatim quotes from Ridge's interview used to illustrate these articles omit informative interactional levels of detail.[1] For example, Hancock's response is filled with disfluencies, delays and other marks of structural *dispreference* such as the long silence before answering (line 03), hesitation (U::m), abandoned components and restarts (thē::), and the 'well' preface (line 04). Hancock's response between lines 04–12 is also littered with repair. After a turn-initial *u::m* and a pause on line 04, he starts to reply (thē::), but abandons this beginning and restarts with ↑W'll. After a 0.2 second gap (line 05), he again abandons development of the prior TCU and starts a new one, with many more repair initiation components (↓#Uh- (in-)# (0.3) W- g-, line 06). Apart from anything that can be inferred from these details, such delays and disfluencies work to extend the time available before a politician is obliged to provide a response. These disfluencies also tend to cluster around particularly troublesome and therefore informative moments in the interaction.

Firstly, Hancock's response, when it finally comes – that there is a *whole ↑s'ries of people* – orients to the preference requirement of the question to supply a number (*How m'ny:*, line 01), but expands the constraints of the question by expanding the categorial component 'Black' contained in the initiating action from a more specific category of *Black people* (line 01) to a broader category of *people from a: (0.3) Black an' maha- minority ethnic background*, lines 07–09). Furthermore, this *maha- minority* repair on line 08 is an example of what conversation analysts call 'same-turn' or 'self-initiated self-repair' (Schegloff *et al.*, 1977), a common type of repair found in naturally occurring interaction that, in this case, pinpoints the sequential location of Hancock's trouble in responding to Ridge's question. Whether the self-repair to *Black an' maha- minority ethnic* (usually contracted to BME) at line 08 is a self-correction from 'majority' to 'minority', or another incidental misspeaking, repair marks this term as a source of specific interactional trouble. Both the terms 'BME' and 'BAME' are deprecated in official guidance (UK Government, 2021; see Aspinall, 2021) because they aggregate groups racialized by different identity categories such as skin color or geographical location, while excluding other persecuted minorities racialized as White such as Gypsy, Roma or Travellers of Irish Heritage (Bunglawala 2019).[2] It is ironic, then, that Hancock chooses, then stumbles over this term in the context of being made accountable, as a White Cabinet minister, for the lack of Black members, before tentatively naming two of his British Asian Cabinet colleagues (*e::r the Chancellor of the Exchequer? (.) the Home Secretary?*, lines 09–10) – notably using their official titles instead of their identifiably Indian names (Rishi Sunak and Priti Patel).

Finally, Hancock's laughter inflection in line 11, produced following his own response to a 'serious' question, resists the premise or trajectory of Ridge's questioning by treating it as laughable (Glenn, 2003: 142–144). Since media reports, quotes and print representations do not usually transcribe delays, disfluencies and repairs, even when politicians are held accountable for their failure to answer a question, they are not always held accountable for the disingenuity and deliberate evasiveness evident in the interactional detail of their answers.

The second example is a leaked audio recording of an off-air conversation in January 2018 between two British Broadcasting Corporation (BBC) journalists, John Humphrys and Jon Sopel, about another journalist colleague, Carrie Gracie. Gracie had resigned from the BBC (a 'bombshell' decision, according to BuzzFeed) the previous week, in the context of revelations about a gender pay gap at the organization. On 12 January 2018, The Guardian newspaper headline stated that '*John Humphrys jokes about BBC gender pay gap in leaked off-air recording*'. Extract 2a is part of an orthographic transcript of the leaked recording published on the news website Buzzfeed (Di Stefano, 2018), followed by Extract 2b, which is the same segment transcribed for conversation analysis.

(2a) Buzzfeed transcript: John Humphrys and Jon Sopel, Jan 2018
Humphrys: 'Ah... Can you hear me Sopel?'
Sopel: 'Humphrys, I can hear you'.
Humphrys: 'Good, slight change of subject — first question will be how much of your salary you are prepared to hand over to Carrie Gracie to keep her, and then a few comments about your other colleagues, you know, like our Middle East editor and the other men who are earning too much...'

| Sopel: | 'I mean, obviously if we are talking about the scope for the greatest redistribution I'll have to come back and say, 'well yes Mr Humphrys, but…''. |
|---|---|
| Humphrys: | 'And I could save you the trouble, because I could volunteer that I've handed over already more than you fucking earn, but I'm still left with more than anybody else and that seems to me to be entirely just – something like that would do it?' |
| Sopel: | 'Don't'. |

(2b) Jefferson transcript: John Humphrys and Jon Sopel, Jan 2018

```
01    Humph:    Ah.h
02              (0.2)
03    Humph:    >↑C'n ↑you 'ear me.<=Sopel.
04              (1.3)
05    Sopel:    ↑.hHumphrys: I c'n £↓hear£ you.
06    Humph:    Good.=slight change of um:: (.) slight
07              change of subject, .hhh um: u- a- first
08              question will be: um how much hhh
09              (0.4) of your salary
10              [#you are prepared t'hand over to]=
11    Sopel:    [   £#.h.h .h .h .h  .h#£      ]
12    Humph:    =Carrie Gracie to keep her, .hhh um::
13              an' th(h)en uh- [- y- a few- a £few£ ]=
14    Sopel:               [ .  hh heh hhe      ]=
15    Humph:    =[comments about (0.2) your- your]=
16    Sopel:    =[       hheh h hh  .heh        ]
17    Hump:     =other [ c o l l]eagues: you know: l- um=
18    Sopel:           [.HHH]
19    Humph:    =like our: o- [our-] [our Middle East
20    Sopel:                  [.HH ] [Yeh,
21    Humph:    =[editor: and .hh the other men who are=
22    Sopel:    [(yeh.)
23    Humph:    =earning too much.=d'you know ↑just- .hh=
24    Sopel:    =I mean ↑obviously- (0.2) ob- obviously
25              if we're talking about- the scope for
26              the greatest redistribution,
27    Humph:    Mmm.
28    Sopel:    .hh I'll have t'come back an' say well-
29              (0.2) ↑ye:s mister Humphrys.=[but
30    Humph:                                 [An' ↑I am:
31              an' I- I- I'd (.) could save you the
32              [trouble because I could volunteer]=
33    Sopel:    [   £#.h.h .h .h .h  .h#£         ]=
```

```
34    Humph:      =[.hh <I've um:> handed over alrea:dy=
35    Sopel:      =[£.HHh£ heh
36    Humph:      =.h more than you fuckin' ↓earn
37                [.hh um:: I'm sti:ll left with more  ]=
38    Sopel:      [      £#.h .h  .h  .h .h  .h         ]=
39    Humph:      =[than anybody e:lse.=an' n- that]=
40    Sopel:      =[        .h .h .h hh #£ .shih        ]=
41    Humph:      =that- seems to be- t'be entirely just.
42                .hhh uhh so(h)mmat like [that,
43    Sopel:                              [£uh heh heh£ heh
44                [ heh #eh eh .h  eh eh ] £.HHHHH£
45    Humph:      [Would do it, d'y'think,]
46    Sopel:      £Don't.[hh£
47    Humph?:            [uhhh. Dear g(h)od.
```

The conversation analytic transcription not only provides more information about what was said, how and precisely when, but also reveals the extensive affiliative laughter particles produced by Sopel throughout Humphrys's talk. This was not included in Buzzfeed's transcript. Sopel's affiliative laughter is audible at lines 11, 14, 16, 18, 20, 33, 35, 38, 40, 43 and 44, including immediately as Humphrys produces *more than you fuckin' ↓earn* at line 36.

A search of the LexisNexis database for reports of the leaked conversation, while formulated in some articles as 'the Humphrys-Sopel exchange' (Daily Mail, 12.1.2018), focused much more heavily on Humphrys rather than Sopel. It was Humphrys's name that appeared in the headlines and his conduct that was the focus of the public outcry (e.g. '*BBC stars at war as several female presenters threaten to walk out after £650,000-a-year John Humphrys is recorded JOKING about gender pay gap*' (Daily Mail, 12.1.2018)). Our point is not, of course, to lessen the offensiveness of Humphrys's conduct, but to show that Sopel might also have been held to account. Media coverage taking into account the co-production of this episode rather than focusing on one individual might also have explained more about the institutional culture and systemic inequalities in gender pay at the BBC that Gracie cited in her resignation.

Together, these two examples begin to reveal the power of conversation analytic methods to expose far more of what happens in social interaction, and to specify and explicate matters of practical, political and ethical accountability. While, of course, neither of our technical transcripts 'contain everything' (the naïve realism arguments mentioned above), the first points to the specific sources of trouble and highlights the form, structure and content of a politician's practices of dissembling in a political interview about race. The second straightforwardly demonstrates the collusion of a second party in an offensive 'hot mic' moment for which only one party was held accountable. Similarly, conversation analysts have systematically shown the serious problems of relying on standard orthographic records of spoken interaction in high-stakes contexts such as legally regulated evidence- and testimony-gathering interactions. In a recent overview, Richardson *et al.* (2022) make the point that, while there are many transcription developments in conversation analytic and related disciplines, these 'have not (yet) translated over to improvements in transcription practices in institutional contexts' and 'there is little recognition in legal contexts of the long realized basic principle of the non-equivalence of spoken and written text' (2022: 1–2).

## The Power to Reveal Variation in Standards

Conversation analysts have regularly exposed the gap between written instructions, diagnostic instruments, guidance, regulations, the letter of the law – and what the actual interactions that are apparently accountable to these texts look like in encounters (e.g. Houtkoop-Steenstra, 2000; Lavin & Maynard, 2001). There is a tacit assumption that in settings where equity is particularly important such as police interviews or healthcare interactions – where encounters are routinely recorded as part of institutional or organizational practice for the public record or for (explicitly inspectable) 'training and quality purposes' – that standardized interactions will reflect the paperwork trails they generate. However, myriad conversation analytic studies have shown how actual encounters deviate from guidance or instruction, and from one encounter to the next, even in experimental or survey research which ostensibly generates standardized 'hard' data compared to the 'soft' accounts of qualitative research, a presumption that Stokoe, Antaki *et al.* (2021) refer to as 'the softness of hard data'. Researchers have identified, for example, 'radical departures' from 'standardized experimental procedures' in research laboratories (Gibson, 2011; Hollander, 2015), the impact of experimenters' talk on 'the trajectory of the experiment' (Wooffitt, 2007), and even how the spoken (re)formulation of standardized (written) questions for gaining research consent shapes participants' responses (Speer & Stokoe, 2014). Without recordings and transcripts, however, we would not know about how the details of interaction – in-breaths, pauses, gaps and delays, self-repair – tacitly convey interactional trouble, preference, affiliation, alignment and so on.

These gaps between guidance and practice can have dramatic and morally worrisome implications for research and procedures with a direct bearing on social justice. For example, in interviews between police officers and suspects – a high-stakes encounter for those involved – one might imagine that police officers follow the letter of the law when it comes to asking questions, reminding suspects of their rights and so on. However, police interviewers routinely deviate from the mandated wording in the *Police and Criminal Evidence Act* (1984) in important ways, such as how they cite suspects' right to remain silent (Stokoe *et al.*, 2016), and how police reformulations of suspect testimony comprise evidence for one of the 'hardest' data categories around: whether they broke the law (Stokoe & Edwards, 2008). These variations in practice are, of course, subject to bias, and may further entrench existing inequalities in law enforcement.

For example, Walker *et al.*'s (2021) analysis of 585 case files of reported rape suggested that there are intersecting inequalities in the trajectory of cases reported to police for survivors minoritized by their sexuality, gender, mental health status, race or ethnic background. However, studies of police case files alone may not show how such inequalities are generated in practice. Using conversation analysis, Richardson *et al.* (2018) analyzed evidence-gathering interviews between police officers and 'vulnerable' adult or child victims of sexual assault and rape. In particular, they asked to what extent police officers followed formal guidance: *Achieving Best Evidence in Criminal Proceedings: Guidance for Vulnerable and Intimidated Witnesses* (UK Ministry of Justice, 2011), which was published as a special measure to enable the best conditions for these groups of witnesses to provide evidence. One instruction in these guidelines is for police officers to establish that alleged victims understand what it means to report their experiences honestly. As the document puts it, police officers are instructed to ascertain whether victims understand the difference between 'truth and lies'. This is what the guidelines say:

*Certain vulnerable adult witnesses*

*Para 3.22   In cases where discussion of truth and lies is appropriate, it is important to demonstrate that the witness understands the difference between the two. The witness could be asked to give examples of truth and lies. If this is not possible, the interviewer can ask some questions about this difference. If such questions are asked, they should follow the guidance set out elsewhere on styles of questioning, and focus on the intention to deceive rather than mere mistakes. After such questions, it is appropriate to conclude with a statement like: 'Please tell me all you can remember about what happened. Don't make anything up or leave anything out. It is very important to tell the truth'.*

(UK Ministry of Justice, 2011: 73)

The guidelines also state that questions about truth telling should not happen 'later in the interview because this might run the risk of the [witness] concluding that the interviewer had not believed what they had said up to that point' (UK Ministry of Justice, 2011: 72). Yet conversation analysis revealed that police officers deviated from the guidance inappropriately in several ways – not only by eliciting confirmations rather than demonstrations of understanding, but also by eliciting multiple demonstrations and confirmations of understanding, and by reintroducing 'truth and lies' conversations at potentially sensitive points in the interview. The latter two cases do exactly what the guidelines warn against – implying dishonesty on the part of the victim, creating opportunities for variations in practice to generate aggregate forms of discrimination and inequality.

As in policing, there is also evidence of structural inequalities in healthcare outcomes that could benefit from more explanatory interactional accounts. The UK government's Marmot Review (2020) shows widening inequalities between different regions of the UK, where intersections between ethnicity and socioeconomic background produce particularly poor health outcomes, although the lack of adequate data and analysis presents a continuing barrier to more informative explanation (Marmot, 2020). In healthcare provision, it is probably also assumed that diagnostic instruments and surveys of the kind delivered by clinicians will be administered as instructed, in a standardized way. However, Antaki and Rapley (1999) analyzed recordings of how a 'Quality of Life' questionnaire was administered by a psychologist to service-users. The questions on the sheet had three response options. The instructions for 'reading the items' were for the psychologist to '*pay close attention to the exact wording*' (emphasis added). But, in the empirical reality of encounters, the psychologists often reformulated those three options into one 'yes/no' question with a positive tilt, which led to service-users responding in particular ways that had consequences for the type and level of support they subsequently received. Once again, these conversation analytic approaches to the detail of talk and social interaction have the power to reveal variations in standards between guidance, procedures and practice, and to highlight opportunities for bias that might explain otherwise opaque inequalities in health outcomes.

This section has exposed three problems that can lead to injustices and inequalities, and three ways in which CA has the power to expose and explain these issues in actionable ways. The first problem is the tacit assumption that, even in mundane settings, people can 'just read out' the words written in a document (including scripts, survey questions, experimental instructions) without succumbing to the interactional imperative.

In fact, apparently 'just reading out' is an interactional accomplishment itself (Stokoe & Edwards, 2007). The second problem is that we do not know how, in the heat of a sequence of talk, people turn guidance into spoken talk. For example, what does *'The witness could be asked to give examples of truth and lies'* look like in actual police interviews? Finally, even though so much of institutional life is now audio- or video-recorded, and thus inspectable, egregious breaches of standards, guidance and even the letter of the law often remain hidden in verbatim transcripts. CA has the power to reveal the inadequacy of standardization and written guidance for securing the assumed validity and equity of institutional encounters.

**The Power to Assess Communication**

The assessment of communication styles and practices is also a common site for bias and discrimination that conversation analytic research has the power to expose. Communication guidance, training manuals and role-play assessment methods can easily reproduce harmful stereotypes because they often draw on assumptions rather than an evidence base about what constitutes good communication practice. The outcomes of communication assessments can be highly consequential for those being evaluated – will they be employed, promoted or fired, depending on how they perform against a list of assessment criteria? This begs questions about what should appear on a list of 'communication skills'. Conversation analysis has the power to challenge and improve the interactional integrity and real-world usefulness of assessment practice.

One of the most common environments for assessing communication is in simulated encounters or role-play, in which simulated interlocutors (including actors) aim to replicate communicative scenarios and those who are being assessed attempt to meet the assessment criteria for effective interviewing, medical history-taking and so on. Yet, conversation analytic research shows that what happens in role-play does not correspond to the institutional encounter it is designed to mimic (Stokoe, 2013a). This means that assessing someone's communication skill based on what they do in role-play is potentially problematic.

For instance, Stokoe (2013a) examined how police interviews with actual suspects compared to interviews with actors playing the parts of suspects in training and assessment sessions. The opening of such interviews is legally prescribed by the Police and Criminal Evidence Act (PACE, 1984). So, in real and simulated interviews, the interviewers' first task is to turn the written law into spoken turns at talk with the suspect, including legal instructions to '*tell the suspect about the recording process*', '*give their name and rank and that of any other interviewer present*' and '*remind the suspect of their entitlement to free legal advice*'. These written directives were formulated differently depending on whether the interview was an assessment with an actor-suspect, or part of the criminal justice process with a real suspect.

One difference, which may seem inconsequential, was that, in real interviews, police were likely to turn the instruction to '*give their name and rank and that of any other interviewer present*' into a statement like, 'I'm PC 3456 Smith based at Anytown police station', whereas in assessment role-plays, they more typically said, 'Um my name is PC 3456 Smith, please feel free to call me Bob'. The latter component of the role-play seems designed to enact other guidance to 'build rapport' and lessen the formality of institutional identifications – while at the same time meet the constraints of formal identifications for the benefit of the tape (Stokoe, 2009).

Furthermore, when more than one interviewer was present, the two officers were more likely to introduce themselves across a compound turn construction unit or TCU (Lerner, 1991), with the first interviewer adding 'Also present is my colleague...' after 'I'm PC ...'. The second interviewer then collaboratively completed the overall action. Stokoe also found that, in real interviews, officers do not typically supply their first name nor issue an invitation to the suspect regarding how to refer to them. Compound TCUs were largely absent in assessment role-plays. That is, each officer took their own full turns to introduce themselves, presumably to ensure that the 'assessable' communication practices were clearly visible and attributable just to them by the observing assessor. In real interviews, ironically, officers work as a team and display this teamwork interactionally.

Why do officers state 'My name is X' when they know they are being evaluated but use 'I am' elsewhere – and does it matter? Atkins (2018) found the same alternative formats in real versus simulated doctor–patient conversation. In real encounters, general practitioners introduced themselves saying, 'I'm Dr X'. However, when being assessed on their consulting skills, they were more likely to say, 'My name is Dr X', to pass their 'objective structured clinical examination' (OSCE). Furthermore, if a candidate used the 'I'm Dr X' format in the simulation, they were likely to be marked negatively for doing so. As Atkins *et al*. (2016) point out, 'the linguistic problems and differences that arise from interacting in artificial settings are of considerable importance in assessment, where we must be sure that the exam construct adequately embodies the skills expected for real-life practice'.

It appears, then, that different occupations are trained to make introductions in the same way by saying, 'My name is X'. Doctors and police officers use this format when being assessed. But they use 'I'm X' in real encounters – with no evidence that this is less effective for the comprehensibility of the action or 'poor communication'. It is therefore difficult to know what underpins the reification into guidance and evaluation of one practice over another. Training, guidance and scripts for, and assessment of, communicative encounters are often apparently built from people's attempts to make explicit their tacit knowledge and build that into guidance and recommendations. This leads to failures in identifying the right 'assessables'.

The point is not that stating, 'My name is' rather than a categorial 'I'm X', or some other way of referring to oneself is intrinsically flawed, or not found endogenously in other non-simulated data. Rather, we argue that prescribing ways of talking falls foul not just of the principle of recipient design, but also the evidence of how people actually talk in any given situation.

This brings us to another example of communication assessment based on simulation. We examined what happens when 'mystery shoppers' telephone veterinary practices with the goal of evaluating the provision of good service – as achieved through conversations with receptionists (Stokoe et al., 2020). The point of mystery shopping as an assessment tool is to evaluate the process of service rather than *post-hoc* scoring on a scale. Unlike the police and general practitioner (GP) contexts, mystery shopping relies on those being assessed not knowing that they are talking to, in our case, a real pet owner or a simulated client.

Our research on mystery shopping pulls together several themes. First, when used in healthcare, mystery shopping studies claim to reveal bad practice, such as that pharmacists deviate from regulatory guidance when selling medicines over the counter. But what guidance are mystery shoppers using to ask for medicines in the first place? The methodology claims to ensure its validity and parity of assessment by training shoppers with scripts, but how the written script is (re)formulated in encounters is unknown. Second, the research showed that mystery shopper calls differed systematically from real calls. Real calls were longer; the reason for the call was different (real callers asked for appointments and treatment; mystery shoppers asked about the cost of services); and the outcome of the call was different (real callers made appointments, requiring the receptionist to navigate the appointment system and meet their needs; mystery shoppers did not).

While a mystery shopper is hard to identify on a one-off occasion, larger datasets revealed stark differences. The implications for equity and workplace assessments are also stark: when mystery shoppers report back to organizations on the communicative competencies of their staff, their reports cannot reflect what staff typically do on the phone and the contingencies they routinely manage. Scripts and reports are based on normative notions of 'good communication' or 'effective service'. Yet staff will be promoted, given bonuses, be mandated for more training and so on based on a deeply flawed assessment methodology (e.g. Miller & Turner, 2005).

We also found that real callers included components that mystery shoppers did not, such as accounts for their requests, or the name, breed and weight of their pet. Only real callers referred to their pet by name, and mystery shoppers were more likely to initiate repair on, delay or otherwise 'stumble' in responding to queries about the pet breed and weight. These small details have implications for the development of conversational AI systems such as Apple's *Siri*, Amazon's *Alexa* and Google's *Duplex* (Leviathan & Matias, 2018) that attempt to emulate naturalistic spoken interaction. There is an emerging body of conversation analytic research that shows how constrained the 'conversations' are in such interactions (e.g. Albert *et al.*, 2019). Our findings suggest that, worse still, even *humans* who are simulating other humans do not produce social actions in the same way when the stakes are different. So, the developers of artificial agents face an even tougher challenge.

Our final example in this section stays with the practice of assessing service provision on the telephone. The use of natural language processing (NLP) and AI to build tools for 'speech analytics' and 'sentiment analysis' has grown exponentially, with many software-as-a-service (SaaS) products on the market to assess service provision at scale. To analyze, say, contact center calls, audio-recordings are uploaded, run through speech-to-text software, and text outputs are assigned codes and scores of various kinds (e.g. positive, neutral, negative; confusion, happiness, anger). This labeling can be applied at different levels of granularity, from a turn-by-turn code to a score for an overall encounter. However, they do not typically capture the micro-analytic details of interaction or concepts such as 'adjacency' – and certainly not conversational AI 'moonshots' like compound TCUs (Stokoe *et al.*, 2021).

In pilot research (Parslow *et al.*, 2021), we were invited to work with a start-up to test out their speech analytics platform. We uploaded audio-recorded telephone calls from institutional settings including general practice. These calls had been transcribed using Jeffersonian conventions and were already analyzed as part of earlier projects (e.g. Sikveland *et al.*, 2016). We then made some basic observations about the accuracy of the platform's speech-to-text transcription, speaker 'diarization' (partitioning and attributing the audio to separate interlocutors), and the kinds of codes attributed to parts of the interaction that comprised an overall service provision score.

212  Part 3: A Final Argument

As an example of the difference between our transcript and the software system output, consider Extract 3. Extract 3a is the Jefferson transcript of a call between a caller (C) and their general practice reception (R); Extract 3b is the SaaS output of the same recording. Both are anonymized. The caller and receptionist are discussing the caller's son.

(3a) Jefferson/GP call
```
01    R:    Ri:ght.
02            (1.0)
03    R:    Uh:::m hh do you feel it's ur:gent.=I've got
04            to ask you this because I can't make the
05            decision.
06            (1.3)
07    R:    [You see.
08    C:    [If you've not got any appointments I can
09            take him to the walk-in centre.
10            (0.8)
11    R:    Are you sure:¿
12            (0.4)
13    C:    Y:eah,
14            (0.9)
15    R:    I c- >I mean< there is that,
16            (0.4)
17    R:    Uh:: or I can put him on a cancellation list,
```

(3b) SaaS / GP call

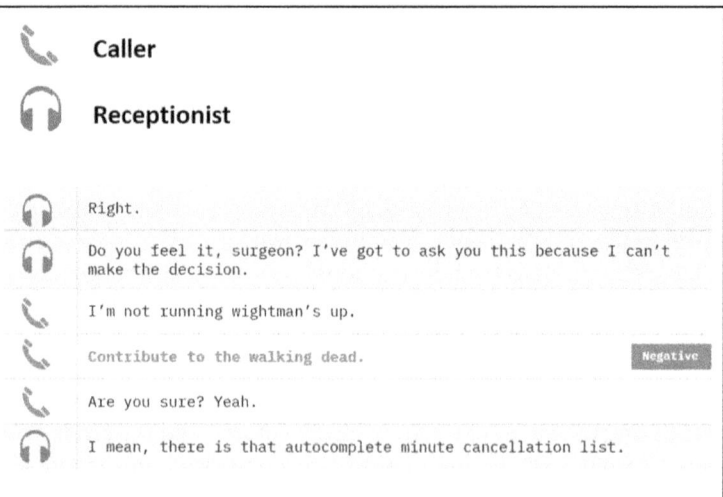

The contrast between the two transcripts is stark. Not only is Extract 3b full of errors, including which speaker is producing which turn (e.g. it is the receptionist not the caller who asks, *are you sure*), but one mistranscription (the caller's solution to take her son *to the walk-in centre* becomes *contribute to the walking dead* and is, perhaps unsurprisingly, tagged as 'negative').

We found many basic errors in transcription, with knock-on consequences for the system's inability to correctly attribute turns, interpret gaps and pauses, handle repair or overlapping talk, and – perhaps most importantly – identify action and sequence. For example, the 'reason for the call' (e.g. *'I've got a bad eye'*; *'my window frame is broken'*) was frequently tagged as 'negative', despite this action in a service encounter having little relevance to service provision. Furthermore, items like *'thank you'* were typically tagged as 'satisfaction' or 'positive', regardless of who produced the turn and its sequential position. Extract 4 is an example from the GP-patient call:

(4) SaaS / GP call

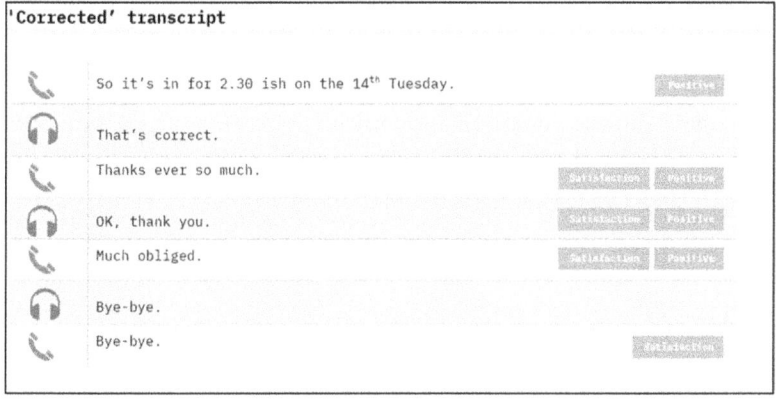

Here, both the caller's and call-taker's *'thank yous'* – despite being composed differently (*thank you*; *thanks very so much*) and formulated twice by the caller (*much obliged*) – receive the same tags. The system makes no distinctions between, say, a pre-closing 'thank you' and appreciation, even as the caller does both things. Since the call-taker's *ok, thank you* is also tagged as 'satisfaction' and 'positive', we can see how scores may be inflated or depressed depending on diarization errors. And, of course, conversation analytic research shows that 'thank you' is an unreliable indicator of customer satisfaction and, depending on its sequential location and who says it first in pre-closings, can actually convey dissatisfaction (Sikveland & Stokoe, 2017).

Like other examples in this chapter, we see how a basic lack of attention to what some regard as 'excessive' and 'surplus' details, as well as a deeply flawed set of assumptions about real conversation and communication, embed themselves into a wide variety of research, assessment and organizational practices. Communications training and assessments are often vital for addressing obstacles to career progression for disadvantaged groups in critical professions such as policing (see e.g. Mayor of London, 2020) where there are persistent unequal outcomes in recruitment, retention and promotion, with significant implications for social justice.

These research findings discussed above, about the differences between simulated versus actual professional settings, have been disseminated in public lectures and science communication environments, leading practitioners to reach out to us to discuss what happens in communication assessment in their organizational contexts. For example, one medic wrote to discuss the implications for inequality in the aforementioned simulation-based OSCE examinations. The medic had observed – and, indeed, research has shown (e.g. Elewa-Ikpakwu & Ayoola, 2020; Wass *et al.*, 2003) – that minoritized medical students perform less well on such (simulated) communication assessments. What might this mean if the assessment situation does not authentically reproduce actual practice and assessment criteria are based on 'examiners' assumptions about what is good communication' (Wass *et al.*, 2003: 800)? Conversation analysis has the power to shine a light on these common flaws in communication assessment practices and the unfair consequences for those assessed.

## The Power of Evidence-Based Communication Training

The final example of the power of conversation analysis is connected to the previous section on communication assessment and focuses on the related issue of communication training. In 2008, Stokoe (2011) began to develop Conversation Analytic Role-play Method, or CARM, which is a communication training method based on conversation analytic research. With Derek Edwards, Stokoe had conducted analyses of initial inquiry (or 'intake') calls into community mediation (and related) services focusing on how identity matters – cashed out in categorial terms, including gender, race, ethnicity, age and class – impacted the trajectory of the dispute between parties (e.g. Stokoe, 2009). These data were collected as part of a project on community and neighbor conflict and dispute.

Towards the end of the project, Stokoe began to focus particularly on whether callers became clients of community mediation organizations by the end of their encounter with a mediator. Such intake calls are treated as separate from and outside of an actual mediation and had previously received no attention from either researchers or the mediation industry, both in the UK and USA. But because community dispute resolution services secure funding partly based on recognized need – on the size of their client base – it became important for mediators to learn what might improve their conversion rates, from caller to client, as Stokoe's research demonstrated (e.g. Sikveland & Stokoe, 2016; Stokoe, 2013b).

Starting with findings about mediation, Stokoe designed a communication training method underpinned by selected aspects of conversation analytic research, often co-produced with organizations who funded the research-to-training cycle. This approach was in stark contrast to traditional forms of training based on simulation or role-play, discussed earlier, since it took research findings about effective practice as its basis. CARM involves identifying examples of more and less effective practices; for example, for describing and offering mediation to skeptical callers. Audio and video extracts from recordings are anonymized and played synchronously with transcripts to enable participants to 'live through' real encounters without knowing what would happen next. Workshop participants discuss what they might do next to handle the situation. For example, if party A makes a particular sort of comment, how might party B respond most appropriately? Finally, party B's actual response is revealed and discussed, and the workshop moves on.

The workshop with the largest reach, delivered to organizations across the UK and USA, started out as a response to a request from community mediators. Stokoe was awarded funding to develop CARM and offer two workshops to mediation organizations, including a 'bespoke' session designed to meet whatever need they had. One asked for a session on hate speech and how to identify and respond to it. To meet this need – and move away from role-play or experience/scenario-based training – Stokoe developed a workshop based on different strands of her research in which age, gender, race and ethnicity categories became live issues in the inquiry calls, as well as accusations and denials of multiple forms of prejudice (e.g. Stokoe, 2003; Stokoe & Edwards, 2007).

To illustrate the CARM approach, Extract 5 comes from a mediation session (not an initial inquiry) in which three parties in a dispute are co-present (Macy, Gary, Henry), with two mediators (M1, M2). This extract is over halfway through a 90-minute session, and the ostensible cause of the dispute is a shared garden space which has been, according to Gary and Henry, 'colonized' by Macy's plants. Here, Macy (MA) is explaining what she sees as the root of the problem.

(5a) KM-3
```
01     MA:    I remember (0.3) uh having a word with Gary
02            about something he accused me of being uh-
03            (0.5) like a Barbra Streisand.
04            Which meant I must be aggressive (0.5) Jewish,
05            (0.3) which I am neither,
```

In the CARM workshop, the audio recording and transcript stop here. Participants discuss questions about what kind of accusation this is (and their evidence for it) and what – if they were the mediator – they may say in response. This case is interesting not least because of the way Macy turns 'Barbra Streisand' into a category (note the indefinite article *a*, at line 02) and unpacks what she takes to be the category-bound predicates that turn the categorization into a possible instance of anti-Semitism.

Most workshop participants – the community mediators – say that their response would be to explore the categorization further, including asking Gary for his account. But this is what happens next.

(5b) KM-3
```
06            (0.4)
07     MA:    Um::
08            (0.4)
09     M2:    I- I think- [I'm not- I'm not sure that=
10     M1:                [Is this helpful?
11     M2:    =this is helpful
```

The mediators, in overlap and in alignment, do not expand upon Macy's accusation but instead negatively evaluate it as something that is not *helpful* to address in mediation.

The participants in the CARM workshop use such cases as the basis for further discussion, including about the nature of mediation itself. Like findings from a survey of mediators reported in Rendon (2007: np), some mediators 'believed that prejudice and discrimination issues are irrelevant distractions from mediation's goal of case resolution, and therefore should be ignored or put aside', while others argued that 'the mediator should meet the issues "head on" by bringing them to the table'. What became possible in CARM sessions, however, was that mediators – sometimes from the same organization – were able to discuss actual cases, and see actual mediator responses, and discover that not everyone shares an understanding of what counts as an '-ism' nor even what the purpose of mediation is.

The '-isms' workshop was initially delivered to mediation centers between 2011 and 2013. It has since evolved, including into a co-produced document by Loughborough University's Discourse and Rhetoric Group and its 'Maia' women's network, led by Stokoe. The one-page guidance, 'How to say when it's not okay: Tackling prejudicial -isms in workplace conversation', is designed as a standalone how-to, as well as providing a quick-reference to accompany the regularly refreshed CARM workshop. The guidance describes eight response types to an '-ism' based on research (e.g. Pino, 2017; Robles, 2015; Stokoe, 2015; Stokoe & Edwards, 2007; Whitehead, 2018). It also foregrounds the fact that what people say they would do to 'be an ally' is not the same as what typically happens in interaction (see also Kitzinger & Frith, 1999).

## Discussion and Conclusion

Since the earliest days of EMCA, a common criticism has been its ostensible lack of what Coser (1975) referred to as 'substance' in his keynote address to the American Sociological Association. This rather dismissive attitude and – for us – unfounded claim has persisted across the decades. Indeed, the title of this chapter is a direct quote from a reviewer who characterized conversation analysis as 'a method in search of a problem'. However, its power to shine empirical light on the pervasive interactional production of social problems of injustice and inequity makes this a description to embrace.

The bringing together of 'critical' and 'conversation analysis' is not new (e.g. Blain, 2020) and, for some in EMCA, the notion of adding 'critical' to 'conversation analysis' will be conceptually flawed, tautological or even oxymoronic. Indeed, although the most-cited debate about conversation analysis versus critical analysis was undoubtedly between Schegloff (1997), Wetherell (1998) and Billig (1999), there have been other long-running debates between ethnomethodologists and conversation analysts themselves about, say, the project of 'feminist' conversation analysis (e.g. Kitzinger, 2000, 2008; Speer, 1999; Stokoe, 2000, 2008; Tennent & Weatherall, 2021; Whelan, 2012; Wowk, 2007).

The aim of this chapter has been to provide evidence that and how conversation analytic methods, research designs and findings provide the strongest possible evidence for understanding and exposing power, ethics and injustice in practice. CA transcription has the power to describe and document, in detail, the co-production of systemic forms of bias, and to empower public debates to hold people and institutions to account. It has the power to show the variation in ostensible 'standards' and highlight how certain deviations from 'standard practice' in communication may lead to unjust and iniquitous outcomes. It has the power to highlight the ways in which communication assessment and simulation training often rely on biased and simplistic assumptions, and can provide evidence as the basis for more accurate, fair, social justice-oriented communication training. Despite Billig's (2019) criticisms of conversation analysis, we agree with his call for 'more examples' and 'less theory'. We underline the importance of examining everyday life 'as it happens' (Boden, 1990). The devil, as we have seen, is in the detail. Finally, we agree with Edwards's (p.c.) proposal that, rather than worrying about our accountability to the rhetoric of 'big questions', we should argue that those who make those critiques should be accountable to our data which shows the workings of real-life inequalities, the myriad practices of exclusion, and the otherwise hidden reality of the damage turns at talk can do.

## Notes

(1) See for instance: https://twitter.com/ridgeonsunday/status/1269537028040990722; https://www.huffingtonpost.co.uk/entry/black-cabinet-matt-hancock-protests_uk_5edc9ffdc5b6aedebbc6a27a
(2) These terms have also been criticized for their use in Diversity, Equity and Inclusion (DEI) initiatives as a euphemism 'used by institutions to signal their recognition of "diversity" whilst simultaneously cloaking and reproducing the racism of the institution' (Skeggs, 2021: 125).

## References

Albert, S., Housley, W. and Stokoe, E. (2019) In case of emergency, order pizza: An urgent case of action formation and recognition. CUI 2019: Proceedings of the 1st International Conference on Conversational User Interfaces, Dublin, Ireland, 22–23 August 2019CUI '19. https://doi.org/10.1145/3342775.3342800
Antaki, C. and Rapley, M. (1996) Questions and answers to psychological assessment schedules: Hidden troubles in 'quality of life' interviews. *Journal of Intellectual Disability Research* 40 (5), 421–437.
Ashmore, M. and Reed, D. (2000) Innocence and nostalgia in conversation analysis: The dynamic relations of tape and transcript. *Forum: Qualitative Social Research* 1 (3). http://www.qualitative-research.net/index.php/fqs/article/view/1020/2199.
Aspinall, P.J. (2021) BAME (black, Asian and minority ethnic): The 'new normal' in collective terminology. *Journal of Epidemiol Community Health* 75.
Atkins, S. (2018) Assessing health professionals' communication through role-play: An interactional analysis of simulated versus actual general practice consultations. *Discourse Studies* 21 (2), 109–134. https://doi.org/10.1177/1461445618802659

Atkins, S., Roberts, C., Hawthorne, K. et al. (2016) Simulated consultations: A sociolinguistic perspective. *BMC Medical Education* 16. https://doi.org/10.1186/s12909-016-0535-2

Atkinson, P. (1988) Ethnomethodology: A critical review. *Annual Review of Sociology* 14, 441–465.

Bankole, M. (2020) Black British citizens want more than complacency from this government. *The Conversation.* Available online: http://theconversation.com/black-british-citizens-want-more-than-complacency-from-this-government-140297

Billig, M. (1999) Whose terms? Whose ordinariness? Rhetoric and ideology in Conversation Analysis. *Discourse & Society* 10 (4), 543–558.

Billig, M. (2019) *More Examples, Less Theory: Historical Studies of Writing Psychology.* Cambridge University Press.

Blain, H. (2020) Discourses in action: operations of race, sexuality and gender in chinese talk-in-interaction. Unpublished PhD thesis, School of Languages and Linguistics University of Melbourne.

Boden, D. (1990) The world as it happens: Ethnomethodology and conversation analysis. In G. Ritzer (ed.) *Frontiers of Social Theory: The New Synthesis* (pp. 185–213). Columbia University Press.

Bunglawala, Z. (2019) Please, don't call me BAME or BME! – *Civil Service.* https://civilservice.blog.gov.uk/2019/07/08/please-dont-call-me-bame-or-bme/

Charmaz, K. and Thornberg, R. (2021) The pursuit of quality in grounded theory. *Qualitative Research in Psychology* 18 (3), 305–327. https://doi.org/10.1080/14780887.2020.1780357

Coser, L. (1975) 'Two methods in search of a substance'. Presidential Address, annual meetings of the ASA, 1974. *American Sociological Review* 40 (6), 691–700. https://doi.org/10.2307/2094174

Di Stefano, M. (2018) Here's the audio recording of John Humphrys and Jon Sopel's 'jokey exchange' about equal pay. *BuzzFeed.News*, 13 January. https://www.buzzfeed.com/markdistefano/humphrys-sopel-audio-recording

Edwards, D. and Potter, J. (2005) Discursive psychology, mental states and descriptions. In H. Molder and J. Potter (eds) *Conversation and Cognition* (pp. 241–259). Cambridge University Press.

Elewa-Ikpakwu, C. and Ayoola, G. (2021) Response to: Double jeopardy: Black and female in medicine. *The Clinical Teacher* 18 (3), 311–311.

Frosh, S. (1999) What is outside discourse? *Psychoanalytic Studies* 1 (4), 381–390.

Gibson, S. (2011) Milgram's obedience experiments: A rhetorical analysis. *British Journal of Social Psychology* 52 (2), 290–309.

Glenn, P.J. (2003) *Laughter in Interaction.* Cambridge University Press.

Harré, R. (1993) *Social Being* (2nd edn). Wiley-Blackwell.

Hepburn, A. and Bolden, G.B. (2018) *Transcribing for Social Research.* Sage.

Hester, S. and Francis, D. (1990) Ethnomethodology, conversation analysis, and 'institutional talk'. *Text* 20 (3), 391–413.

Hollander, M.M. (2015) The repertoire of resistance: Non-compliance with directives in Milgram's 'obedience' experiments. *British Journal of Social Psychology* 54, 425–444.

Houtkoop-Steenstra, H. (2000) *Interaction and the Standardized Survey Interview: The Living Questionnaire.* Cambridge University Press

Jefferson, G. (2004) Glossary of transcript symbols with an introduction. In G.H. Lerner (ed.) *Conversation Analysis: Studies from the First Generation* (pp. 13–31). John Benjamins.

Johnston, O., Wildy, H. and Shand, J. (2021) Projecting student voice by constructing grounded theory. *Australian Educational Researcher* 48, 543–564.

Kitzinger, C. (2000) Doing feminist conversation analysis. *Feminism & Psychology* 10, 163–193

Kitzinger, C. (2008) Developing feminist conversation analysis: A response to Wowk. *Human Studies* 31 (2), 179–208.

Kitzinger, C. and Frith, H. (1999) Just say no? The use of conversation analysis in developing a feminist perspective on sexual refusal. *Discourse & Society* 10 (3), 293–316. https://doi.org/10.1177/0957926599010003002

Lavin, D. and Maynard, D.W. (2001) Standardization vs. rapport: Respondent laughter and interviewer reaction during telephone surveys. *American Sociological Review* 66 (3), 453–479. https://www.jstor.org/stable/3088888

Lerner, G.H. (1991) On the syntax of sentences-in-progress. *Language in Society* 20 (3), 441–458. https://doi.org/10.1017/S0047404500016572

Leviathan, Y. and Matias, Y. (2018) Google duplex: An AI system for accomplishing real-world tasks over the phone. *Google AI Blog.* https://ai.googleblog.com/2018/05/duplex-ai-system-for-natural-conversation.html

Mayor of London (2020) Action plan—transparency, accountability and trust in policing. Greater London Authority. https://www.london.gov.uk/publications/action-plan-transparency-accountability-and-trust-policing

Miller, G. and Turner, S.H.R. (2005) Applying the mystery shopping technique: The case of Lunn Poly. *Tourism Research Methods* 119.

Ochs, E. (1979) Transcription as theory. In E. Ochs and B. Schieffelin (eds) *Developmental Pragmatics* (pp. 43–72). Academic Press.

Oliver, D.G., Serovich, J.M. and Mason, T.L. (2005) Constraints and opportunities with interview transcription: Towards reflection in qualitative research. *Social Forces* 84 (2), 1273–1289. https://doi.org/10.1353/sof.2006.0023

Parker, I. (2005) *Qualitative Psychology: Introducing Radical Research.* Open University Press.

Parker, I. (2012) Discursive social psychology now. *British Journal of Social Psychology* 51 (3), 471–477.

Parslow, S., Stokoe, E. and Albert, S. (2021) Using conversation analysis to challenge the notion of emotional tone in sentiment analysis. *International Pragmatics Conference.*

Pino, M. (2017) I-challenges: Influencing others' perspectives by mentioning personal experiences in therapeutic-community group meetings. *Social Psychology Quarterly* 80 (3), 217–242

Potter, J. and Hepburn, A. (2005) Qualitative interviews in psychology: Problems and possibilities. *Qualitative Research in Psychology* 2, 38–55.

Previtali, F., Nikander, P. and Ruusuvuori, J. (2023) Ageism in job interviews: Discreet ways of building co-membership through age categorisation. *Discourse Studies* 25 (1), 25–50.

Rawls, A.W., Whitehead, K.A. and Duck, W. (eds) (2020) *Black Lives Matter: Ethnomethodological and Conversation Analytic Studies of Race and Systemic Racism in Everyday Interaction.* Routledge.

Rapley, T.J. (2001) The art (fulness) of open-ended interviewing: Some considerations on analysing interviews. *Qualitative Inquiry* 1 (3), 303–323.

Rendon, J. (2007) Facing prejudice in mediation: What should the mediator do? Available online: https://www.mediate.com/articles/rendon3.cfm

Richardson, E., Stokoe, E. and Antaki, C. (2018) Establishing intellectually impaired victims' understanding about 'truth' and 'lies': Police interview guidance and practice in cases of sexual assault. *Applied Linguistics.* https://doi.org/10.1093/applin/amy023

Richardson, E., Haworth, K. and Deamer, F. (2022) For the record: Questioning transcription processes in legal contexts. *Applied Linguistics.* https://doi.org/10.1093/applin/amac005

Robles, J.S. (2015) Extreme case (re) formulation as a practice for making hearably racist talk repairable. *Journal of Language and Social Psychology* 34 (4), 390–409.

Sarangi, S. (2018) Modes of en'gaze'ment and analytic accountability in discourse and interaction studies. *Language and Social Interaction Working Group*, 8th Meeting.

Schegloff, E.A. (1997) Whose text? Whose context? *Discourse & Society* 8 (2), 165–187. https://doi.org/10.1177/0957926597008002002

Schegloff, E.A., Jefferson, G. and Sacks, H. (1977) The preference for self-correction in the organization of repair in conversation. *Language* 53 (2), 361–382. https://doi.org/10.2307/413107

Sharrock, W.W. and Anderson, R.J. (2017) Has ethnomethodology run its course? Available online: https://www.sharrockandanderson.co.uk/wp-content/uploads/2019/10/Run-its-Course-VII.pdf

Sikveland, R.O. and Stokoe, E. (2016) Dealing with resistance in initial intake and inquiry calls to mediation: The power of 'willing'. *Conflict Resolution Quarterly* 33 (3), 235–253. https://doi.org/10.1002/crq.21157

Sikveland, R.O. and Stokoe, E. (2017) Enquiry calls to GP surgeries in the United Kingdom: Expressions of incomplete service and dissatisfaction in closing sequences. *Discourse Studies* 19 (4), 441–459. https://doi.org/10.1177/1461445617706999

Sikveland, R.O., Stokoe, E. and Symonds, J. (2016) Patient burden during appointment-making telephone calls to GP practices. *Patient Education and Counselling* 99 (8), 1310–1318. https://doi.org/10.1016/j.pec.2016.03.025

Singh, A. (2020) Matt Hancock names two asians when asked to identify black cabinet members. *HuffPost UK*, 7 June. Available online: https://www.huffingtonpost.co.uk/entry/black-cabinet-matt-hancock-protests_uk_5edc9ffdc5b6aedebbc6a27a

Skeggs, B. (2021) Necroeconomics: How necro legacies help us understand the value of death and the protection of life during the COVID-19 pandemic. *Historical Social Research/Historische Sozialforschung* 46 (4), 123–142.

Speer, S.A. (1999) Feminism and conversation analysis: An oxymoron? *Feminism & Psychology* 9 (4), 471–478. https://doi.org/10.1177/0959353599009004013

Speer, S.A. and Stokoe, E. (2014) Ethics in action: Consent-gaining interactions and implications for research practice. *British Journal of Social Psychology* 53 (1), 54–73. https://doi.org/10.1111/bjso.12009

Stokoe, E.H. (2000) Towards a conversation analytic approach to gender and discourse. *Feminism & Psychology* 10 (4), 552–563. https://doi.org/10.1177/0959353500010004018.

Stokoe, E.H. (2003) Mothers, single women and sluts: Gender, morality and membership categorization in neighbour disputes. *Feminism & Psychology* 13 (3), 317–344. https://doi.org/10.1177/0959353503013003006Stokoe 2011

Stokoe, E. (2008) Categories and sequences: Formulating gender in talk-in-interaction. In K. Harrington, L. Litosseliti, H. Saunston and J. Sunderland (eds) *Gender and Language Research Methodologies* (pp. 139–157). Palgrave.

Stokoe, E. (2009) Doing actions with identity categories: Complaints and denials in neighbour disputes. *Text and Talk* 29 (1), 75–97. https://doi.org/10.1515/TEXT.2009.004

Stokoe, E. (2011) Simulated interaction and communication skills training: The 'Conversation Analytic Role-play Method'. In C. Antaki (ed.) *Applied Conversation Analysis: Changing Institutional Practices* (pp. 119–139). Palgrave Macmillan.

Stokoe, E. (2013a) The (in)authenticity of simulated talk: Comparing role-played and actual conversation and the implications for communication training. *Research on Language and Social Interaction* 46 (2), 1–21. https://doi.org/10.1080/08351813.2013.780341

Stokoe, E. (2013b) Overcoming barriers to mediation in intake calls to services: Research-based strategies for mediators. *Negotiation Journal* 29 (3), 289–314. https://doi.org/10.1111/nejo.12026

Stokoe, E. (2015) Identifying and responding to possible '-isms' in institutional encounters: Alignment, impartiality and the implications for communication training. *Journal of Language and Social Psychology* 34 (4), 427–445. https://doi.org/10.1177/0261927X15586572

Stokoe, E. (2020) Psychological matters in institutional interaction: Insights and interventions from discursive psychology and conversation analysis. *Qualitative Psychology* 7 (3), 331–347. https://doi.org/10.1037/qup0000162

Stokoe, E. and Edwards, D. (2007) 'Black this, black that': Racial insults and reported speech in neighbour complaints and police interrogations. *Discourse & Society* 18 (3), 337–372. https://doi.org/10.1177/0957926507075477

Stokoe, E. and Edwards, D. (2008) 'Did you have permission to smash your neighbour's door?' Silly questions and their answers in police-suspect interrogations. *Discourse Studies* 10 (1), 89-111. https://doi.org/10.1177/1461445607085592

Stokoe, E., Hepburn, A. and Antaki, C. (2012) Beware the 'Loughborough School'? Interaction and the politics of intervention. *British Journal of Social Psychology* 51 (3), 48–496. https://doi.org/10.1111/j.2044-8309.2011.02088.x

Stokoe, E., Edwards, D. and Edwards, H. (2016) 'No comment' responses to questions in police investigative interviews. In S. Ehrlich, D. Eades and J. Ainsworth (eds) *Discursive Constructions of Consent in the Legal Process* (pp. 289–317). Oxford University Press.

Stokoe, E., Sikveland, R.O., Hamann, M.G.T., Albert, S. and Housley, W. (2020) Can humans simulate talking like other humans? Comparing mystery shoppers to real customers in service inquiries. *Discourse Studies* 22 (1). https://doi.org/10.1177/1461445619887537

Stokoe, E., Albert, S., Parslow, S. and Pearl, C. (2021) Conversation analysis and conversation design: Where the moonshots are. *Medium*, 3 June. https://elizabeth-stokoe.medium.com/conversation-design-and-conversation-analysis-c2a2836cb042#:~:text=Conversation%20analysis%20and%20conversation%20design%3A%20Where%20the%20moonshots%20are,-Professor%20Elizabeth%20Stokoe&text=Conversation%20has%20been%20described,different%20facets%20of%20life%20accomplished.

Stokoe, E., Antaki, C., Bracher, M., Chrisostomou, L., Henderson, E., Jones, G. and Stewart, S. (2021) The softness of hard data. *Medium*. Available online: https://elizabeth-stokoe.medium.com/the-softness-of-hard-data-475743d8a2f2

Tennent, E. and Weatherall, A. (2021) Feminist conversation analysis. In J. Angouri and J. Baxter (eds) *The Routledge Handbook of Language, Gender, and Sexuality* (pp. 258–271). Routledge.

Thornberg, R., Halldin, K., Bolmsjö, N., Petersson, A. (2013) Victimising of school bullying: A grounded theory. *Research Papers in Education* 28 (3), 309–29. https://doi.org/10.1080/02671522.2011.641999

UK Government (2021) Writing about ethnicity. Available online: https://www.ethnicity-facts-figures.service.gov.uk/style-guide/writing-about-ethnicity#bame-and-bme

Walker, G. (2012) Phonetics and prosody in conversation. In J. Sidnell and T. Stivers (eds.) *The Handbook of Conversation Analysis* (pp. 455–474). John Wiley and Sons.

Walker, S.-J.L., Hester, M., McPhee, D., Patsios, D., Williams, A., Bates, L. and Rumney, P. (2021) Rape, inequality and the criminal justice response in England: The importance of age and gender. *Criminology & Criminal Justice* 21 (3), 297–315. https://doi.org/10.1177/1748895819863095

Wass, V., Roberts, C., Hoogenboom, R., Jones, R. and Van der Vleuten, C. (2003) Effect of ethnicity on performance in a final objective structured clinical examination: qualitative and quantitative study. *British Medical Journal* 326 (7393), 800–803.

Wetherell, M. (1998) Positioning and interpretative repertoires: Conversation analysis and post-structuralism in dialogue. *Discourse & Society* 9 (3), 431–456.

Whelan, P. (2012) Oxymoronic and sociologically monstrous? Feminist conversation analysis. *Qualitative Research in Psychology* 9 (4), 279–291. https://doi.org/10.1080/14780887.2011.634360

Whitehead, K.A. (2018) Managing the moral accountability of stereotyping. *Journal of Language and Social Psychology* 37 (3), 288–309.

Wooffitt, R. (2007) Communication and laboratory performance in parapsychology experiments: Demand characteristics and the social organization of interaction. *British Journal of Social Psychology* 46 (3), 477–498. https://doi.org/10.1348/014466606X152667.

Wowk, M.T. (2007) Kitzinger's feminist conversation analysis: Critical observations. *Human Studies* 30 (2), 131–155.

Yu, B. and Sterponi, L. (2023) Toward neurodiversity: How conversation analysis can contribute to a new approach to social communication assessment. *Language, Speech, and Hearing Services in Schools* 54 (1), 27–41.

# Index

African American English (AAE) 184
Artificial Intelligence (AI) vii, 198, 211
Account xxi, xxviii, xxxiii, 33–34, 46,
    55, 86, 107–109, 124, 150, 163,
    165, 169, 175, 179, 181–183,
    185–186, 189, 199, 202,
    204–205, 207, 211, 216
Adjacency pair xxxiv, 7, 93
Affiliation (affiliating, affiliative)
    xxvi, 33, 35, 38, 140, 146–147,
    151, 205
  Disaffiliation (disaffiliative) 36,
    51–52, 150, 184, 191
Afrikaans 96–98, 101
Albert, Saul vii, xx
Alignment (aligning, align) 10, 95, 99,
    102–103, 105, 107–108, 112,
    135, 146, 149, 190, 205, 216
  Disalignment 112, 182
  Misalignment 95, 102, 105–106,
    108–109, 164–165
  Realignment 105
Anti-racist xv, xxi, 157, 174, 176,
    191–192
Asymmetry 9–10, 182

Billig, Michael xvi, 4
Black viii, xxi, xxvii–xxviii, 92,
    112, 116, 157, 159, 161–163,
    170–172, 175, 177–178, 181–
    184, 187–190, 192, 200–202

Categorial shorthand 15, 127
Category member 38, 116
Category work 38, 80–81, 85

Category-bound activity 175, 184,
    186, 191
Category-bound predicate 216
Category-bound right 134
Change-of-state token 41, 45, 186
Closing 15, 63, 91, 93, 95–96, 99,
    103, 105, 144, 146–147,
    149–151, 190,
  Closing phase 102, 105
  Pre-closing 213–214
Conditional relevance 53
Contiguity principle 38
Conversation Analysis (CA,
    Conversation analytic) viii, ix,
    x–xvi, xxvi, xxxiii–xxxiv, 1–2,
    14, 28–29, 51, 71, 134, 197–199,
    207–208, 214, 217
  Applied CA 8, 110
  Critical CA xiii, xvi, xviii, xx, 1,
    4, 8, 10, 52, 96, 110, 116–117,
    137, 158
  Institutional CA 11
  Interventionist CA 110
Conversation Analytic Role-play
    Method (CARM) ix, 214–217
Corpus of Language Discrimination in
    Interaction (CLDI) 51
Correction 13, 39, 184
  Other-correction 44
  Self-correction 44, 184, 201
Critical Discourse Analysis (CDA)
    xxxv, 115

Delegitimize xxv, 15, 116, 119, 121,
    123–124, 126, 127

Deontic authority xxvi, 134–137, 139–141, 144, 146–147, 150–152
Discursive Psychology (DP) 9, 197
Diversity x, xiii, xix, 177, 179, 218,
Double consciousness viii, xxxiv, 171, 175
Durkheim viii, xvii, xxvii–xxviii, xxx

EMCA 217
Emergency call 15, 93, 95
English as a Second Language (ESL) 28–30, 32, 39, 42, 50, 136–137, 146–147
Epistemological 27
Epistemics (epistemic) 3
  Epistemic authority 135, 143
Essentializing 10
Ethnographic (-observations, -interviews) xvii, 3, 28, 50
Ethnomethodology (EM, ethnomethodological) xvi, xxvi, xxxiv, xxxvii, 2–3, 116, 174, 197
Equality xv, xxvi, xxviii, 7, 116–117, 123–125
  Inequality xv–xvii, xix–xx, xxiv, xxvii–xxix, xxxvii, 1, 4, 7–11, 14–16, 27, 46, 96, 110, 134, 172, 207, 214
Equity xix, 28, 205, 208, 210, 218
  Inequity xxxvi, 217
Exclusion (exclusionary) xv–xvi, xxxvii, 4, 7, 11, 13, 46, 92, 116–117, 138, 140, 151, 218
Expansion 56, 93, 95, 100, 102–106, 110, 144, 147, 150
  Pre-expansion 93
  Sequence expansion 104
Extreme case formulation (ECF) 35, 107, 146–147, 178, 182

Formulation xxi, xxiii–xxiv, xxviii, 15, 50, 71–72, 74, 79, 80, 82–83, 85–89, 107, 119, 122, 135, 156–159, 164–172, 178–179, 182, 184, 205
  Reformulation 135, 206
Foucault xxxiii, xxxvi

Garfinkel, Harold xvi, xxxiii, 156
Gender xvi–xvii, xx, xxv–xxvi, xxxvi–xxxvii, 1, 4–5, 9–10, 66, 116–117, 123–127, 187, 202, 204, 206, 214–215

Hawaiian xxiii–xxiv, 15, 71–89
Heritage, John xxxiii
Heteronormativity (heteronormative) 8, 12, 116, 127
Hyperanglicization 50

Inclusion xix, 116, 127, 133, 218
Indexicality (indexical) 49–50
Indexical inversion 27
Institutional power xxiii, xxvi, 15, 88, 133–134, 136, 151–152
Interjacent (interjacently) 56, 63
Interview data 199
Intersubjective 99
-isms 198, 217

Jefferson, Gail xxxiv, 2
Justice viii, xxviii, xxxiv, 162, 170, 198, 206, 209, 214, 218
  Injustice xviii, xxxvii, 1, 4, 8–9, 12, 14–16, 27, 198, 207, 217

Laughable 202
Linguistics (linguist) vii, viii, ix–xi, xvii, xx, xxix, xxxv–xxxvi, 4, 52

Marginalize (Marginalized) xvii–xxiii, xxv–xxvii, xxx, 3
Mediation 214–217
Membership Categorization Analysis (MCA) x, 1, 9, 74, 76, 116–117
Membership Categorization Device 174
Minoritized 13, 206, 214
Mock language xxii, 49–52, 64–65, 68
Mock Asian 50, 65
Mock ESL 50
Mock Spanish 50, 65, 68

Naturalized 34, 46, 50
Neutrality 72, 76–77
Next-turn proof procedure 71, 74

Other xxv, 15, 115–128
Other-repetition 51

Preference (preference organization)
  xx, xxiii, 44, 175, 184, 187,
  190–191, 201, 205
  Dispreferred (dispreference) xxvi,
    107, 151, 167, 184, 201
  Preferred turn shape 182

Race-based entitlement 177–179,
  183–184, 189
Racial incompetence xxi, 174, 176–192
Racialize (racialized, racialization) xv,
  xvii, xxii, xxvii, xxix, xxxiv,
  27–28, 34, 36, 49, 51–52, 57,
  61, 63–64, 66, 68, 116, 157–159,
  169, 171, 175, 178–179, 181,
  183, 186–187, 192, 202
Raciolinguistic (raciolinguistically) xxi,
  xxiii, 14–15, 27–47
Racist rendition xxii, 15, 49–68
Recipient design (recipient-designed)
  185, 210
Reference form 109
  Categorical reference 109
Repair xxiii, 14, 34, 39, 41, 45–46, 51,
  54, 60–61, 103, 146, 167, 192,
  201–202, 211, 213
  Other-initiated repair xxii, xxiii,
    66, 182
  Self-repair xxvi, 44, 141, 143, 151,
    165–166, 184, 201, 205
  Self-initiated repair 103
  Self-initiated self-repair 201

Reported speech xxiv, 15, 71–72, 74,
  76, 85–89, 165
Routine trouble 95, 98, 100
  Non-routine trouble 95, 98, 105

Sacks, Harvey xvi, xxxiv, 2, 12, 76

Schegloff, Emanuel xvi, xxxiv, 4
Self xxviii, xxx
Self-select 53
Semantic pejoration 49
Sequence (sequential) xvi, xxi–xxii,
  xxiv, xxvi, xxviii–xxix, 9–12,
  16, 39, 44–45, 53–54, 56–57, 66,
  93, 103–104, 106, 116, 135–
  137, 140, 143–144, 146–147,
  149–151, 208, 213
  Sequence termination 53–54
Service receipt 94–95, 106–107
Sociology (sociological, sociologist)
  vii–x, xvii–xx, xxvii–xxx,
  xxxiii–xxxv, 2–3, 97,
  176, 200
Stance xxvi, 32–34, 51, 76, 87, 121,
  135, 149–151
Stokoe, Elizabeth ix–xx, 197
Subjectivity 197

Tag question xxiv, 10, 94, 98–100,
  102–104, 106, 109, 111–112
Talk-in-interaction 1, 8,110
Turn-Constructional Unit (TCU) 32,
  169, 201
  Compound Turn-Constructional
    Unit (TCU) 209, 211
Terminal particle 94, 102,
Trouble source 41, 44–46
Turn-by-turn talk 60
Turn-taking xxi, xxiv–xxv, 5, 9–10, 12,
  71, 88, 175

Wetherell, Margaret xvi, 4
White (Whiteness) xvi, xxi, xxii–xxiii,
  xxvi–xxviii, 14–15, 27–29,
  32–34, 36, 39, 46, 50, 66, 92,
  116, 157–159, 163–164, 171,
  175–176, 178, 181, 186–187,
  190–191, 202
White Public Space 49, 51–53, 67

For Product Safety Concerns and Information please contact our EU Authorised Representative:

Easy Access System Europe

Mustamäe tee 50

10621 Tallinn

Estonia

gpsr.requests@easproject.com

www.ingramcontent.com/pod-product-compliance
Ingram Content Group UK Ltd.
Pitfield, Milton Keynes, MK11 3LW, UK
UKHW021835210426
5322IPUK00021B/307